Madeleva

MADELEVA

A BIOGRAPHY

GAIL PORTER MANDELL

STATE UNIVERSITY OF NEW YORK PRESS

Published by
State University of New York Press, Albany

© 1997 State University of New York

Printed in the United States of America

For information, address State University of New York Press,
State University Plaza, Albany, N.Y. 12246

Production by M. R. Mulholland
Marketing by Nancy Farrell

Library of Congress Cataloging-in-Publication Data

Mandell, Gail Porter, 1940–
    Madeleva : a biography / Gail Porter Mandell.
      p. cm.
    Includes bibliographical references and index.
    ISBN 0-7914-3439-7 (hardcover : alk. paper). — ISBN 0-7914-3440-0
(pbk. : alk. paper)
    1. M. Madeleva (Mary Madeleva), Sister, 1887–1964. 2. Nuns—
United States—Biography. I. Title.
BX4705.M25663M37   1997
271'.97—dc20
[B]   96-36300
                                            CIP

10 9 8 7 6 5 4 3 2 1

CONTENTS

ILLUSTRATIONS

Acknowledgments

Thanks go to the many whose knowledge, wisdom, and encouragement helped me to complete this biography. The Sisters of the Holy Cross helped me in countless ways, generously giving their time, sharing their memories and experience, and opening their files to me. Particular thanks go to Sr. Miriam P. Cooney, CSC, who spent hours telling me about Sister Madeleva, instructing me on the details of convent life, and reading and responding to successive drafts of the manuscript. Sr. M. Elena (Malits), CSC, deserves credit for first suggesting the biography to me, and I owe thanks to Sr. Frances B. O'Connor, CSC, former president of the congregation, who graciously approved the project. Sr. Bernadette Marie (Downey), CSC; Sr. M. Alma (Peter), CSC; Sr. M. Gerald (Hartney), CSC; Sr. Basil Anthony (O'Flynn), CSC; Sr. Mary Jeanne Finske, CSC; Sr. M. Gertrude Anne (Otis), CSC; and the late Srs. Maria Concepta (McDermott), CSC; and Maria Assunta (Werner), CSC, contributed valuable information and insight at crucial stages in my work. Sr. M. Rosaleen (Dunleavy), CSC, who was director of the archives of the Cushwa-Leighton Library at Saint Mary's College during most of the time I worked on this project, offered sustained help and guidance. Without her extensive knowledge and cooperation, always cheerfully given, I could not have completed my research. Sr. M. Campion (Kuhn), CSC, similarly welcomed me to the general archives of the Congregation of the Sisters of the Holy Cross. Sr. Kathleen Moroney, CSC, invested hours of her busy schedule tracking down copyrights for me. When she became president of the congregation, Sr. Catherine O'Brien, CSC, handled my requests for permissions with consideration and speed. I am grateful, too, to Sr. Rachel Callahan, CSC; Sr. M. Francesca (Kennedy), CSC; Sr. Jean Klene, CSC; Sr. M. Rose Anne (Schultz), CSC; Sr. Patricia Mulvaney, CSC; and Sr. Ann Donnelly, CSC, all of whom offered encouragement and help along the way. I deeply appreciate the unrestricted access to material and the complete freedom to tell Madeleva's story in my own way entrusted to me by the Sisters of the Holy Cross.

The members of Sister Madeleva's family also supplied invaluable information, especially regarding her family background and her earliest years. Carol Cooper Wolff, who had served as a member of the Arntz Family History Committee and personally conducted a number of interviews with family members, generously supplied otherwise unobtainable information. Mary Lucia Wolff Stevenson's recollections of her paternal grandparents and their children gave me a lively sense of Madeleva's family life, as did the letters graciously supplied by Col. Julius Frederick Wolff, Jr. Mrs. Hoene Petersen, a family friend, kindly shared with me her memories of the Wolffs.

Numerous friends and colleagues at Saint Mary's College read and made extensive comments on the manuscript and often helped in other important ways. Dr. Ann Loux deserves special recognition and thanks for her characteristically thorough and insightful evaluations of drafts, delivered with her inimitable mix of enthusiastic encouragement and absolute honesty. Long conversations with Dr. Bruno Schlesinger shaped my sense of Madeleva and of Saint Mary's and Notre Dame at an earlier time; I thank him for those as for so much else, and thank as well his wife, Alice, who along with Bruno read and commented on various chapters of the book. Among others to whom I owe special thanks are Dr. Richard Allen; Dr. Kate Shoup; Jeanne Rodes; Dr. Phyllis Kaminski; Dr. Keith Egan; Br. Bernard Donohoe, CSC; Dr. Linnea Vacca; and the late Joe Bonadies, with whom I spent a beautiful July morning truly seeing the campus as he recalled the history of every garden and grove. Dr. John Shinners and Dr. Philip Hicks, my colleagues in the Humanistic Studies Department, offered encouragement and advice, as did President William A. Hickey and Vice President and Dean of Faculty Dorothy M. Feigl. Librarians Julie Long and Robert Hohl helped with research, and Bill Weymouth prepared copies of photographs for my use.

A special word of gratitude goes to my former and present students, as well, for their interest and encouragement, especially to Moira Murphy, who spent a summer researching aspects of Sister Madeleva's biography as part of a SISTAR grant from Saint Mary's College. Her intelligent research and astute observations helped me shape the story of Madeleva's life, as did the comments of Peggy Abood, Tracy Hartzler-Toon, and many others over the course of the seven years I spent writing and researching this material.

I wish also to acknowledge and thank the alumnae and friends of the college who responded to my request for information and remembrances of Sister Madeleva. Their help made the book infinitely richer. My sincere thanks go especially to Sr. Mary of God, OP; Marian Marshall Hemphill; Mary L. Norris; Carrie Powers Powell; Mrs. Terrence Merkel; Dorothy Thiel Lafeber; Susan Klmer Martin; Mrs. Arthur Petersen; Vincent Ferrer McAloon; Mr. and Mrs. William E. Cotter, Jr. and their family; Fr. Thomas Heath, O.P.; Bill Kavanaugh; and the late Ed Fischer.

I am grateful to my husband, Daniel N. Mandell, who put his considerable philosophical and theological wisdom at my service. Our conversations echo throughout this book. My friend and former colleague Dr. Penny Brooke Jameson traveled to Madeleva's hometown with me and offered her knowledge and experience as a psychologist when I needed it (not only to understand my subject!). My mother, Genevieve Henneman, and my mother-in-law, Elizabeth Mandell, read parts of the biography and urged me to finish, as did my friends Kathleen Hohn Dahm and Dr. Susan McGury. Dr. Dana Greene of Saint Mary's University of Maryland offered sage advice when I needed it, and my beloved teachers Sr. Marion Bascom, RSCJ, and Sr. Mary O'Callaghan, RSCJ, along with Sr. Margaret Williams, RSCJ; Sr. Cyrill Gill, OP; and Rev. Didicus Dunn, OP, cap., helped me fill gaps in my knowledge. Jacqueline Dougherty, Assistant Archivist of the Province Archives Center of the Indiana Province of the Congregation of the Holy Cross, and Rev. James E. McDonald, CSC, Asst. Provincial of the Indiana Province, were also very helpful.

For permission to quote from or otherwise use materials as noted, I am indebted to the following individuals and organizations: The Congregation of the Sisters of the Holy Cross for permission to quote from the published and unpublished works of Sr. M. Madeleva Wolff, CSC, collected in the Congregational Archives and Records of the Sisters of the Holy Cross, specifically including *American Twelfth Night and Other Poems, Collected Poems of 1946, Conversations with Cassandra, My First Seventy Years, The Four Last Things, A Question of Lovers and Other Poems, Penelope and Other Poems, A Song of Bedlam Inn and Other Poems, A Christmas Song*, and *Addressed to Youth*, and for permission to quote from other letters and records in the Congregational Archives; The Archives of Saint Mary's College for unrestricted permission to quote from materials and to reproduce photographs in their collection; the Congregation of Holy Cross, Indiana Province, for unrestricted permission to quote from the correspondence of Rev. Cornelius Hagerty, CSC, and Rev. Charles L. O'Donnell, CSC, housed in the Saint Mary's Archives, and from "Design for a House" by Rev. Charles L. O'Donnell, CSC; the Province Archives Center of the Indiana Province of the Congregation of Holy Cross for permission to quote from letters to Rev. Cornelius Hagerty, CSC, from Sr. M. Madeleva Wolff, CSC, dated 5 May 1922, 12 Feb. 1926, Feast of the Ascension, 1920 and for permission to publish photographs from their collection; the Bancroft Library, University of California, Berkeley, for permission to quote at length from the unpublished letters of Sr. Madeleva collected among the Benjamin H. Lehman Papers (Banc Mss C-H 155) in their archives, for permission to quote from the unpublished letters of Benjamin H. Lehman in the Saint Mary's College Archives, and for permission to reproduce a photograph of Benjamin H. Lehman from their collection; the Archives of the University of Notre Dame for permission to quote from a letter of Sr. Madeleva to Rev. Charles L. O'Donnell, CSC, collected in the presidential papers designated UPCO 5/62; Curtis Brown, Ltd. for permission to quote from unpublished letters dated 13 Mar. 1959, 27 Apr. 1959, and 3 Oct. 1963 by C. S. Lewis to Sr. Madeleva copyright © C. S. Lewis Pte. Ltd 1997; the Marion E. Wade Center, Wheaton College, for permission to quote from a letter dated 3 Oct. 1963 by C. S. Lewis to Sr. Madeleva; Marjorie Hall Walsh Witherspoon for permission to quote from her unpublished master's thesis: "Sister Madeleva, Lyric Poet"; Dr. Mary Ellen Klein for permission to quote from her unpublished doctoral thesis: "Sr. M. Madeleva Wolff, CSC: A Study of Presidential Leadership 1934–1961"; and Carol Cooper Wolff for permission to quote from "A Chronological History of the Familie Arntz" and other materials supplied by her.

Finally, I am most grateful to the Lilly Endowment, Inc., of Indiana for the Faculty Open Fellowship that allowed me to begin work on this project, and to Saint Mary's College, which supported my work with two sabbatical leaves and a SISTAR grant.

Preface: At Last

"So here it is at last, the distinguished thing."

—Henry James, on his death.

Asked about her future plans, the old woman, approaching eighty, replied: "I'm mainly interested in getting ready to see God."[1]

The woman who spoke these words to a Saint Louis newspaper reporter was at the time a well-known poet and scholar, recently retired from the presidency of Saint Mary's College at Notre Dame, Indiana. The time was just before Christmas 1961, and Sister M. Madeleva Wolff, CSC, was on one of her frequent lecture tours, during which she would talk to a group of college students about poetry and read a few of her own lyrics, or deliver a lecture with a whimsical title such as "Adventures in Inner Space" to a group of high-minded businessmen, or pose to a convention of Catholic educators the conundrum: "How Christianizing Is Christian Education?" Always on such trips she would meet with friends and former students and, particularly in the last years, when her reputation was at its highest, with reporters who sought her opinion on everything from life in a convent to *Sputnik.* In her medieval widow's weeds and her fluted wimple with its flowing veil, she made her way out of trains and taxis and into such unlikely places as the New York studios of the National Broadcasting Company, or the Arizona retreat of long-time friends, writer and diplomat Clare Boothe Luce and husband Henry, founder of Time-Life Enterprises.

By this time in her life, Madeleva's image had crystallized and, like an icon, superseded the woman behind it. Those who still remember her, especially those who saw her from the distance that a certain fame—even a modest amount—imposes, tend to remember her as she was then, an impression caught by and forever fused with the remaining photographs from the last years: her face pale—preternaturally pale—but still firm and smooth, and her features composed, but her gaze piercing. As she aged, her speech had become measured, marked by long pauses, and her demeanor increasingly reserved and dignified, even though she was no less engaged and attentive. Gradually, almost imperceptibly, she had adapted to life in the public eye. She played her part well: that of professional nun, academic grande dame, and daughter of the muses.

Madeleva joked lightly about her "double" constitution, inherited from her parents, August and Lucy Wolff, who both lived long into their nineties. In spite of recurrent spells of insomnia and mysterious sloughs of depression and fatigue that began in her youth and persisted into old age, Madeleva contemplated a long and active life. After all, at ninety, her parents had still climbed ladders to wash their second-story windows and put up preserves from their own garden. They had even taken the long train trip from northern Wisconsin to Saint Mary's to surprise—indeed, flabbergast—their daughter with a visit.

Nevertheless, even though—or perhaps precisely because—Madeleva had resigned herself to the possibility of extreme old age, meditatively she had directed much of her adult life toward its final moment. She contemplated death in her poetry and, one presumes, in her prayers; spoke and wrote of it often; and always idealized it. To imagine death, she borrowed the familiar terms of Saint Francis of Assisi; death became "Sister Death." In an early poem of that title, the "doorway" of death is "love's architrave" where the King waits for her arrival. In another, "The Theme," her bridegroom Christ promises to embrace her with "death's fierce kiss." During a hospital stay when she was in her early forties, she wrote what became her best-known poem on death, "Details for My Burial," in which she left instructions for the proper preparation of her final "consecrate cell." She impishly gave the poem to her uncomprehending doctor, who assured her with chagrin that such instructions were premature.[2] If one believes the poetry, Madeleva spent her whole life: "Waiting—ah! who could guess,—waiting for death, my lover."[3]

Yet when it arrived, death took her by surprise. Madeleva made time in her busy schedule to go to the Leahy Clinic in Boston for what promised to be a simple surgical procedure, removal of a gall bladder that had been giving her problems. The day before surgery, July 22, 1964, which was also the feast day of her patron saint, Mary Magdalen, she snuggled into a new blue robe that she had just removed from its gift wrapping, surveyed her numerous bouquets, read the many telegrams from well-wishers, and chatted with those who came in person to visit her. According to friends who were with her that day, "She was in a most happy frame of mind."[4]

After surgery, Madeleva seemed to be recovering well, and her doctors predicted a reasonably quick convalescence. Two members of her congregation visited her that afternoon and found her in good spirits, alert and looking well. They were so reassured they left for Indiana later that day. But at dawn on Saturday, July 25, she died. The official cause of death was recorded as "septicemia": blood poisoning. The attending physician, Madeleva's friend for many years, wrote to her superiors that her death, which had surprised him no less than they, resulted from a "very rare complication of this type of surgery." He concluded his medical report on a personal note: "I soon grew to love her and admire her for the many fine things for which she stood."[5]

Madeleva left behind her an intellectual and spiritual legacy: over twenty published books, including thirteen volumes of religious poetry and an autobiography, and a thriving college which she had led for almost thirty years and that could no longer be defined apart from her influence. In its obituary, *The New York Times* lauded her wide-ranging accomplishments as a poet, essayist, scholar, and educator, citing in particular her establishment in 1943 of the School of Sacred Theology at Saint Mary's, the first of its kind for women and laymen.[6] She left the sense, even in those who knew her only slightly or by reputation alone, that someone special, not to be replaced, had gone.

On the sweltering Sunday afternoon that Madeleva's body was brought back to Saint Mary's, the convent bells tolled and an honor guard of sisters lined the long drive to the entrance of the main college hall, where her casket lay in state for two days until the burial. Hundreds packed the solemn requiem mass in the convent church and followed the funeral procession to the community graveyard.

And so Sister Madeleva passed away, and after her one by one went those still left who knew her best. Few remain to visit her grave under the canopy of a flowering tulip tree. Those who chance upon her portrait on the wall of the classroom building named for her now see a stranger. Madeleva anticipated this eclipse in one of her poems, "Concerning Death":

> DEATH: The moon does not change.
> Tonight a shadow shuts from me its borrowed beauty!
> This will be divinely true of you when you are dead.[7]

She suggests that beyond the shadow of death lies the person who does not change but lives each moment of her life, regards it curiously, and savors it delightedly, everlastingly present.

1

The Harness-Maker's Daughter

The woman known as "Madeleva" most of her adult life was baptized on June 2, 1887, at the Church of Saint Mary in Cumberland, Wisconsin. As the priest poured baptismal water over her head, the daughter whose birth on May 24 to August Frederick and Lucy Arntz Wolff had been recorded at the Barron County Court House became "Mary Evaline." From the beginning, the Roman Catholic church sealed her identity.

Lucy Wolff saw to that. August was Lutheran, his confirmation certificate a cherished possession that hung on his bedroom wall.[1] But Lucy was an ardent Catholic, who attended daily mass in the tiny mission church when the priest was in town. She made time to launder altar linens and mend vestments for the priest, who had no other help. Once, on her hands and knees, she singlehandedly laid a heavy carpet in the sanctuary of the church. After mass on the one or two Sundays a month when it was offered, she opened her kitchen to the families who came in from the surrounding territory, fortifying them with hot coffee and toast for the rough trip home.

Lucy's immigrant parents had brought their Catholicism with them from their native Westphalia, which was at the time a province of Prussia. Even in their early years in the Wisconsin wilderness without church or priest to help them, the Arntz family had practiced their religion faithfully.[2]

Lucy's father, Peter Joseph Henry Arntz, and her mother, Hendrina Bernadina Schmitz, known as "Dina," had left their home near the Dutch border for the Wisconsin frontier shortly after their marriage in 1848. Seventeen years older than his wife, who was barely seventeen when they married,[3] Peter Arntz had traveled widely before his marriage. As a young man, he settled for a time in Dutch Guiana, but returned to his native Germany a few years before his marriage. Something of a linguist, he spoke five languages fluently.

As his travels suggest, Peter shared the Arntz family penchant for adventure. In family lore, an older brother, Werner, was notorious because, to avoid arrest for smuggling, he allowed himself to be bricked up for three days in a kiln on the family farm. Indeed, as a youth Peter himself probably participated in clandestine forays into France and Belgium for silk thread, an illegal activity in which the Arntz family engaged with clear conscience, despising as they did their Prussian conquerors.⁴ But if the family had ways of replenishing their dwindling resources (the profit from one such expedition had been enough to complete a new barn), they also had an inclination for living beyond their means. In his lifetime, Peter had seen the family wealth squandered and the farmstead and brickyard that supported it sold. Of seven children in the family, only the two sisters, one of whom became a nun (and, eventually, superior of her convent), chose to remain in Europe; all the males emigrated to America.

Peter's young wife, Dina, had also suffered a decline in family circumstances. Raised in comfort and given an expensive education, she had to cope with abrupt changes after her father, a retail merchant, died when she was fourteen. He left his wife with three daughters to support, of whom Dina was the oldest. Dina soon met and married Peter Arntz in her native town of Emmerich, just across the Rhine from Kleve, where Peter had gone into business after his return from South America. Most likely hoping to regain something of past prosperity and at the same time to escape worsening political oppression, the newly married couple joined the swell of emigrants, two among more than a million Germans who left their native land for America between 1844 and 1854.

Dina bore their first child three months after she and Peter arrived in Wisconsin. Over the next twenty-five years, twelve more children followed. The fourth child, Lucia, who became simply "Lucy" when she started school,⁵ was the first to be born at the family's new homestead on the Lemonweir River, a few miles from its juncture with the head of the Wisconsin River. The year before Lucy's birth on January 8, 1854, Peter built a sawmill there. The area was still mostly pine forest, sparsely populated by Winnebago Indians. For the first year and a half of their stay, Dina went without seeing a single white woman.⁶ Needing help, she employed some of the native American women, teaching them to sew in a European manner with a needle and thread.

The oldest Arntz children had only each other for companions. Eventually, however, Peter's younger brother Heinrich and his wife, Johanna, settled close by. Other immigrants came as well, some German, but most Irish. The Arntzes established close ties with their neighbors, and the younger generation eventually intermarried.

Lumber became the family business until the mid-1860s, when, out clearing roads for his logging teams, Peter was stranded in a fierce snow storm that froze both his feet. He spent three months recuperating; for the rest of his life, he was lame. His accident, and the end of the easy supply of timber when the area became more densely settled, caused him to devote himself entirely to farming, with hops for the brewing industry as his chief crop. About this time, he took one of his sons with him to explore the Nebraska Territory, traveling to Omaha and Lincoln, but decided against moving his growing family to a new frontier.

Well educated and used to status in the community, Peter Arntz assumed the role of leader among the other settlers. He used his teams of horses, the only ones in the area, to fetch provisions for nearby families from the closest town, forty miles distant. According to his daughter Lucy, he saw that each family had what it needed, even if it meant supplying the poorest families from his own goods.[7] His wife, Dina, also commanded respect; she impressed those who met her as a "lady."[8] Even in the backwoods, the couple established a home for their children marked by pious religious observance and polite formality.[9]

Along with the rest of the family, Lucy worked hard. She recalled, "I had to work indoors and out, do all the serving for a family of twelve—wash, iron, cook, milk six and seven cows twice a day, make butter, cheese, etc. In those days, we could not buy ready to wear clothing of any kind. We had to make men's underwear as well as for ourselves. Then Sunday morning we often had to walk $4^1/2$ miles to Mass by 9:30 or 10 and often fasting. Those were pioneer days."[10] In the family, Lucy was famous for her bread making. She also became a surrogate mother to the youngest children, Eva Louisa and Werner Peter, born in 1870 and 1873, respectively. She later named two of her own children after her young charges.

The children from the Lemonweir community attended a country grade school, but those like Lucy who wanted a high school education had to board during the week in New Lisbon, some fifteen miles from home. Apparently, Lucy's parents were willing to sacrifice her much needed labor as well as the price of board in town so that she could attend the only secondary school in the area. After graduation, she returned home for several years to teach in the country school she had attended.

In her mid-twenties, still unmarried, Lucy took a job as clerk in Isaac Alsbacher's general store and harness shop in Mauston, eight miles cross country from home.[11] There, she met August Wolff. Even though he was almost four years her junior and had little to offer except his character, they began keeping company while they worked together at the store.

August, known to those outside the family as "Gus," had come to Mauston in the fall of 1879, just after his twenty-second birthday, to practice his trade of harness making. Like Lucy, August was used to hard work. He had been making his own way since he was eleven, when his formal schooling ended and he took a job in a heading and stave mill for fifty cents a day.

August was the oldest child of Louisa Wolff, born to her on September 10, 1857, in Brallentin, Pomerania. He never knew his father and in fact, may never have known the truth of his birth—that his father was a single man whose family objected to his marrying Louisa because she was not "good enough for him," her family being "too poor" and of a "low class."[12] Three years after August's birth, Louisa had twins by a married man. She gave all three of her children her maiden name, Wolff. Reputedly, the father of the twins gave her the money that she used to emigrate after her marriage to Christian Engelke, a widower with two children of his own. Together, they had a daughter before they left Germany for Richwood, Wisconsin, in 1866. Five more children were born to them there.

The family arrived in Wisconsin knowing nothing of English, dependent entirely upon relatives to help them get started. Within a year, Chris Engelke had a job in the mill where his stepson August would later work for a time, and was able to build a house for his family on a small plot of land where they could garden. Life at home was not easy. August, who was nine years old when the family emigrated, attended school briefly, in desultory fashion, obtaining most of his education at a Lutheran Sunday school. At thirteen, he left home for good, moving to nearby Watertown, where he found work as chore boy in a hotel.

Within a few months of his arrival in Watertown, Paul Herzog, a harness maker, hired August as his apprentice. The boy worked in Herzog's shop for four years. During this time he formed a close friendship with a fellow harness maker, Gus Weitz. Both young men moved to Madison early in the summer of 1876.

Always a sober youth, August preferred hunting and other outdoor activities or, alternatively, reading and drawing, to less temperate pleasures. He particularly enjoyed sketching trees, leaves, and flowers in notebooks that he carefully preserved. The five months he spent in Madison made him "education-conscious," and the University of Wisconsin became the "single symbol of higher learning" for him.[13] Later, he would send all three of his children there.

In November 1876, in spite of the depressed economy that followed the Panic of 1873, August quit his job in Madison because his employer insisted he work on election day. A series of temporary jobs in Wisconsin and western Michigan followed. It was during this three-year period that he took a job with August Ruengling in Baraboo, Wisconsin. While he was working in the harness shop, so the story goes, Johnny, the youngest son of his employer, ran off with a traveling show. August later delighted in telling his family how his employer sent him and another Ruengling son to track down and bring home the delinquent teenager—who later became famous as one of the Ringling Brothers, owners of "The Greatest Show on Earth."[14]

August wanted a shop of his own, and after three years of steady work for Alsbacher in Mauston, he set out to find a place to establish himself and, now that he and Lucy were planning to marry, a family. After Aberdeen, South Dakota, and then Grand Rapids, Wisconsin, failed to satisfy him, he wrote a friend who had settled in Cumberland, about sixty miles north and west of Eau Claire. A brother-in-law of Isaac Alsbacher, an engineer with the Chicago, Saint Paul, Minneapolis, and Omaha Railway, had first told August about the village, which he had platted a few years before. According to all reports, it was growing rapidly as a lumbering town, thanks to the railroad and a new sawmill. August visited Cumberland, arriving May 1, 1883, judged the prospects for the harness business to be excellent, and decided to stay. He opened his shop in rented quarters on the main street three weeks later.

In 1883, northwestern Wisconsin was still logging country, although the once dense virgin forests were dwindling fast. First named "Lakeland" (and still known as the "Island City"), Cumberland occupies a small island just off the southeastern shore of Beaver Dam Lake, which connects with a chain of lakes extending some sixteen miles to the northwest. Along these lakes, Chippewa Indians lived in scattered villages. Italians brought in to build the railroad lived with their families in a colony to the south of Cumberland. Also to the south lay a German settlement, and to the east, a smaller French colony. The newly incorporated village had a population of fewer than one thousand inhabitants. Nevertheless, within its limits the year that August Wolff opened his store were twenty-four saloons[15] and at least two brothels, along with several hundred frequently intoxicated woodsmen. The town's reputation in those early days put it in an unholy quartet: Hurley, Hayward, Cumberland—and Hell.[16]

This was the place to which August Wolff brought his pious bride eight months later. The day after Christmas, he had returned to southern Wisconsin to marry Lucy Arntz. The ceremony took place on

New Year's Day 1884, at the Catholic church in Lyndon, the town closest to the Arntz farm. Afterward, the couple traveled over the snowy roads to Mauston by sleigh, where they expected to take a train to Cumberland the same day. Instead, through no fault of their own, they spent the night in jail. They would tell the story many times to children and grandchildren. Because of the frigid weather, all train service had been canceled. Lucy's older brother Will was the sheriff in Mauston; his home, where they spent the night, was also the county jail. And so it happened that they spent their wedding night there. Their only honeymoon was the trip home, which took a full week because of blizzards and drifts along the line. That week, the temperature fell as low as fifty-two degrees below zero.[17]

Initially, the couple set up housekeeping in the same building as the store they rented. There on November 19, 1885, their first child was born. Julius Frederick was named for the father August had never known.[18] Within three years they had bought first their own store, and then a two-story, white frame house on the property just behind it. The couple's second child, Mary Evaline, called Eva (pronounced "Eh'vuh") or sometimes "Sis," was born a month after the family moved into their new home. Two more children followed: Werner Peter (nicknamed "Vern"), on October 25, 1889, and a third son, Leo, who died soon after birth on December 23, 1892.

An early photograph of Eva shows a big-eyed baby who stares intently down the eye of the camera. She appears small, delicate, fine boned, but wiry nonetheless. Her large, pale eyes and abundant, dark hair are her most distinctive features, even as an infant. As an older child, newly confirmed, she stands straight, shoulders back, feet apart and planted solidly on the ground. Her gaze in both pictures is the same—penetrating and wary. Both record the image of an intense, intelligent, self-possessed child.

Eva spent much of her childhood with her brothers, out of doors, playing what were then boys' games. She did her best to keep pace with her brother Freddie, her favorite and constant companion even though he was a year and a half older than she. All three children were close, but in those early years a special bond formed between the first two.

For Eva, as for Freddie and Vern, the lake that encircled the village became the most important feature of the landscape and dominated the memory of her early years. About to be taken for a boat ride, two-year-old Eva surveyed the huge expanse of water and announced decisively to her parents, "I don't want to get into that big tub."[19] She

FIGURE 1.1

Fred and Eva Wolff, c. 1888

Courtesy of Saint Mary's College Archives.

FIGURE 1.2

Eva Wolff, c. 1892

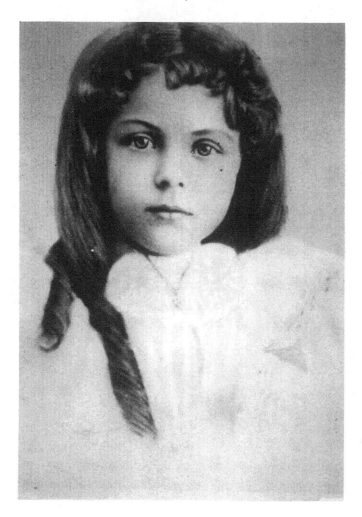

Courtesy Saint Mary's College Archives.

changed her mind, however, and for the rest of her life she loved to be in and on the water. At a young age, she learned to swim by using a small board to support herself as she kicked, and she soon challenged herself to swim across the narrow part of the lake and back. Almost as soon as she could walk, she learned to ice skate. She was always one of the first on the ice, certainly the first girl, often before

FIGURE 1.3

Fred and Eva Wolff's Confirmation, c. 1898. Vern is seated;
Rev. Stephen Leinfelder is standing behind.

Courtesy Saint Mary's College Archives.

the ice was hard, liking best "the thrill of spinning off with the ice cracking under every stroke."[20]

Other early memories were of the Chippewa Indians, who came often to her father's shop to sell deer hair and buckskins. Old Cutlip, the chief, particularly impressed her, perhaps because of the unsightly scar that gave him his nickname. As the only native American who could speak even a little English, Cutlip did most of the trading for the tribe. He often startled Lucy and her children by peering through the windows of the house, looking for her husband.[21]

As children, Eva and her brothers turned their father's workshop into a playroom. The pungent smell of rolled up leather, the feel of thickly knotted rope, the crack and whistle of long horse whips, and the sounds of bells—sleigh bells, cow bells, and sheep bells—stayed with Eva for life. The children rode the horseless saddles their father had for sale and played in the empty wooden boxes in which buffalo robes were shipped.

Almost as soon as they could talk, the children learned the names of trees, flowers, animals, and birds. On Sunday afternoon drives into the country in a horse and buggy on loan from the livery stable, Lucy and August would identify the trees and growing crops that they passed; on the way home, they quizzed the children to test what they had learned. In the large yard that enclosed their house facing Back Street and the store facing Front (now Main) Street, Lucy, the farmer's daughter, had a kitchen garden that included not only vegetables but also berry bushes and fruit trees. She also cultivated herb and perennial gardens. The children helped tend these, Eva bearing particular responsibility for the asparagus bed and strawberry patch. Her special love, however, was the trees. She set for herself the goal of climbing every tree in the yard, the elms excepted. On summer mornings, Lucy would hear the voice of her second child calling from among the green leaves, "Mama, find me!"

Eva also remembered winter Sunday afternoons in her childhood, when her father would hold her on his lap in the chair they called "our big chair" and read aloud to her. He preferred poetry, which he clipped from newspapers and magazines and pasted in scrapbooks, and as Eva grew, he included editorials, which he also enjoyed. He often read cartoons and humorous sayings to her. He himself had a shy, sly sense of humor that showed itself in conversation (he told the children, for example, that other cheese was fit only for mousetraps, but Wisconsin cheese was for men).

Sometimes August told Eva and her brothers stories of his boyhood in Pomerania—of running barefoot to the brook near his cottage to wash his dirty feet, then leaping home from one flagstone to the next to keep his feet clean; of carrying water to the workers in the field at the age of six or seven; of a trip on foot with his mother to a nearby village to visit relatives; of carrying grist to a windmill to be ground. His single relic of those days was a photograph of the thatch-roofed stone cottage where he had lived with his mother's family. He told his children stories of his early days in Wisconsin, when the family was so poor that they had only one kerosene lamp, a great luxury, which they used so sparingly that two quarts of oil lasted an entire winter. He had seen oranges in the stores, he told them, and had heard of their wonderful taste, so when he finally got a nickel, he went to buy one. Not yet speaking English, he could only point to what he wanted. So the storekeeper gave him the fruit he had chosen—a lemon.[22] As Eva later said many times, through his reading and storytelling, August stimulated his little daughter's imagination and prompted her lifelong love of language.

Sundays were the only days the family had together in their early years in Cumberland. Because of the large and constant demand of the lumber industry for harness, August's business grew rapidly. By the late 1880s, he employed five harness makers in his shop. Business was so good that he could help his half-brother, Chris Engelke, purchase his own shop in North Branch, Minnesota. He also set up several branch shops near Cumberland, which required him to be gone most of every week. Often, he spent only Saturday nights and Sundays in Cumberland, using most his time there to oversee the home business.[23]

Lucy was left alone to run the house, to care for the children, and to deal with the shop as best she could. She also earned extra money for the family with her skill as a seamstress, sewing not only for her own family but for others as well. According to those who knew her, she coped admirably in spite of a fragile constitution. One week away from her thirtieth birthday when she married, she must at times have wondered whether she would ever have a home and family of her own, especially if she compared herself with her older sister Mary, who married at nineteen. Lucy now had a growing family and gave herself to them as energetically as her husband was devoting himself to his business.

To help with the housework and the children, Lucy took in a series of young women in return for room and board. One of them, Lizzie Tyrrell, later remembered Mrs. Wolff as one of the best housekeepers and cooks she had ever met. "The house was spotlessly clean," Lizzie recalled, and Mrs. Wolff made "the most delicious bean soup in which buttered croutons floated." She remembered, too, little Freddie and Eva, who was still using a high chair. Lizzie presented the family with a photograph of herself with her hair arranged in long, beautiful curls. Eva later loved to look at it in the family album, and wore her own thick hair similarly curled when it was not plaited in long braids.

Lizzie left when a nephew of the Wolffs came from Germany to live with them and to learn the harness trade.[24] He was only one of many relatives who came to Cumberland to stay with the Wolffs in their spare bedroom off the kitchen. Two of August's half-brothers, Chris and Fred Engelke, joined the Wolff household while they learned the harness trade, and his unmarried half-sister, Amelia, came in the early 1890s to help Lucy with the household. Later, Lucy's youngest sister, Eva, moved to Cumberland for several years.

The Christmas season of 1892 imposed itself with special force on Eva's young mind. Freddie had recently turned seven, Eva was five, and Vern, three. Their mother, almost thirty-nine, had just given birth prematurely to a fourth child, hastily baptized Leo, after the reigning pope, and she and the new baby lay close to death. A nurse brought the perfectly formed infant for the children to see. They next saw him, ready for burial, in his small, white coffin. On Christmas Day, Eva caught sight of the parish priest, the doctor, and her father gathered at her mother's bedside. In the dining room, the little girl sat sobbing, unnoticed until the family's washerwoman found her and asked her what was wrong. "My mama is so sick," she answered, "I'm afraid she is going to die."

At some point during the crisis, Eva saw the priest look at her and her brothers and heard him tell the doctor: "We can't let this little woman die."[25] The child's perception of priestly authority as extending even over life and death was confirmed by subsequent events. Even though she was bedridden until the spring, Lucy recovered, to live past her ninety-fourth birthday. Her childbearing years, however, were over.

Another powerful childhood memory was of the forest fires that raged out of control every autumn, owing in part to the tinder-like pine slashings left in the woods after logging. A village six miles north of Cumberland was wiped out by fire in September 1894, the same day that an even larger fire destroyed the town of Hinckley, Minnesota, where Lucy's brother Ed was living. Two years later, when fire devastated the area just south of Cumberland, Lucy organized relief efforts, collecting and distributing clothing and food to survivors, an activity in which her daughter, then nine, would have taken part. On September 29, 1898, fire swept into Cumberland itself, destroying more than thirty homes and businesses. It came within fifty yards of the Wolff property.

Eva's childhood in the northern Wisconsin woods gave her a complex awareness of nature. She feared its devastating fires and storms, but she felt at home in nature, too. She knew most of the vegetation and wildlife of the region by name, and understood what could be used as food and, if need be, medicine. She also knew how to fish and to use a gun and liked to hunt with her father and brothers. At the same time, most likely through her father's love of literature, she developed the capacity to contemplate nature with a poet's eye and ear, to see the beauty in woods and wildflowers, and to listen for the music in the cries of orioles and deer.

In Cumberland, human nature, too, revealed itself to the young girl in all its complexity. How incongruous Eva's pious, orderly family must have seemed beside the boisterous woodsmen with whom they shared life in the small town. Living on Main Street, serving the public, the Wolffs came in daily contact with all segments of the community. Even if they retreated into their private world in the house behind the shop on rowdy Saturday nights, they could not effectively shield themselves or their children from routine drunkenness and violence. Eva grew up disliking town life; she longed to live on a farm as her mother had.[26]

While the children were still small, the family began taking biennial trips south to visit grandmothers. (By then, Lucy's father, Peter Arntz, and August's step-father, Christian Engelke, were dead.) On the first of these trips, the family stopped overnight at a hotel in Madison. There August and Lucy had a good laugh at the independence of their little daughter, then about three. Taken to the dining room before the others by a maid, Eva promptly ordered her favorite foods, chicken and strawberries, for breakfast.

This same trip supplied the daughter, years later, with her own good laugh at the innocence of her parents. August and Lucy decided to drop in at the governor's office, where they proudly introduced themselves to the governor and received in return a guided tour of the capitol building from him while Vern, a baby at the time, took a nap on the couch in his office.

Eva's paternal grandmother still wove her own linen from flax that she had grown and spun into thread; she also turned into rugs the big balls of rag that the Wolff children helped their parents tear and sew into strips on winter evenings at home. Eva regarded the giant loom with fascination and spent hours watching her grandmother work. At the Arntz farm, their young uncles, who kept the farm going, gave the children rides on the big work horses.

On one of their last visits to her old home, Lucy took her daughter, about twelve then, to all the places she had loved at Eva's age. Together, they climbed to the highest bluff above the Lemonweir River, where they found a single pink moccasin flower growing from the rock. As mother and daughter returned home, they stopped wordlessly for one last look at the lovely late afternoon light; a whippoorwill's call broke the silence. For Eva, that time was "the most complete" she ever shared with her mother.[27]

As Eva came to realize, her mother's characteristic economy and efficiency extended beyond material things to her emotions and to her relationships. Lucy parsimoniously measured out praise and rarely spoke the tenderness she felt. As on that late summer afternoon walk with her daughter, others had to interpret Lucy's silence by attending to her actions. However, her harsher judgments could be swift and spoken in no uncertain terms. The children called their mother, not altogether fondly, "our little dictator," and in retrospect, Eva referred to her as "severe" and "exacting," recalling that her mother's response to her children's achievements was invariably something like "And what should I expect?" or "You should have done better."[28] Consequently, as she grew up, Eva pressed for perfection, convinced that she had never done well enough, no matter how others might praise her. But she also learned to accept criticism patiently, without holding a grudge.

Eva developed her mother's eye for detail, which made Lucy such a splendid housekeeper and hard taskmaster, and with it the critical acuity it generated. As Lucy said about herself, she expected value for money spent;[29] her daughter did likewise. Eva admired and sought to imitate her mother's "pluck," as she called it, and a certain superiority she identified as "gentility,"[30] in spite of the lack of anything remotely aristocratic in her mother's background. Possibly, the disparity in education and breeding between her mother and her father and their respective families as well as between her mother and most others in the backwoods community in which Eva grew up gave her the notion that her mother was somehow a class above those around her. No doubt, her mother's sense of her own superiority added to such an impression.

Even as a little girl, Eva began to manifest refined tastes. Given a choice of gifts from a maternal uncle's store, she chose Spode ware, impressed both by its beauty and by its reputation for quality. She received "six of everything, plates big enough for bread and butter service and cups for demitasse."[31] The imaginary teas she served transported her to a world far beyond Cumberland, with its vulgar tastes and rough ways.

Eva also imitated her mother's religious devotion. On the eve of her first Communion, the child for the first time refused the glass of beer with which her German family, children included, customarily ended the day. When her father asked her the reason for such uncharacteristic asceticism and she stumbled for an answer, her mother urged,

"Let her alone, if she wants to do this." The next morning, Eva asked her mother to braid her long chestnut hair so that she might avoid any vanity on this day, which she regarded as the most important of her life so far.[32]

From her father, Eva learned a different type of devotion. When his young daughter objected to feeding a vagrant who had come to the door, on the grounds that he ought to be working, August invited him into the house, sat him at the head of the table, and served him first.

Growing up, Eva Wolff absorbed her parents' complementary and sometimes contradictory qualities: her father's light touch and capacity for play along with his humble, childlike charm and sweet gentleness; and her mother's shrewd intelligence, steely determination, and profound reserve.

2

I Go to School

I seek a teacher and a rule . . .

—Sr. Madeleva, "I Go to School"

Eva was prepared for the sacrament of Holy Communion, which she received with tightly braided hair, by Father Stephen Leinfelder. He had studied in Rome before being sent to the Wisconsin missions, and his facility with languages particularly impressed the child, who grew up understanding German but unable to speak it fluently. Not only did he say the mass in Latin but he also read the Epistle and Gospel and made announcements to his parishioners in English, French, German, and Italian. His European education served him well as he ministered to his congregation of immigrant families.

Because Cumberland shared its priest with numerous other villages, formal religious instruction was infrequent and, at best, minimal. Catechism classes for the children were held only occasionally.[1] Nevertheless, Father Leinfelder made a special effort with the first communicants. Making use of the only space available to him, he sat the children on the kneelers in the church and had them use the pews as desks. As he dictated, the children, most of them no older than seven, copied down the essentials of Eucharistic theology, which he told them to transcribe in ink at home and then memorize. As did each of the others, Eva dutifully recited what she had learned before the next dictation. This, and the instruction that preceded her confirmation at age eleven, was the only religious training she received as a child except for what her mother could provide, aided by textbooks ordered from Chicago.

Hungry for more, Eva tried to read copies of the *Homiletic Review*, which the priest had stored in the Wolffs' attic, but she could make nothing of them. Disgusted with herself, the eight-year-old child wondered whether she would ever be able to read anything without illustrations and dialogue.[2]

On the whole, Eva found her secular education more satisfying, even though it began badly. At six, when she started first grade at the only school in Cumberland, a small public school a block from home, she was more than ready to begin. According to her mother, Eva, like her brothers, had been "book and pencil crazy" from her earliest years.[3] However, she later remembered that first day of school in September 1893 as both frustrating and humiliating, if not without humor.

As she told the story later, the day began well enough, with a worried mother entrusting her frightened son to the care of the self-assured, although younger and smaller, Eva. She was no sooner assigned her seat in the classroom—second row, third seat from the back—than she tackled what was clearly the first assignment, printed on the board and ready for copying, without waiting for instructions. She could already read and understand it: "The cat is black." She took up her chalk in her left hand, which she naturally favored, and carefully, neatly, copied the sentence on her slate, starting from the right, with the "k," and moving to the left. But instead of the praise she anticipated, her teacher, Miss Williams, reversed the child's expectations: "Yes, but now, dear, suppose we take the pencil in the other hand and begin at the other side of the slate and the other end of the sentence."[4]

To the little girl, the experience must have been something akin to Alice's passage through the looking glass. It dawned on her that "[t]he the cat is still black, but I must say so with my right hand, traveling horizontally from left to right." Even in old age, the woman who had been Eva Wolff found her mind returning on sleepless nights to this first experience of learning. Her sense of the world had been subtly but essentially altered. The world itself might remain the same, but Eva's relationship to it had changed. The obvious, the natural, and the spontaneous were subtly undermined. Perspective became relative. An authority outside the self must be appeased if not internalized.

From the time she started to use a spoon, Eva's preference for her left hand had been obvious. The "feud," as she put it, between left and right was one she first associated with the dinner table. Her mother insisted she eat with her right hand. School settled the matter; she learned to write with her right hand, although from then on she became ambidextrous—in her words, "equally awkward with both hands."[5] She could sew with either hand, but could use a scissors only with her left. In any emergency, she reverted to the use of her left hand.

The child adjusted to a turned-around world. School became a source of stimulation, adventure, and delight for her. Years later, she remembered each of her teachers by name, so important had they been to her and so deeply had they impressed themselves on her young mind. She strove to imitate them, as in the case of her fourth-grade teacher, Miss Anderson, upon whose distinctive handwriting, "precise, tailored, vertical,"[6] the child modeled her own. With intense pleasure, she recalled the accoutrements of learning: the chalky slates of the earliest grades, the thick lead pencils of the next years, and, superseding them, the "Spencerian pens, ink, and small inkwells and glossy paper"[7] of the later grades. Each classroom had its own shelf of books; Eva chose as her first withdrawals *Dolly Dimple Fly Away* and, perhaps remembering her father's acquaintance with young Johnny Ringling, *Toby Tyler or Ten Weeks with a Circus*.

For Eva, school itself was in many ways the other side of the looking glass. The books and ideas she discovered there carried her beyond the rough-hewn lumber town where she spent the first eighteen years of her life. Later, from a distance, Eva liked to emphasize the rustic charm and quaintness of Cumberland, but as she grew, she must have experienced its limits at every turn. In her youth, Cumberland existed because of timber; essentially, it was a mill town, with four sawmills in operation at the time her parents settled there. In the early 1880s, the village had, in addition to its score of saloons, a few stores only, most of which traded in essential provisions and clothing; one hotel, Merchant's, and a boarding house or two; a blacksmith's shop and livery stable; and perhaps a dozen other small businesses, including after 1881 a newspaper office.

While Eva was growing up, drunkenness and violence in Cumberland were curbed thanks to a strong-armed town marshall, who quite literally beat the rowdiest of the lumberjacks into submission and limited the number of saloons on the island to five.[8] Still, life in Cumberland was by modern standards primitive. Even the main streets were unpaved and consequently impassable in inclement weather; a plank sidewalk, interrupted by steps when the street sloped, lined Front Street. In dry weather, heavy dust and in rain, tracked-in mud from the streets made housekeeping a perpetual chore. Not until 1897 were the streets lit by gas light. The next year, an electric power plant was built in Cumberland, finally making electric light available, and by 1900 telephone service with the outside world was established. The town had no sewer system until the 1920s.

August Wolff was instrumental in improving the small community. He spent fifteen years as a member of the city council and twice served as mayor of Cumberland, first in 1900 for a two-year period, and again from 1920 through 1922. During his years of public service, he actively worked to provide the city with a deep-well water supply, electric light, water, and sewer systems, and paved streets. Shortly after the turn of the century, and in large part during August Wolff's tenure as mayor, a spate of public building occurred in Cumberland, even though its days as a logging center were essentially over, and farming, in particular dairy farming, was fast becoming the chief industry of the area. In the first five years of the new century, a new high school went up, including a gymnasium, as did a public library, and even an opera house. August himself broke ground for a new brick building, which still stands, to house his store; he moved into it at the end of November 1902.

In spite of such changes, the island city was remote from what increasingly interested Eva—the world of ideas and culture introduced to her in the six-room, white frame schoolhouse she attended until, between her junior and senior years, the new high school was completed. The girl profited from the rigor and imagination that characterized American public education of the period, even in so isolated a place as Cumberland, where resources and facilities were limited. Both the curriculum she followed and the teachers she encountered, "schoolmarms" in the best sense of the word, lifted her out of her provincial surroundings.

Eva met perhaps the best of these teachers, one of the "great teachers" of her life, when in the fall of 1898, at eleven, she started the seventh grade. Mrs. Kavanaugh was unusual in that, instead of remaining unmarried as did most teachers of the day, she was a widow with one child who returned to teaching after her husband's death. At a crucial stage in Eva's development, this woman took charge of her education for two years, introducing her and her thirty or so classmates to a variety of subjects above and beyond the prescribed course of studies: among them, stocks and bonds, algebra, physiology, Shakespeare, Latin, mythology, and etymology.[9]

Mrs. Kavanaugh practiced the most advanced pedagogical theory of her day, allowing her pupils to learn by doing. She brought the town doctor into the classroom to demonstrate human anatomy with the aid of a human skeleton and with a new X ray machine, which the doctor turned on the children themselves; she also imported the village butcher to exhibit calves' brains, hearts, and lungs. She herself procured and taught geography from the best relief maps available, impressing upon her students the global awareness they would need as they crossed the threshold into the twentieth century, which she emphasized would be theirs to make and mold. Graduating from the grades, Eva "lived to learn, so learning to live richly."[10]

Because she skipped a grade, either the fifth or sixth, Eva was barely thirteen when she was graduated from the eighth grade. She may have been exempted from an entire year's work because of superior achievement, or the curriculum of the fifth and sixth grades may have been condensed into a single year of work because of a lack of teachers or facilities. In any case, she remembered herself as always the smallest and the youngest in her class.[11]

The summer before she entered high school, her father, the new mayor of Cumberland, chose his daughter to deliver from memory a thirteen-page speech at the town's official Fourth of July festivities. Looking perhaps ten instead of thirteen, the girl stood in a leafy bower erected for the occasion to deliver her declamation. Her high-pitched voice rang out clearly through the open air. She did not miss a word, or so she recalled over fifty years later.[12] In describing herself as a child, here as elsewhere, Madeleva stressed her smallness and her youthfulness, thereby implicitly emphasizing her vulnerability, albeit a vulnerability tempered by precociousness.

Possibly the protective, admiring attitude of the adult toward herself as a child reveals something of the unconscious perceptions of the child at the time. Eva's battle against insignificance began early. She would find a way to release the power that she recognized in herself and that her parents also saw and fostered. Against all likelihood, against all expectation, tiny Eva would make her mark. As she did that Independence Day, she would amaze everyone.

Typically, Madeleva describes herself as a new high school student as being too small for the big desks; for the first year, her feet did not reach the floor. She writes, "The boys found this amusing until we began to work on algebra and Latin together. After that, they stopped teasing the littlest girl in high school."[13] In 1901, at the start of her sophomore year, the enrollment in the Cumberland High School totaled fifty-eight pupils, of whom twenty-four were boys and thirty-four were girls. They were taught by a principal, who changed at least once during Eva's high school career, and two full-time teachers.

As had her brother Fred, two years ahead of her in school, Eva registered for the "Modern Classical Course," composed of college preparatory classes, instead of the more practically oriented terminal program. According to her high school transcript, she completed a surprisingly varied curriculum for so small a teaching staff. Her studies comprised four years of Latin (including the works of Caesar, Cicero, and Virgil); the equivalent of three years of English composition and literature; and two years each of German, mathematics (primarily algebra and geometry), history (including ancient, English, and

FIGURE 2.1

Eva Wolff at age sixteen.

Courtesy Saint Mary's College Archives.

American), and science (divided among physics, botany, and physical geography); as well as a single course in civics. In a system in which the lowest passing grade was seventy-five she consistently earned grades in the middle nineties, with her lowest mark an eighty-seven in advanced algebra and her highest, a ninety-seven both in ancient history and in solid geometry. During these years, the studies that challenged her the most were Latin and German.

Like most adolescents, Eva as a high school student was uncomfortable with ambiguity. Consequently, she found the rectitude of mathematics deeply satisfying and, given her growing sense of the uncertainties of life, consoling. She treasured so rich a store of right answers. However, her English classes failed to satisfy her, perhaps because of her teachers, who roused her indignation with their sarcasm. The entire class of students retaliated against one exceptionally offensive English teacher by refusing to look at his face while he taught, concentrating instead on his high-top shoes.[14]

Eva resisted the approximations of literary composition and criticism. As she put it later, "I could not learn from my teachers exactly what was wrong with a composition, even a sentence. . . . The comment on my paper, 'Try to improve this sentence,' left me completely adrift."[15] Nevertheless, she continued to love to read, her nose always in a book. She read her way through most of the English classics, including a large dose of Sir Walter Scott.

In line with the expanded social role of schools advocated by educators at the end of the nineteenth century, Cumberland High School sponsored a number of extracurricular activities in which Eva participated. She particularly enjoyed the debate team and speech and drama contests, almost certainly taking part in the first league declamation contest held in nearby Rice Lake in 1901. Such contests were major events of the school year; most of the student body attended county and regional finals, in which Eva often competed.

Senior year, Eva won the female lead in the class play; but to her chagrin, she was cast opposite a leading man who was at the time carrying on a real-life romance with another girl. Still loving sports of all kinds, Eva played basketball according to boys' rules in the new gym. A photograph of the time shows her and a classmate outfitted in their thick woolen uniforms that included a sailor collar and cuffs, bloomers, and long, dark stockings. As a spectator, Eva avidly supported the high school football team, traveling with her classmates to away games. "The Island City Student," a monthly school newspaper, had been established in 1899, to record such events.

Eva had nothing but praise for her high school principals. They were responsible for most of the extracurricular activities of the school, in particular those connected with debate. During her high school years, Eva thrilled to the reenactment of the Lincoln-Douglas and

Webster-Haynes debates organized by one of her principals. In addition, the principal customarily opened each class day with a talk on some general educational topic, and during free periods often read to the assembled students from popular writers of the time. During the year she would spend in Cumberland after she finished high school, Eva participated in a form of continuing education when she met several afternoons a week with the last of her principals, J. H. Ames, and two of her classmates to read the works of Shakespeare.

Eva was graduated from high school on June 8, 1904, just a few weeks after she turned seventeen. As part of the commencement ceremony, each of the eight graduates recited an essay, written and memorized for the occasion. Eva's was titled "German Ballads and Folk Songs" and included her first attempt at poetry, a translation of some of Goethe's verse. She then received her diploma, and as she wrote

FIGURE 2.2

The Wolff Family. Front row: Lucy Arntz Wolff and Eva.
Back row: Vern, August, and Fred.

Courtesy Saint Mary's College Archives.

later, "The school year was over. . . . Our parents had never promised us money. They had always promised us an education. I had some now. I was ready for more."[16]

But more education for Eva would require money, of which the Wolffs had little extra in 1904. Lucy often told her children that their father "pulled wax threads" for all they had.[17] Certainly his harness business had thrived in Cumberland, but the need for a larger shop, recently completed, had consumed most of the family savings. Also, Eva at barely seventeen was considered too young to leave home for college. Fred was just finishing his first year in engineering at the University of Wisconsin. After his graduation from high school two years before, he had taken a year off from school to work as a clerk in Cumberland. Now Eva would do the same.

Eva probably clerked in her father's shop when he needed help. Because of her mother's continuing poor health, Eva also did most of the shopping, meal planning, and housekeeping for the family, which included her parents, her fifteen-year-old brother Vern, and herself; Fred returned to the University for his sophomore year. The one chore she detested was the laundry, which she eventually turned over to a girl her father hired to help her.[18] She enjoyed the rest of the work, even though her own health was not robust. She suffered from severe headaches, which had plagued her since childhood, and experienced occasional attacks of insomnia and fatigue.

That year, Eva and her friends found excitement in the motorboats and automobiles that had lately made their appearance in Cumberland. She "did more than a fair share of riding in both."[19] Lucy did not approve. She guarded her young daughter jealously and tormented her with restrictions, which Eva, as strong-willed as her mother, defied.[20]

Chafed by her mother's demands, Eva was doubly eager to leave home for Madison in the fall. The University of Wisconsin promised not only more of the learning for which she longed but also more of the independence she craved.

3

Away from Home

This country, sweet Sire, whither thou has sent me
Is passing lovely and fair to see;
It should, in truth, if aught could, content me
Away from home and apart from Thee.

—Sr. Madeleva, "A Young Girl Writeth to Her Father"

No less than Eva Wolff's own determination and talent, her parents' selflessness and broad-mindedness brought her to Madison that fall. Eva had the advantage of having been born to a woman who had gone off on her own to attend high school, who held a job outside the home for a decade before she married, and who knew what it was to long for wider horizons. She also had a father who, thanks to his stay in Madison thirty years before, deeply respected the University of Wisconsin and willingly sent his children there for the education he himself never had, though he certainly wished for it.

The Wolffs counted on their older son to watch out for their only daughter. Fred's presence must have made the decision to allow Eva to continue her education so far from Cumberland easier, even though the parting was painful. Many years later, a former neighbor recalled how sad Eva's family was when she left home—as though she were an only child.[1] Her departure stands as something of a small miracle given her mother's uncertain health and the financial strain on the family at the time, together with the prevailing attitude toward the education of women as at best superfluous and at worst threatening to a woman's primary role of wife and mother.

Public opinion of the time regarded coeducation as a dubious, even dangerous, experiment both in high schools and in colleges, but particularly the latter. In an article published in *Munsey's Magazine* in March 1906, David Starr Jordan, then president of Stanford University, felt called upon to defend coeducation against the charge that it injured educational standards. He dismissed the widespread fear "that the admission of women to the university would vitiate the masculinity of its standards, that neatness of technique would impair boldness of conception, and delicacy of taste replace soundness of results," and concluded: "It is thorough training, not separate training, which is indicated as the need of the times."[2] In spite of such opinion, the fact remained that most of the elite educational institutions of the period were single sex.

Women had first been admitted to the University of Wisconsin in 1866, twelve years after its first class was graduated. For the first few years, women received their education separately within the institution, but by the time Eva entered, few distinctions were made between male and female students, who numbered about one-quarter of the student body. Indeed, men and women frequently boarded in the same houses, sometimes sharing adjacent rooms. A Women's Self Government Association existed to "further in every way the unity of spirit of women in the university";[3] however, there was no established system by which the opinion of women students could be transmitted to the faculty.[4]

Like most of the other women students, Eva would be living in the city in a rented room. A rapidly expanding student body, now numbering more than three thousand, coupled with a disastrous fire that had destroyed a number of campus buildings, rendered the remaining facilities inadequate. Chadbourne Hall, the single dormitory for women, housed barely one-seventh of the female student population. Perhaps another seventh lived in sorority houses. The rest had to find their own accommodations wherever they could, without university help. Male students were also on their own. Fred returned to off-campus housing, which he shared with a group of male friends.

Under its new president, distinguished geologist and educator Charles Richard Van Hise, the university was beginning its ascent to national prominence as one of the premier state universities. Two years before Eva arrived, Van Hise had assumed the presidency of his alma mater, advocating the democratization of knowledge. He regarded the university as a continuation of the public secondary school system, and its reason for existence, to serve the needs of the people of the state. In addition to establishing a system of extension courses throughout Wisconsin to continue the education of farmers and their wives, the university under Van Hise was broadening its offerings, particularly in the areas of the sciences and agriculture.

When the Wolff children matriculated there, the university offered free and open admission to any resident who had completed with credit a high school curriculum, or who could pass an entrance examination. Consequently, Fred and Eva paid only ten dollars each a semester for fees. Their major expense was the cost of room and board, which at that time averaged about five dollars a week per person with a private family.

Compared with Cumberland, whose population was less than 2,000, Madison must have seemed a metropolis to eighteen-year-old Eva. The city was growing; in 1900 its population was close to 20,000, and by 1910, it would exceed 25,000. Eva had of course been through Madison before on trips south to visit relatives, but living in the capital offered an exciting array of intellectual, aesthetic, and social possibilities.

Built on a hilly isthmus between two lakes, Mendota and Monoma, Madison was beautiful, then as now. The capitol building sat in a park and crowned the summit of a hill in the heart of the city; broad, tree-shaded avenues radiated from it. State Street, lined with shops, ran directly west from the capitol to the university, a mile distant. University Hill rose one hundred feet above deep, clear-watered Lake Mendota; the campus covered a wooded tract that stretched for a mile along the lake's southern shore.

Eva registered for classes on September 25, 1905, intending to pursue a major in mathematics. In addition to the required math courses, she enrolled in rhetoric, medieval and modern history, French, and German courses. When she attended her algebra and trigonometry classes, she noted without undue concern that she and one or two others were the only women in the large lecture hall. Her entire education had been coeducational, and she felt confident of her ability to match wits with the best male.

In her rhetoric course, Eva at last learned to write well by writing three themes a week and analyzing them with the help of her professor. Her history course, of greatest interest to her, introduced her to medieval culture. She studied medieval art and architecture as well as the ideas and institutions of the period, focusing on religious institutions; she researched and wrote a term paper on the *Rule* of Saint Benedict. The course uncovered the historical roots of her Catholic faith and introduced her to its intellectual tradition. It was a heady experience.

For the first time, Eva had "books, the reasons and the leisure to use them."[5] She spent long hours in the university library, housed at the time at the foot of University Hill in the Wisconsin Historical Society Building. Her transcript of "A"s and "B"s, with the exception of a single "C" in algebra, reflected the energy she devoted to studying. Pursuing her high school interest in speech and drama, she joined the oratory club, and during her freshman year, entered the dramatic division of at least one declamation contest.

Perhaps the greatest pleasure of the year, however, came from the time Eva spent with her brother Fred. Ever since they were small children playing the same games, they had enjoyed each other's company and shared an easy intimacy. At home, when Eva suffered from her periodic migraines, Fred was always the one who massaged them away.[6] With alacrity, he undertook his charge to look after her and went out of his way to include her in his social life.

The looks of brother and sister contrasted strikingly. Fred stood five inches taller than Eva, who had grown to her full height of five feet four inches. His hair was light brown, on the verge of blond, whereas hers was dark with reddish highlights, and his face was as angular as hers was round and soft. He had inherited the square Arntz jaw, but his coloring and his big-boned frame were his father's. His sister had their mother's thick, glossy hair, her pale, clear skin, and her small bones.

Eva just missed great beauty. She knew the power of physical attractiveness without having to bear it as a burden. Her face was a perfect oval, her eyes large, blue-gray, and pleasantly wide-set, her nose well-shaped, and her mouth small with full lips—the "rose buds" much admired at the time. Others perceived her to be pretty, and she thought of herself as such,[7] although her teeth, which protruded slightly, flawed the regularity of her other features. In photographs she rarely parted her lips; Gioconda-like, she mastered the half-smile.

Eva's face and figure were very much in line with and modeled on the taste of the time. With her abundant hair, long neck, full bosom, and small waist, the Gibson Girl look suited her, as did the fancier, high-necked lace dresses, handmade by her mother, that she reserved for special occasions. She wore clothes well and loved them.[8]

Fred and Eva spent most of their leisure time together. With mutual friends, they often gathered at the apartment of a young couple, Frank and Clare Shroeder. Frank was a classmate of Fred, also an engineering student, who had married in his sophomore year. Clare became like an older sister to Eva while she was in Madison. Around the Shroeders' piano, with the help of a violin or two, the young people made music and danced. An older couple, the McCabes, opened their home to the group of friends once a month for dances. When the time of his Junior Prom arrived, Fred took his sister instead of a date.

Whatever the weather, Eva and Fred took long walks together, often to the university farm, where they befriended a deaf and dumb graduate student who took them on tours and allowed them to taste the cheeses made in the dairy. Both brother and sister enjoyed poking around used bookstores. They went to lectures in French and German and frequently attended concerts together. When Sarah Bernhardt came to Madison in a touring production of *Camille*, Eva, a thespian herself, wanted desperately to see her performance; she feared, however, that the play was censored by the church, and her conscience kept her away. The next day, she and Fred lined up to watch the "divine Sarah" drive through the university section of town.

During this year, both Eva and Fred bore witness to the efficacy of their mother's religious training. With their Catholic friends, many of whom were Latin American and Filipino, they formed a group who together attended mass and met with the Catholic chaplain for instructions in Catholic dogma. The young men collaborated with the priest to purchase a former fraternity house as a Catholic student center. It became the first Newman Club, the prototype of an organization that now ministers to the needs of Catholic students on most secular campuses.

The religious instruction Eva received, however, did not satisfy her. The attacks of mild depression that she first experienced in high school persisted through her year in Madison. She felt uncertain about her choices and vaguely dissatisfied with the direction her life was taking. Life was pleasant enough, school was interesting, she had friends and a family she cared about, and others seemed to find her attractive and good company—but something essential was missing. She felt incomplete, but powerless to remedy, or even to identify, the lack.

Late one night, in the spring of her freshman year, a strong wave of discontent washed over her as she sat on the side of her bed, brushing her long hair. She had just come home from a dance, where she had had a good time, and was getting ready for bed. Suddenly the thought struck her, "There must be more to life than just this." She seemed to be merely skimming along the surface of life, unable to break through to its depths; meaning eluded her. It occurred to her that if life had no more to offer, she ought to commit suicide.[9]

Dispirited, the young woman returned to Cumberland for the summer. There, she took up again with her high school friends, meeting to talk, dance, and motor by automobile and by boat. She and a group of her friends, both male and female, rented a houseboat for two weeks, sleeping little, spending the nights in conversation and the days in the sun so that she came home tanned and hungry for sleep. Time drifted by, and she with it.

One afternoon Eva stopped by the local drugstore, where she picked up a copy of *McClure's* magazine, a literary journal that combined fiction with essays of broad interest, and flipped through its pages. With a sense of portentousness, she noticed an advertisement for a liberal arts college for women, Saint Mary's College at Notre Dame, Indiana. She paid forty cents for the magazine, hurried home with it, and sat on the back porch reading and rereading the brief description with mounting excitement. "If this makes a difference in my life I shall always remember it," she told herself.[10]

At the time Eva knew nothing about the college, but soon after, when her mother mentioned her daughter's return to Madison in the fall, Eva found herself announcing that she intended to go instead to Saint Mary's. About to pin up her hair into a knot, Lucy in her amazement let her long hair fall about her shoulders. "What do you think your father will say?" she asked. "Oh, he will let me go," Eva answered.[11]

Perhaps it was the idea of a woman's boarding school, with its connotations of gentility and exclusiveness, that appealed to Eva, the daughter of "superior" Lucy and the granddaughter of Dina Arntz, whom even the most uncouth farmhand recognized as a lady. The connection of the college with a convent would have enhanced such appeal by lending it a European air. Or, quite possibly, Lucy's daughter responded to the religious nature of the institution, anticipating answers to questions her mother had taught her to ask: "What does God mean for me to do? What does God want of me?"[12] Whatever the reason or combination of reasons that led Eva to her precipitous decision, the idea of Saint Mary's stirred something in her, something beyond the surface she abhorred.

Eva wrote a long letter of application to the college, in which she self-consciously described herself as a modern young woman, independent and accustomed to an active social life, but nevertheless interested in transferring to Saint Mary's. As if to put her in her place, the letter of acceptance came addressed not to her but to her parents, written in an elegant handwriting that thrilled the entire family. August showed the letter to his customers. Lucy began to be excited at the thought of her daughter attending a convent school.

The added cost of a private boarding school must have been a concern to the family. Whereas a year at the University of Wisconsin cost a total of perhaps $150, including fees, room and board, books, and transportation, the annual cost of a Saint Mary's education would be more than three times as much. To make it possible, Fred volunteered to drop out of school for a year;[13] he found a job as an engineer with the Chicago, Milwaukee, and Saint Louis Railway. It was settled. Eva would transfer to Saint Mary's in September.

4

Finding Peace

Never has human love held me in tranquil thrall,
For not to human love does peace belong.

—Sr. Madeleva, "As One Finding Peace"

Beyond the stone gateway to Saint Mary's, a wide avenue shaded by overarching maples and sycamores spanned the quarter mile from the highway to the nearest building. Late in the afternoon of September 8, 1906, Eva Wolff drove up the avenue in a horse-drawn cab. Woods and fields lay to her right; on her left, far below, flowed the Saint Joseph River. Just ahead was Collegiate Hall,[1] newly built in modified Elizabethan style of stone and cream-colored brick, where she would live and attend class. Beyond that, to the south and west, lay the Church of Loretto, the buildings that housed the academy, both secondary and elementary (or "minim") grades, and the convent of the Sisters of the Holy Cross. Eva immediately liked what she saw. As she never had in Madison—or Cumberland, for that matter—she felt she had at last found the place where she belonged.[2]

Two days after Eva's arrival, the semester began. To her consternation, she was placed in freshman English with the promise of advancement to the sophomore course if her work warranted. She protested, to no avail. However, she feared that her Latin class would be too difficult for her and transferred into a class on water colors, a decision she later regretted.[3] She continued her study of French and German and enrolled in logic, chemistry, piano, and Christian doctrine. Her plan to major in mathematics she put aside for the time being.

The following Sunday, along with the rest of the student body, Eva took part in the first of many Saint Mary's religious ceremonies in which she would participate, a sung high mass that at once celebrated the opening of the academic year and honored the feast of Our Lady of Dolors, the titular feast of the Sisters of the Holy Cross. Any young woman from mission country would have been overawed by such a mass—an exotic liturgy offered by the bishop of Dacca, Bengal, and measured with music, perfumed with incense, lit with scores of candles, and colored by vibrant vestments. Gathered in the cavernous church would have been members of the community of nuns then living at Saint Mary's, numbering in the hundreds, and as many as two hundred and fifty students in all branches of the school, ages five through twenty-two.

In spite of an immediate predilection for her new surroundings, adjustment to life in a convent school was not easy for Eva. As she had warned the directress in her letter of application, she was used to being on her own. In Madison, she had come and gone as she pleased, accountable to no one except her brother Fred. At home, she was usually able to get her own way when it mattered to her, even with her demanding mother. Now, she suffered under a stringent discipline that was a modified form of the convent rules and customs.

At Saint Mary's Eva's every move was monitored. She could not leave campus unless accompanied by a chaperon. She could not receive visitors unless they were members of her immediate family, and then only on Wednesday afternoons between 1:30 and 4:30 P.M. Even her letter writing was confined to one hour a week, to those approved in advance by her parents. Excessive contact with home was discouraged. Apart from the summer months, the only vacation period was two weeks at Christmas. Students who chose to spend the holiday at Saint Mary's did so at no extra charge.

Unable to take many of the apparently arbitrary rules seriously, Eva proceeded to procure forbidden sweets (only fresh fruit was allowed in packages from home), to host surreptitious gatherings in her room, and to engage in unauthorized conversations during quiet hours. Used to cutting classes when she pleased, she soon decided to spend a day outdoors; presumably the fall weather was too fine to consider spending the day inside. When she was missed, the prefect of studies sent another student to find the truant and bring her to class. Eva responded, "Tell Sister Claudia that I am not going to class today." Later in her office Sister Claudia confronted the delinquent: "Why did you come here to school if you did not expect to keep the rules?" Eva's honest defense was that some of the rules were, in her opinion, foolish.[4] She soon earned a reputation as a scapegrace.

Also used to the easy association of the sexes at the University of Wisconsin, Eva regarded the restricted social life at Saint Mary's with ironic amusement, as the scrapbook she kept at the time suggests. On a page labeled "Men I Met While at College," she pasted a single photograph: of the white-bearded college gardener. Any excursion to Notre Dame required a good reason and, according to the rules, a chaperon. Approved social contact between the two student bodies was kept to a minimum. Even fancy dress balls at Saint Mary's were for women only; Eva's dance cards were filled with the names of her female friends.

At Saint Mary's, in an environment designed by women for women, Eva, who had grown up without sisters, discovered the pleasures of female society. She learned what it means to share with others one's unspoken, sometimes unrecognized preferences, often dismissed as inconsequential by the larger society of her day precisely because they were "feminine." At Saint Mary's, Eva's delight in clothes, for example, which might otherwise have been dismissed as frivolous or vain, assumed new importance as a form of self-expression and also self-definition. Like the rest of the students, she wore a simple uniform of a dark blue blouse and matching floor-length skirt for classes and a white blouse and black skirt for Sundays and special occasions, but she could express her individual taste in her party dresses and traveling clothes.

Through the influence of the young women she met, many of whom came from wealthy, cultured backgrounds, Eva began to refine her tastes. She discretely studied and imitated the taste, bearing, manners, speech, and laughter of the women she met. She no doubt observed the psychological power over others that comes from a well-cut coat or a knowledge of the intricacies of etiquette, and without seeming to, perhaps without realizing she was doing so, cultivated such control. She was aided by a knack for fitting in, whatever the circumstances, perhaps developed in those early years spent keeping up with her male playmates. She also had much to recommend her to her privileged peers: her good looks, her adaptability, her common sense elevated by a lively wit, and her talent for pleasing others when it mattered to her.

For friends Eva chose, and they chose her, some of the brightest, most talented women on campus, including young women both older and younger than herself. As a transfer student, she found herself mixed in academically and socially with both first-year students and those from the upper levels. The friends she made became "the dearest" of her life.[5] She filled her scrapbook with photographs of the group she referred to as "Dix and the bunch," identified in her mind with Dixie Stout from Denison, Texas. The group included among others Eva's lifelong friend Evarista Brady, from Pittsburgh,

FIGURE 4.1

"The Bunch." Eva is third from left.

Courtesy Saint Mary's College Archives.

Pennsylvania, several years younger than she. Evarista later married
a mutual friend from Notre Dame, Bill Cotter, who jokingly referred
to the two Evas and their friends as his "pinup gals," perhaps because of a snapshot of the group lined up like chorus girls, with the
long skirts of their uniforms raised risquely above their ankles. For
fun, they paddled canoes around newly excavated Lake Marian, had
picnics on the island in its center, played lawn tennis, and took walks
along the river.

       Two separate events in the fall of her first semester at Saint Mary's
profoundly affected Eva and combined to mark a turning point in
her life. Had one or the other not occurred, she might have ended
up a stylish career woman or the cultivated wife of a well-to-do
professional.

       The first of these happenings was the annual religious retreat
conducted late in October for the students, that year by a noted Dominican friar, Father Bertrand Conway, OP. During the days of the

retreat, all other activity stopped while the students attended a series of sermons focused on their spiritual lives. These talks would have addressed the questions about the purpose of life that had shadowed Eva's year in Madison, and they were undoubtedly delivered with mounting intensity by an accomplished speaker whose religious vocation was dedicated to preaching.

During the three or four days of the retreat, the young women kept almost complete silence, devoting themselves entirely to prayer and meditation on the topics of the talks. The purpose of the retreat was conversion from the world to God; the heady ambience of prayerful silence alone did much to promote such change. One of its most potent effects was to offer each young woman a taste of convent life at its most rarefied. For the extent of the retreat, each participant was drawn imaginatively into the atmosphere of the cloister, a world apart from the college even though their buildings and courtyards were contiguous. The identification of the students with the nuns was often strengthened and their empathy increased as a result of the retreats.

The effect on Eva was just what Father Conway and the nuns would have hoped. She wrote later, "To me it opened spiritual worlds of which I think I must have had some intuition, for which I know I had an immense and clamorous hunger."[6] Most exhilarating was her realization that religion could be more than emotion. Beyond the piety of her mother lay an intellectual tradition accessible to the mind. The frustrated desire of the eight-year-old Eva to comprehend the contents of *The Homiletic Review* renewed and redirected itself. She could, after all, use her mind to understand and worship God. Grown-up Eva began to regret her willfulness, her many blind choices, and above all, her lack of seriousness about what mattered most as she now saw it— the state of her soul. She envied those whose natural goodness and tractability suited them for the life of the convent. She herself felt unworthy, disqualified by her own misdoing.

The second decisive event was her meeting with Sister M. Rita Heffernan, CSC. By Thanksgiving, Eva had satisfied her teachers that her studies at the University of Wisconsin had in fact prepared her for sophomore classes at Saint Mary's. In spite of her at times capricious conduct, her name appeared on the honor roll at the end both of her second and of her third months at the college (although only occasionally after that, owing to low marks in deportment). After the holiday, she received permission to transfer into the sophomore English course, taught by Sister Rita.

For years Eva had harbored the adolescent fantasy of finding a mentor. Like many young women, she longed to meet a wise older person, full of experience, charm, and taste, who would see in her rare possibilities and transform the duckling into the swan. For some females, the fantasy centers on a man who will first fashion the young girl into a better self, then marry her. However, Eva harbored another form of the dream, longing to find, as she put it later, "a wonderful woman who would have a profound influence on my life."[7] The minute Sister Rita walked into the classroom that day in late November, Eva knew she had found the person she was looking for. This was the woman Eva wanted to become, someone in possession of beauty, intelligence, culture, and goodness.

When Eva met her, Sister Rita was forty-six. The nineteen-year-old Eva surmised that she and her teacher were about the same height and appraised the older woman as "dark-eyed, straight-featured, quiet-mannered."[8] Something of the dazzling beauty for which Sister Rita was noted in her youth remained—the fine bone structure, the brilliant eyes, the vivid coloring. Rumor among the students had it that several artists had requested permission to paint and photograph her, and that the portrait of the Blessed Mother on the medallion used by Ave Maria Press at the University of Notre Dame was modeled on Sister Rita. Whatever the truth of such whispers, Sister Rita avoided any appearance of vanity; according to others in the convent, "her reserve and elusiveness made even a snapshot the rarest of all treasures."[9]

Adding to Sister Rita's mystique in Eva's eyes was the information that she had just returned from a trip through Europe with another member of the order, Sister Irma Burns, and their good friend Elizabeth Jordan, the editor of *Harper's Bazaar*. Along with recent course work at Harvard University, Sister Rita's travels constituted an impressive, if improvised, graduate education. When Eva met her, Sister Rita was just beginning a series of lectures on her foreign travels. She later used these as a basis of a fictionalized account of her journey (published as *Schoolgirls Abroad*[10]). Eva discovered that this "quiet-mannered" woman was a published poet, and that among her friends, she numbered not only Miss Jordan but also many other writers and poets, including novelist Henry James, who had lectured at Saint Mary's the previous spring.

This paragon had been born Louise Heffernan in Albany, New York, on September 22, 1859. Her father, promoted to brigadier general for gallant conduct in the Civil War, moved the family to Salt Lake

City when Louise was fifteen. Both she and her sister attended the new academy which the Sisters of the Holy Cross had just opened there. Louise won the first school prizes for scholarship and good conduct. At seventeen, she entered the convent at Saint Mary's, the mother house of the American branch of the order.[11] When Eva met her, she taught English and sponsored the student literary magazine, *Chimes*. In a community that was blessed with many exceptional women, Sister Rita became a star.

As she had been doing since her arrival at Saint Mary's three months before, Eva called Sister Rita's attention to herself by resisting orders. Asked by her new teacher to write a lyric poem as a class assignment, Eva announced, "But I cannot write poetry." Sister Rita was unmoved. "And I don't know what to write about," she added. Sister Rita advised her that perhaps giving thought to the subject might solve that problem.[12] Harking back to her high school graduation essay, which had been devoted to poetry in German, Eva decided to translate another of Goethe's poems.

In spite of its inauspicious beginning, her literary career was launched. By the spring of her sophomore year at Saint Mary's, Eva was publishing both prose and poetry regularly in *Chimes*. The first piece she published, titled "Snap-shots," appeared in November 1906 under her initials, a thin disguise considering that she was the only E. W. in college. She mused: "If there is one place in which we may see ourselves as others see us it is in our Kodak books. . . . The world is, in a sense, a vast Kodak and we are all being constantly 'snapped' upon the minds of those with whom we come in contact. How many of us, I wonder, if we could look into some of those mental Kodak books, would recognize ourselves in the impression we have made there?"

Her themes on the Maha-Bharata and *King Lear* appeared in subsequent issues, along with an essay on "Listening and Culture," in which she argued that listening brings knowledge, and "upon the acquisition of knowledge follows culture, one of the special aims of college life." She advised her reader, "It is well to remember that culture really begins with listening."

Eva began to publish her poetry in *Chimes* at the end of her sophomore year; the first to appear was a religious poem on spring titled "From Death to Life." Many followed, and by the close of her junior year, her verse was winning prizes.[13] She later published in a national magazine the poem that she identified as the first she ever wrote, "A Song for a Man."[14]

You, man, have a home and a wife and a child; what song do
    you sing?
I have a mate on her nest with a little blue egg under each gray
    wing,
And for joy of this thing I sing.

Sing to my brooding bird-wife of the skies above her,
Sing of the birdlings now soon to awake 'neath the soft breast of
    her,
Sing at dawn, at the dusk that I love her, I love her!
A bird on the nest with a little blue egg under each gray wing
Is a simple thing;
For the heart of a woman, the soul of a child, O man, what
    rapturous song do you sing?

What began as an onerous duty, and then offered itself as a way
of emulating her "ideal woman," soon became for Eva an obsession.
Writing poetry absorbed and elated her. At night she lay awake, trans-
lating her experiences and perceptions of beauty into verse.[15] Although
many of her first poems were conventional and, by her own admission, full of platitudes, they showed talent and consequently roused
Sister Rita's interest. In the early poems that survive, an image now
and then stands out, as when in "From Death to Life" Eva speaks of
"winter's winding sheet"; but the promise of the earliest verse does
not lie in its fresh imagery but rather in the young poet's ability to
develop a theme over several stanzas and in her capacity to compose
a musical line. Rarely does rhythm or rhyme seem forced, even if both
are often predictable. The conversational tone that characterized her
later verse is already apparent in much of the early verse. Before the
year was out, Eva changed her major to English. Unknown to her,
Sister Rita was already predicting to others in the community that she
had found in Eva Wolff the person who would replace her.[16]

When summer came, Eva had ample evidence that thanks to
Saint Mary's and to Sister Rita the transformation she desired was
underway: she was becoming a "lady." Stopping at Madison on her
way home, her friends there noticed distinct differences in her manner
and style. Her hairdo, her grooming, and even her way of carrying
herself had altered, and for the better, they assured her. Eva was developing grace and style.

Such changes intimidated her Cumberland friends, who responded stiffly at first, holding themselves aloof. Her family too was

a bit taken aback by this elegant young creature who descended upon them, with her French newspapers from which she could read fluently and her arch insistence that Mama and Papa and Vern all converse with her in German at the dinner table.

The old Eva soon emerged; she was not a snob, although she did desire to improve herself. All affectation fell away as she roughed it for two weeks at a cottage on the lake, then traveled out to the Mesabi Range to stay a few weeks with Fred, who was working that summer as a mining engineer before his return to Madison in the fall. She fell back into her old, easy friendships with the Cumberland crowd. The only difference was that she now attended mass as often as she could, and contrary to the custom of the time, took Communion every time she went.

Eva's relationship with her family, and in particular with her father and brothers, remained as affectionate as ever. With the men in the family she continued to share a love of the outdoors. With them she was "one of the boys"; together, they camped, hiked, and hunted that summer as they always had. At the same time, she thought of her father as far from typically masculine. She often described him as "artistic" and identified him as the person in the family most sensitive to beauty.[17] He had been the first to teach her to love poetry, and by his example, he also taught her gentleness and humility, typically considered female virtues. August and his younger son, Vern, who resembled his father temperamentally, were meek, mild men—at times too much so in the opinion of strong-willed Lucy, Fred, and even Eva herself.[18]

When Eva wrote about her father later, she idealized him and their relationship, magnifying his virtues and making a blessing of his simplicity, which must have been starkly apparent to her that summer, after her experience at Saint Mary's. In actuality, his lack of formal education (his few surviving letters betray his rudimentary knowledge of spelling and grammar) and of polished manners (he ate in public from his knife)[19] must have embarrassed his daughter as they did his wife, especially now, when the young woman was trying hard to improve herself. But if she ever felt that her mother had married beneath her or that her father was in any way not good enough for her mother—or for herself—she never expressed anything other than love and admiration for him. Perhaps to ward off possible criticisms of him, loving him as she did, she began in later years to speak of him as "saintly"—always easier from a distance—thus exempting him from judgment according to worldly standards.

However, Eva was inordinately proud of the worldly accomplishments of her brothers, both of whom eventually earned degrees from the University of Wisconsin and became engineers. Her brothers in turn treated Eva with a mixture of camaraderie and courtliness. They recognized her as their equal, and in many ways their superior—a judgment with which her parents seemed to concur, given their allocation of family resources.

Back at Saint Mary's for her junior year, Eva found intense and increasing delight both in reading and in writing verse. She discovered the work of three contemporary poets, the premier Catholic poets of the time: Alice Meynell, Coventry Patmore, and Francis Thompson. Of the three, who had been close friends, two were converts; all were mystics. Beyond the veil of their poetry, religious mystery shimmered at its most alluring.

A young woman who lived across the hall from Eva regularly invited her over to read aloud from Patmore's poems by the light of pink candles reserved for the occasion. Privately, Eva read Sister Rita's poetry, which also spoke of divine love.

When Eva herself wrote, she frequently composed poems that paralleled the paradoxes of nature—death and birth, winter and spring—with the religious mysteries of the death and resurrection of Christ and their promise of new spiritual life. In "From Death to Life," she wrote:

> Spring comes, and with one magic touch
> Rolls back the stone of winter's powers;
> In notes of joy the robin sings
> The resurrection of the flowers.

Even the early poems that are not explicitly religious often address religious themes, such as the transitoriness of earthly life. Most are romantic in attitude, dwelling for example on the sweetness of sadness. One such poem, "A Spray of Mignonette," published in *Chimes* in the fall of 1907, speaks of "The sighs that were echoes of pleasure,/ The joys that were half of regret," and recalls the "fragrance" of "sorrows I would not forget."

Filled with longing, though for what she could not yet say, Eva found herself stealing down to Sister Rita's classroom in the evenings to ask for help, then turning back before she reached the door.[20] She began rising at 5:30 every morning to attend mass with the nuns and to receive Holy Communion. Always the extrovert who preferred to have a companion in whatever she did, she found a friend willing to accompany her in this act of devotion, in this case the youngest sister of a bishop. It no doubt added to the appeal of the mass that

Sister Rita would be there and that Eva would see her and be seen by her.

Eva's infatuation for her teacher complicated but ultimately fed into an older, deeper desire: to discover God's will and to do it. In "The Universal Call," published in *Chimes* in February 1908, she wrote:

> Whene'er the voice of Him we love and fear
> Shall summon us, in eagerness may we
> Obey the call.

Although in this poem she wrote explicitly of the death and resurrection of the body, she chose a metaphor that applied as well to the disposition of one's earthly life, the "call" or "vocation" that signified one's life work and deepest self.

Poetic and religious experience merged for the young woman and offered a way to satisfy her desire for something deeper. That desire had sent her first to mathematics, in search of fulfillment she had once identified as "certainty." Still unsatisfied, it had troubled her during her year in Madison. It brought her, at least in part, to Saint Mary's and drew her to Sister Rita and to the study and practice of literature, which she had formerly disdained. Now it led her in search of a more active spiritual life.

Unlike the speaker of one of Francis Thompson's poems, "The Hound of Heaven," who felt himself hunted "down the days and down the nights," Eva perceived herself to be God's pursuer, asking again and again, "What do you want of me?" and promising in advance to accomplish whatever it might be. All she wanted was a clear summons. Throughout that year she prayed daily for two things: the conversion of her father and knowledge of her vocation in life.

At twenty, Eva seems not to have been averse to marriage. Her parents' marriage was to all appearances a happy one, even if her mother and father were unequal in important ways, such as family background and education. This inequality surely elevated Eva's view of women by emphasizing their importance in the family, but it does not appear to have undermined her view of men and marriage. In fact, growing up, Eva enjoyed male companionship, and as an adult she continued to form strong bonds with men.

Later, Madeleva confessed to having been "popular with the boys"[21] when she was young and hinted that had she chosen to, she could have married. Her perfectionism no doubt would have made finding a suitable mate difficult. In any case, likely candidates in Cumberland were few, although she spoke of having "boy friends" there.[22] She was surrounded by eligible men in Madison and also at Saint Mary's. In spite of rules designed to keep the all-male population of the University of Notre Dame at a proper distance, many of Eva's classmates, like her friend Evarista Brady, managed to meet and later marry their male counterparts from across the road. As for Eva, it seems that during her student days, she knew and admired a number of men and they returned the favor, but she fell in love with none of them.

For whatever reason, Eva began to turn away from marriage as a possibility. Not that she necessarily rejected marriage in and of itself; like most young women of her generation, she no doubt knew and as a matter of course accepted the fact that a woman's choice of a profession almost certainly entailed celibacy, at least while she actively pursued her career. However, Eva was about to make a choice that would of its very nature exclude forever the possibility of a husband and children of her own. About that loss she probably felt a sense of regret; she liked and would continue to enjoy male companionship, and as she grew older she doted on children. Nevertheless, what she was looking for, human love alone could not satisfy.

5

An Unlikely Candidate

"God [does] not make sisters out of girls like me," Eva had thought after her first retreat.[1] Such an admission suggests that, like most of her contemporaries, prevailing notions of courtship and marriage colored Eva's image of religious life. As a suitor chose his prospective mate, God called those who would enter the religious life. The most one could do was to try, as Eva was trying, to draw God's attention to her readiness and willingness. To this extent, the religious vocation might be seen as analogous to the Catholic concept of 'grace,' by which one becomes open to faith itself—it is a gift from God, dependent on divine will, although the individual must freely choose to accept it. Eva expected that God, the Perfect Lover, chose only the best, of which Sister Rita was a prime example. Eva began to desire such a call, but felt herself unlikely to receive one.

On Memorial Day, 1908, flushed from the honor of reciting her prize-winning commemorative poem at the festivities held at the University of Notre Dame, Eva stopped by the classroom of one of her teachers, most likely Sister M. Eugenie De Orbesson, who taught her French. As they talked, Eva glanced out the north window of the classroom and saw a group of young nuns at recreation. "I wonder what I will be doing ten years from now?" she mused aloud.

"I suppose if you thought that you might be a sister you would be furious," the nun answered.

Astonished that the suggestion should come from someone who knew exactly what the reality meant, Eva stated emphatically that, on the contrary, she would be happy, very happy, but added, "I know that I could never be a nun."

Several days later, walking along the bank of the river, she and the nun continued their conversation. When Eva spoke of her desire to do anything God wanted of her, if only she could find out what it was, Sister said simply, "That is all that one needs for a religious vocation." In an instant, those words quelled Eva's doubts.[2] The little book on vocation that the nun gave her brought certainty. The choice was made: God's, hers. To Eva her will and God's had become indistinguishable.

When in a few weeks Eva met her family in Madison, where they had assembled for Fred's graduation from the University of Wisconsin, her mother sensed a change in her daughter in spite of her fashionable merry widow hat and smart outfit. She had spent the time on the train devouring a history of the foundation of the Sisters of the Holy Cross at Saint Mary's,[3] given to her on her departure by its author, Sister Rita.

Eva read that from humble beginnings in France in 1841, when four women joined the order founded seven years earlier by Abbé Basil Moreau, the Congregation of the Sisters of the Holy Cross had grown to nearly one thousand members in the United States alone. They ministered in academies, schools, hospitals, and orphan asylums across the country. Eva read the stirring stories of women such as feisty Mother Angela, founder of Saint Mary's, who early in 1861 led a team of Holy Cross nuns to nurse the Union wounded in the Civil War, and in the middle of the next decade trekked to Salt Lake City to found a hospital and a school there. Holy Cross sisters continued to care for the sick, educate the young, and mother the orphaned, living and working together in a concerted effort to do God's work.

Three hundred and more sisters had already finished their life's work and lay in the cemetery behind the convent at Saint Mary's. In the words of Sister Rita, the hope of the congregation lay in "placing before the young the noblest ideals for the building up of the perfect life."[4] The image of a society of vigorous, passionate women working together for the good of God and humankind must have been irresistibly attractive to the young woman who had once considered suicide the only rational alternative to a meaningless existence.

Eva was convinced that in convent life she would find what she desired; however, she did not tell her family of her intentions until after she received a letter of acceptance to the novitiate, sometime during that summer of 1908. They received the news badly. Fred was dismayed at her decision and disgruntled at not having been taken into his sister's confidence. Although Lucy swallowed her objections and piously accepted her daughter's decision, August was distraught. Not a Catholic, he saw no value in such a way of life. Looking for an explanation, he interpreted her decision as a failure on his part and asked her the harrowing question, "What have I done to you to make you want to leave home forever?"[5] Only her quiet younger brother, Vern, showed signs of understanding her determination.

Eva decided not to tell any of her friends that she was planning to enter the convent. She feared that she might be asked to leave and, if it came to that, she preferred to have them think she had dropped out of school. She surreptitiously began to collect the things she would need as part of her religious "trousseau," which included bed and table linens as well as underwear and stockings. She must also obtain outer garments of the prescribed style along with the plain white linen collars and long white veil that distinguished the dress of the first stage of the novitiate, or "postulancy." For grooming, she would need only a hair brush and a tooth brush. In addition, she was expected to contribute as much as her family could afford toward her upkeep in the novitiate, an expense that must have taxed August to the extreme, compounding his sense of deprivation.

With a secret awareness of the poignancy of each event, Eva spent her last summer in Cumberland. She turned down any invitation that seemed to her too festive or "ultrasocial," as she put it,[6] but she spent time at a lake cottage with her female friends. Her male friends wondered at her sudden inaccessibility. At the end of the summer, she put on her prettiest dress, a new ball gown of blue voile and taffeta that she had worn to Fred's senior ball in Madison, and with Vern as her escort, went to her last dance.[7] Shortly after, she left for Saint Mary's, where instead of returning to classes she was scheduled to enter the novitiate on September 14, the feast of the Holy Cross.

On the train, Eva wept most of the way to Chicago. Parting from her family had made her miserable. Her father had been grief stricken and Fred, full of reproaches. As she changed trains for South Bend, she mailed her father a hasty note, "Dear Papa, If you want me to I will come home. Sis."[8] Prudently, she did not telephone. By the time her father received the note, she was safely within the convent walls.

First, however, Eva had to undergo the unanticipated ordeal of sharing the two-hour train ride from Chicago to South Bend with many of her closest friends, on their way back to school. They assumed that she, too, was returning for her senior year. She felt suddenly awkward in their company, reluctant to join in their gossip but unwilling to announce publicly that she was on her way to the convent, not the college. Modesty and a sense of decorum kept her silent; her decision was too personal to discuss with anyone except her spiritual advisors and her closest kin.

In South Bend, Eva excused herself lamely when her friends invited her to ride with them from the train to campus; she could not tell them that she had to find a shoe store that sold the black, high-topped shoes she needed to complete her new wardrobe. With her

package in hand, she took a lonely cab ride to Saint Mary's, where she
directed the driver to Augusta Hall, which housed both the novitiate
and the convent, instead of to familiar Collegiate Hall.

There, Eva was welcomed by Mother Barbara Long. As mistress
of novices, Mother Barbara bore primary responsibility for initiating
aspirants into the religious life and assessing their suitability for it.
Over the coming months, before formal acceptance into the order as
a novice, Eva would test her decision. She would also be on trial.

Shortly after her arrival, Eva dressed herself in the simple habit
of the postulant, thus symbolizing her changed status. She who, in her
own words, had "lived for clothes"[9] had left her brightly colored party
dresses and gold jewelry behind in Cumberland; forty years later, her
mother still had them, carefully preserved, wondering what to do
with them.[10] From now on, Eva was to write, beads were the only
jewelry she wore.[11] As on the occasion of her first Communion years
before, she steeled her will and exerted her capacity for self-denial and
asceticism. The will of her superiors, she believed, would reveal God's
will for her.

According to the custom of the congregation, one of the first
conversations between the postulant and her novice mistress concerned
her responses to a questionnaire completed as part of the application
process. The new arrival was expected to discuss her reasons for entering religious life (which Eva had summed up on the questionnaire
as "the desire to serve God,"[12]) and confess any impediments such as
illegitimacy or chronic illness. If there were family or personal secrets
to be revealed, this was the time to tell them.[13]

The postulancy, which lasted only three months in Eva's case,
was a time both of separation and of initiation. She left behind her
family and friends and her old ways and habits in order to begin to
identify with an entirely new set. As aspirants to the religious life, Eva
and the other postulants along with the novices lived in a community
separate from the nuns who had taken final vows, but they kept the
convent schedule. Eva rose daily at five, attended mass shortly after,
and throughout her day, which ended each night at nine, engaged in
various short periods of prayer. In fact, the schedule she kept as a
postulant did not differ markedly from the schedule she had been
voluntarily keeping the year before when, as a student, she began
attending daily mass. In the convent, she did her share of manual
work, but she spent most of her time in classes, learning the rules and
pious exercises of religious life.

The *Rules* and the *Constitutions*—that is, the written laws and
customs of the congregation—stressed detachment and obedience,

virtues that Eva had always found difficult to practice, but toward the attainment of which she now bent her considerable will. Particularly daunting to the gregarious young woman must have been the rules that instructed her to "hold in horror particular friendships," to "shun all demonstrations of affection," and in all things to renounce her own will and judgment in favor of the rules and constitutions and the will of her superiors.

The detachment from her friends that Eva had practiced on the train ride from Chicago to South Bend had made her uncomfortable, but she as well as her superiors saw it as necessary if she were to center her life on God and achieve a tranquil spirit. Eva lived within one hundred yards of Collegiate Hall, but her path seldom crossed that of her college friends; if it did, she avoided mingling with them. As she and they realized, she now lived in a separate world.

Even Sister Rita kept her distance. Until Eva was a full-fledged member of the community and her adherence to its rules had become habitual, her relationships with others, even other nuns, must be limited and carefully monitored.

Although Eva feared and her family hoped that once she had tried convent life she would find herself unsuited for it, she persevered. On December 10, 1908, in a chapel decorated as for one of the feasts of the church, August and Lucy Wolff watched from a distance as their only daughter and seven other postulants gathered in the sanctuary of the church dressed in bridal array. Right Reverend Bishop Alerding spoke to them and the assembled congregation on the scope and influence of Catholic education, and exhorted the new novices to practice courage and perseverance.[14] The postulants withdrew into an adjoining room where they were stripped down to their underwear, shoes, and stockings, and dressed in the habit of the novice, similar to that of the professed nun except for the white veil that the novice wore during her first year. As part of this ceremony, Eva sacrificed her long chestnut hair, which for the first time in her life was cut short.

From the hands of the bishop, each new novice received a copy of the books that would guide her in her new life: the *Directory*, or prayer book; the *Rules*, by which she would live as a Sister of the Holy Cross; and the Little Office of the Blessed Virgin, a collection of prayers that she would recite daily. The bishop then pronounced her new name to the assembled congregation with the following words: "He who will be victorious, says our Saviour, shall receive of me a new name: behold a new one which I give you on His part, to enable you to overcome the devil, the world, and yourself."[15] When he came to Eva Wolff, he announced, "Hereafter, you will be called Sister Mary

Madeleva." As with the bride who takes the name of her bridegroom, Eva's new name signified that a transformation had occurred. What a later age might interpret as a denial of her identity she regarded as its revelation.

The new Sister Madeleva was pleased and honored by the name chosen for her by her superiors, which she heard for the first time that day. It represented "a combination of the names of the mother of God, Magdalen, the friend of Christ, and Eve, the mother of mankind"[16]— a spectrum of feminine experience. It also subsumed without obliterating her earlier identity, "Eva," which she had borne for the first twenty years of her life.

That day, the Magdalen ("Madeleine" in its French form) became Madeleva's special patron, and her feast day, July 22, became Madeleva's own. After the ceremony, August teased his daughter, calling her "Model-Eva."

Madeleva later described at length the transformation effected in her by the ceremony she had just undergone:

> Nun, Religious, Sister—whichever name you wish—is not merely a woman in a "cloke ful fetys" and "ful semelypynched ... wimple," nor even a woman upon whom the religious life has been superimposed, but a woman whose life has undergone a change more subtle and entirely spiritual than marriage but quite as real. . . . The forces by which this change is effected are two: the first, a mystical but most real relation between the soul and God; the second, the rules and customs and religious practices of the particular community in which the individual seeks to perfect that mystical relation. These determine almost entirely, apart from the personality of the individual, the manners, the deportment, the whole external aspect of the religious.[17]

Although the first year of the novitiate was customarily reserved entirely for religious training,[18] scarcely a month after Madeleva received her habit, she was asked by Mother Barbara Long, her novice mistress, to teach an English class in the academy. Surprised—she had not yet finished her last year of college—she promised to do her best. "You always do your best," Mother Barbara replied curtly. These few words of praise from the exacting and taciturn novice mistress deeply gratified the young novice, raised by her demanding mother to expect none. Fifty years later, Madeleva recalled those words with pleasure.[19] Implicitly, the assignment affirmed her superior's unspoken confidence in her intellectual ability and spiritual maturity. Before, the young

FIGURE 5.1

Madeleva as a Young Nun

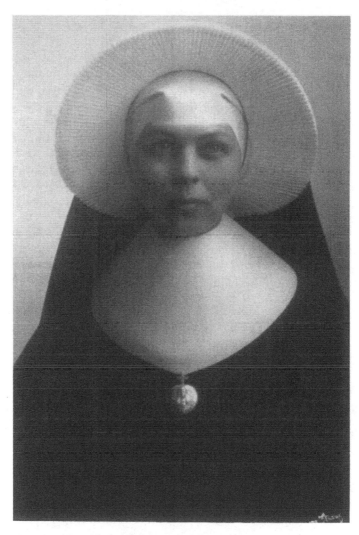

Courtesy Saint Mary's College Archives.

woman had wondered what work she was suited for, and had prepared herself to accept any assignment, including a life of sweeping floors and washing dishes. Teaching had not entered her mind. Now, her future was unfolding, in advance of her desire but very much to her liking.

The morning following her conversation with Mother Barbara, with no time to prepare herself—indeed, with textbooks she had never seen before—Madeleva found herself facing a class of high school students only a few years younger than she. The haste with which she became a teacher no doubt concerned her, if for no other reason than her perfectionist desire to do everything thoroughly and well. She also knew that the *Rules* of the Sisters of the Holy Cross stipulate that the first duty of the sister teacher is to know her subject and how to conduct her class. To this end, the *Customs and Reminders*, which regulate details of the common life of the convent, stresses the weight of responsibility the teacher bears and, in fact, sets aside prescribed hours for class preparation.[20] Eva also knew that her first duty was obedience. Unless her superior somehow exceeded her authority or failed in her own duty, the dedicated nun would take her command as an expression of God's will.

Simultaneously, Madeleva continued to immerse herself in the intense intellectual and spiritual initiation into religious life that characterized the first year of the novitiate. During this period, her first responsibility (one not always easily reconciled with her duties as a teacher) was, according to the *Rules*, to deepen her interior life, to "walk in God's holy presence, love prayer, [and] overcome [her]self"— in short, to learn to live the contemplative life.

During Madeleva's time in the novitiate, Mother Barbara as her novice mistress became the most important person in her life. A key figure in the convent community, the novice mistress guides and shapes its new members, acting as instructor, guardian, and disciplinarian. She teaches the young nuns to interpret the *Rules* by which they live a life of prayer; she examines them on their understanding of the spiritual life and the customs and constitutions of the community; she scrutinizes their actions; and she chastises and corrects them when they fail. According to the *Constitutions* that governed the Holy Cross order early in the twentieth century, the novice mistress had to be at least thirty-five years old and no fewer than ten years beyond final vows. One of the superiors of the congregation, she held an ex officio position on the chapter, its chief governing body, headed by the mother superior of the congregation.[21] The novice mistress assumed almost total responsibility for every aspect of the lives of her novices, heading the small community that they formed within but separate from the larger one.

When Madeleva became a novice, Mother Barbara was fifty-three years old and had been a member of the order for almost thirty-five years. Her Irish brogue betrayed her foreign birth. As Madeleva suggested in later references to the woman, Mother Barbara could be, in her opinion, dour, demanding, and overbearing, traits that a position which gave her almost absolute authority over the lives of her charges in no way mitigated. However, she seems to have recognized Madeleva's promise as a future leader of the congregation and to have given her encouragement and recognition.

During Madeleva's days in the novitiate, Mother Barbara included her in a small group devoted to a study of the Scriptures. Under her tutelage, Madeleva read the Bible for the first time; indeed, for the first time, the young woman held an English translation of the Bible in her hands, one sent her by her brother Fred as a Christmas gift. The poetry of the sacred text thrilled her. It became for her one of the most important influences on her own writing.[22]

Madeleva's congregation recognized and soon used her talent for writing. As part of her duties in the novitiate, Madeleva received instructions to compose poetry for various occasions. Mother Barbara, in particular, encouraged her to write. Some of her earliest poems were written to commemorate various church feast days, among them Christmas, Easter, and Pentecost.[23] Her poems, which had begun as class assignments, continued as acts of obedience, prompted by the exigency of the moment. As she described it later, the need to write was at this time external; she had no time—and, most likely, no desire, with much of her energy focused on community life—"to write for the sake of writing."[24]

In all likelihood, her superiors would have condemned such a desire, had it existed, not only as inappropriate but as dangerous in one dedicated to life in a religious community. The *Rules* implied that individual activity must be subordinated to the needs and goals of the community; consequently, artistic expression, inherently connected with self-expression, was particularly suspect. Nevertheless, Madeleva soon realized that her poetry fed her spiritual meditation, an activity she found essential to her development as a religious person, and grew from it in turn. In many of the early poems that remain, the poet meditates on nature as a way to contemplate the divine; thus, red tulips become a homely manifestation of Pentecostal flames, and the sun becomes a figure of the tabernacle and the moon of "the elevated host."[25] Her own experience convinced her that an individual talent such as writing could in fact enhance the spiritual development of the nun.

In the act of composition itself Madeleva discerned parallels to the rigors of religious life, seeing similarities in the austerity and discipline required by each. She was to say later, "I know of no discipline more merciless, more demanding than the writing of good verse—even if it doesn't reach the levels of great poetry."[26] In the elimination of the superfluous and the search for the essential, the act of writing mirrored her religious quest. From such abnegation, a certain purity, or cleanness of heart resulted, which she considered to be a prerequisite to inspiration of any kind.[27]

Unexpectedly, Madeleva found her new life not only compatible with but in fact conducive to creativity and artistic expression. As she liked to joke, her experience proved the wisdom of Wordsworth's assertion: "Nuns fret not at their convent's narrow room." Her cell was her "room with a view," from which the ardent young nun looked outward and inward, and in both directions saw infinite possibilities.

Because she had spent less than three months as a postulant, Madeleva remained in the novitiate longer than the usual year. In August 1910, the exchange of the black for the white veil signified her transition from sequestered novice to scholastic. In this interim between the novitiate and final vows, the nun traditionally receives training for her eventual ministry. In Madeleva's case, she had been teaching English in the academy for over a year before the scholasticate. To those classes were added English courses in the college, although the young nun was still completing course work for her baccalaureate degree. The reason for this precipitous assignment was the death of the teacher and mentor who had beckoned her into religious life, Sister Rita.

6

LEARNING HOLY INDIFFERENCE

Late in life, Madeleva wrote of Sister Rita, "We had planned hours and walks together when my novitiate would be over. . . . I never knew her in the intimacies of community life. She remains still my dream-lady."[1] Little more than fifty, Sister Rita died early on the morning of July 23, 1910, following her fourth surgery in as many weeks for intestinal cancer. On the day before her death, which was the feast of Mary Magdalen and Madeleva's feast as well, word came from the hospital that Sister Rita could not last through the night. She herself sent a message to her former pupil that "she had almost gone to God that day to pray for [her]." That Sister Rita's last full day of life should also have been the feast of her religious namesake comforted Madeleva, inclined to see the hand of Providence at work. She must have felt that her patronesses had joined forces to guide and protect her.

But the sense of loss lingered. Madeleva consoled herself with relics of her teacher. In the front of her copy of Sister Rita's *A Story of Fifty Years*, which Madeleva had read so avidly on her train ride to Madison two years earlier, she pasted one of the rare photographs of Sister Rita along with a poem her teacher had written on death. On the fly leaf, she copied out a passage that reminded her, "When one we love dies his place is forever vacant. . . . but enough of him remains to make it profanation to put another in his room." She inserted between the pages a small leaflet that contained, along with a brief biography of Sister Rita, a description of her funeral mass. With more than twenty priests in attendance, Father John Cavanaugh, CSC, the president of the University of Notre Dame, had presided at the requiem, which was sung by a Gregorian choir.[2]

Three professors of English from the University of Notre Dame, Reverends Leonard Carrico, Michael Quinlan, and Charles L. O'Donnell, were assigned to teach part-time at Saint Mary's in the fall of 1910 to replace Sister Rita. When Madeleva learned that she would join them as partial replacement for her former teacher, her sentiments must have resembled those expressed in an editorial in *The South Bend*

FIGURE 6.1

Rev. Charles L. O'Donnell, CSC

Courtesy Indiana Province Archives Center.

Tribune: "In the death of Sister Rita Saint Mary's loses a lovable, Christian woman whose place in the academy and in the world cannot be filled as she filled it."[3] Once again, Madeleva would "do her best" as, at age twenty-three, she began her career as a college teacher.

Over the next few years, Madeleva taught a range of courses at a variety of levels, from the introductory to the most advanced. To her literature classes were added others in philosophy, necessitated by the sudden death of another brilliant young nun, Sister M. Eleanore Sturgis, head of the philosophy department. Within a few years, Madeleva was also teaching Scripture; by then her teaching assignment was entirely in the college. She also oversaw various extracurricular activities of her students.

Never a slave to precedent, Madeleva quickly began adding texts to her syllabi that she herself loved and wanted to teach. Some of her first additions were from the works of Dante and John Henry Cardinal Newman. With what became her trademark as a teacher, she began each of her courses with an appeal to the "Word" by reading the opening of John's Gospel. "I love words because I love the Word," was her justification, one that she applied to writing poetry as well.[4]

During her first decade as a teacher, in the years between 1909 and 1919, Madeleva carried a heavy work load. Most of that time, she not only taught but also took classes, to complete her training as a novice and to finish requirements for first an undergraduate then a master's degree. In addition, she lived the life of a religious, with its daily rituals of prayer and reflection.

No matter how busy Madeleva was, and she was often busy to the point of exhaustion, she managed to find time to write poetry and essays, to read—even if it was only to skim a book—and to converse with others. She felt keenly the demands of having to lead a religious, professional, and personal life,[5] and at times expressed wistful envy of those who had chosen a contemplative order given entirely to solitary prayer and meditation.

Never a passionate lover of novels or fiction, Madeleva sought relaxation by reading each evening from the plays of Shakespeare, sometimes finishing a play a day. Doing so would have kept her in touch with a store of fond memories—of the time she had studied Shakespeare in Cumberland with her high school principal, during the year between high school and college; and of the Shakespeare class she had taken as a sophomore from Sister Rita.

For other recreation, Madeleva had available to her more possibilities than she could possibly choose but many of which she felt a desire or an obligation to participate in, among them not only the activities planned within the convent, which might include an occasional picnic or other outing, or the celebration of a special feast day, but also a lively schedule of intellectual and aesthetic events sponsored by the college. The members of convent, college, and university communities as well as the many visitors to both campuses offered abundant opportunity for stimulating human contact. Often, Madeleva felt grateful for the religious rule of silence that preserved a measure of solitude in her active life.[6]

During these years, Mother M. Pauline O'Neill was in the second decade of her thirty-six-year presidency of the college. Made directress of the academy in 1895, she oversaw its transition to a baccalaureate degree-granting institution within the first three years of her administration. Mother Pauline ran the college like a tiny kingdom: she personified it, and it reflected her ideals, values, and tastes. In rapt terms, a contemporary recorded her impression of this regal woman: "Tall and erect, rather slender, her beauty of figure and grace of carriage make her very distinguished-looking, while her well-shaped hazel eyes, clear and kindly, with the fine lines of nose and chin and shapely mouth, mark her as exceedingly good-looking. In her countenance one reads straightforward thinking, balanced judgment, and strength of character. Possibly one of the first things you would remark in her is her poise, a perfect blend of assurance and restraint—the mark of cultured ease."[7]

The college thrived under Mother Pauline's direction, which Madeleva studied closely. She listened to and read the older nun's frequent addresses to students, parents, and faculty, in which Mother Pauline traced convent education back to the days of Abbesses Hilda of Whitby and Hroswitha of Gandersheim. She took note of Mother Pauline's decision to send off her faculty, almost all of whom were sisters, to prestigious universities, both Catholic and secular, to further their educations. She was aware of Mother Pauline's own travels abroad and of her acquisition, arranged through one of the Holy Cross priests in Rome, of copies of the paintings of the Italian masters for the college. Madeleva would later exhibit the same kind of ingenuity and resourcefulness that enabled Mother Pauline, with a limited budget, regularly to supplement the curriculum of the college with ongoing lecture series and cultural programs.

Mother Pauline's most ambitious enterprise was to bring, in the fall of 1911, grand opera to Saint Mary's: *Il Trovatore*, sung by a stock company from Chicago. Over the years, she sustained a steady procession of lecturers, visiting professors, and performers, bringing to campus such personages as novelist Henry James, poets William Butler

Yeats and Joyce Kilmer, Secretary of War (and soon-to-be president of the United States) William Howard Taft, Mayor John F. ("Honey Fitz") Fitzgerald of Boston, and artist Eliza Allen Starr, who began the art department at the college.

Of most significance to the young teacher and writer Madeleva was journalist Katherine Conway, an editor of the *Boston Pilot* and the *Republic*, a newspaper owned by her friend "Honey Fitz," whose daughter Rose would marry young Joseph P. Kennedy in 1914. Miss Conway was a frequent visitor to campus before she accepted a position as visiting professor. She was a successful career woman at home in the competitive world of journalism and publishing and at the same time an ardent Catholic who sought temporary refuge in the sheltered environment of the college and nearby convent.

Miss Conway took up residence at Saint Mary's in the fall of 1911 to teach courses in church history, Scripture, and contemporary literature.[8] Madeleva was appointed girl Friday to the distinguished journalist. Over the five years that Miss Conway was in residence at the college, Madeleva had almost daily contact with her. In addition to her other duties in the college and the convent, the young nun ran errands for Miss Conway, read proof for her, commented on the editorials for various newspapers that she continued to write, and listened to the older woman's assessment of the mounting political tension in Europe. Madeleva called her association with Miss Conway a "rich apprenticeship."[9] Vicariously, she gave the young nun a glimpse of the world she had renounced and introduced her to its ways.

In their conversations, Miss Conway revealed details of her early life: how, as a young woman, she had left her home in Rochester, New York, for Boston to become a writer and to contribute as a laywoman to the intellectual life of the church. She reminisced about her friendship with writer Louise Imogene Guiney, whose work was well known at the time, with whom she had lived after her arrival in Boston.

Most likely it was Miss Conway who introduced the young nun to an essay by Miss Guiney, "La Sainte Indifferente," which in retrospect Madeleva credited with deeply influencing her philosophy of life and inspiring some of her best poetry.[10] It revealed to her the idea of holy indifference and supplied her with the paradoxical image of the "relaxed grasp," which she adopted as her motto. The saint of holy indifference, she read, "will never tighten his fingers on loaned opportunity; he is a gentleman, the hero of the habitually relaxed grasp."[11]

The ideal combined attributes and attitudes that Madeleva prized and struggled to attain, most significantly the acceptance and enjoyment of God's creation (made all the more precious by the acknowledgment that it is fleeting) together with an ultimate detachment from worldly things. Such magnanimity, at once worshipful and courteously self-effacing, combined holiness with good breeding. In the concept of the relaxed grasp, the qualities of saint and lady merged.

As Madeleva made her perpetual vows as a Holy Cross sister on August 15, 1914, her idea of the relaxed grasp surely helped her make sense of the sacrifices she was making willingly—of family ties, of her girlhood identity, of the possibility of marriage and children—and also of the sacrifices that had been required of her—of the friendship of Sister Rita, most of all. Valuing these things, she graciously chose to relinquish them because of faith in a more profound reality. She had come to believe that what others might regard as diminution would reveal her essential self.

Miss Guiney had supplied Madeleva with a description of the process: "Of all his store, unconsciously increased, he [the saint of holy indifference] can always part with sixteen-seventeenths, by way of concessions to his individuality, and think the subtraction so much concealing marble chipped from the heroic figure of himself."

During these years, Madeleva understood that God meant her "to live without props." As she put it, God was turning her natural independence into "an asset rather than an obstacle."[12] In her opinion, convent life furthered her independence and individuality by paring away her dependency on such unnecessary "props" as personal possessions, satisfactions, and diversions.

Madeleva expressed that individuality most obviously in the poems she wrote as a young nun. They remain as evidence of her interior life and depict a passionate relationship with God. By the time of her final profession, she had a growing sheaf of poems, many of which speak of Christ as a lover who meets her secretly and comes and goes swiftly and unpredictably. "Awakening" describes one such meeting, in which the speaker confronts God "spoiled of Divine disguise . . . with naught between . . . He whom my soul desires!" In the poem, Christ meets her in a "morning tryst," and for "One timeless breath the veil was drawn." In language and images evocative of those of mystical writers such as Teresa of Avila and John of the Cross, these poems express a love of God that is physical, intense, and absorbing. Because Madeleva consciously equated her poetry with prayer, the ecstatic quality of the early verse seems to have applied to her prayer life as well.

"After profession, the religious becomes a person of consequence," states one of the histories of the congregation.[13] With her vows, Madeleva's time of trial ended and she entered fully into the life of the community of which she was now a permanent member, with all its obligations and freedoms. Chief among the privileges granted to her was the opportunity to travel, including regular visits home. At least once every two years, she could if she wished return for several weeks to Cumberland to stay with her parents.

Traveling in the company of an older nun, Madeleva visited Cumberland in the summer of 1915 for the first time since she had entered the convent seven years earlier. She faced many changes. The house in which she had grown up had been sold. She and her companion stayed with her parents in their apartment above the harness store, where they had moved after all their children had left home. Fred was now newly married and living in Minnesota; and, following his graduation from the University of Wisconsin, Vern was working in Michigan. The family must have seemed sadly diminished with them gone.

Over the years, August and Lucy had reconciled themselves to their daughter's decision to become a nun. As she had seen for herself when they returned to Saint Mary's for her profession of final vows, her parents were "now happy with and for her."[14] But the reunion in Cumberland confirmed the profound differences between Eva Wolff and Sister Madeleva. Walking the streets of the little town, she felt as if for the first time the power of her changed identity. She never forgot the reactions of some of the townspeople to her habit, such as those of the devout Italian immigrants who showed their respect by kissing the hands of the two nuns, and the Chippewa Indians who brought them a tribute of wild berries.[15]

The following summer, Madeleva traveled to Lake George, to the summer retreat of the Sisters of Saint Joseph, most likely because she needed rest that she was unable to get at Saint Mary's. Travel acted on her like a tonic. She hiked up Prospect Mountain and boated on the lake. During her stay, she struck up a friendship with young Eddie Maginn, who ran the motor boat for the nuns; the two of them matched wits by composing poetry extemporaneously. Years later, they teased each other about the fun they had once had together. She reminded the man she still called "Eddie," who in the intervening years had become the bishop of Albany, "We were young once, were we not, Bishop?" He responded that if he caught a seminarian of his "matching sonnets with a beautiful young nun on any lake," he would certainly "fire" him without hesitation.[16]

That summer—the summer of 1916—Miss Conway left Saint Mary's to return to Boston. Before she went, she delivered a series of lectures on the war in Europe. She then turned over her courses to her apprentice Madeleva, now twenty-nine, who at the same time became head of the English department at the college.

During most of her years of teaching, Madeleva was also a student. Until 1912, she had continued to take undergraduate courses;[17] by 1916, at the request of Mother Pauline, she had begun work in a special master's program in English offered by the University of Notre Dame. The program consisted of summer courses both in pedagogy and in literary study and criticism taught on the Saint Mary's campus by Notre Dame professors to young Holy Cross sisters, of whom Madeleva was one. Although the University did not yet regularly admit women students, this experiment paved the way for the admission of female religious into regular summer sessions in 1918.

In courses she took between 1910 and 1918, the year in which she completed her master's degree in English, Madeleva came to know two men, Charles O'Donnell and Cornelius Hagerty, both priests, both only a few years older than she, who singled her out. At some risk, they opened themselves up to her in friendship, as she did to them. As Madeleva was well aware, the *Constitutions* of her order warned sisters to be careful in their relationships with priests; they must never visit them except in matters of necessity or business, and never alone. They should be "respectful to all priests, familiar with none." Nevertheless, a lively and mutually beneficial collaboration existed between the male and female members of the Holy Cross congregation located respectively at Notre Dame and Saint Mary's. Working closely together, sharing similar interests and occupations, individuals inevitably became not only colleagues but friends.

Both Fathers O'Donnell and Hagerty were as committed to their vows as Madeleva was to hers, and all three individuals respected the rules and cherished the ideals by which they had freely chosen to live. When they met, all were still in the first flush of religious life, the men newly ordained, and Madeleva still in the novitiate. Her relationship with each man proved long-lasting and complex, and it enriched— even though it sometimes complicated—the celibate lives involved.

Charles O'Donnell and Cornelius Hagerty had entered the Holy Cross seminary at Notre Dame within a day of each other in September 1899. "Con" Hagerty was then two months shy of his fourteenth birthday, and Charles O'Donnell, two months from turning fifteen. Both had been born and raised in Indiana, both were the offspring of Irish immigrants, and both became priests and completed doctoral degrees within a year of each other. Even in appearance, the two men

FIGURE 6.2

Rev. Cornelius Hagerty, CSC

Courtesy Indiana Province Archives Center.

shared similarities: both were of medium height, with athletic builds. Each in his own way was an eloquent speaker, Father Hagerty noted for the intensity and vehemence of his delivery, Father O'Donnell for the beauty of his voice and diction and the subtlety of his wit.

Temperamentally, the two men differed dramatically. Whereas Charles O'Donnell was a master of self-restraint and ironic under-statement, Con Hagerty's impatience could be consuming, his outspo-kenness bold to the point of rashness, and his opinions absolute. Charles O'Donnell was a scholar and a poet, cultured, with refined tastes, who in spite of a lively sense of humor tended to moodiness and depres-sion. Con Hagerty was a philosopher cast in the mold of Peter Abelard. His battles were external, his grievances legion, and his victories often Pyrrhic. Father O'Donnell vented his frustrations by penning limer-icks and doggerel. Father Hagerty spent his pent-up energy navigat-ing the rapid rivers of northern Indiana and southern Michigan. He was an avid outdoorsman who took chances and enjoyed narrow escapes.

Because both priests frequently said masses for the sisters in the convent chapel, Madeleva probably knew them first from a distance. In the fall of 1910, she became a colleague of Father O'Donnell when he began teaching one of Sister Rita's advanced English classes and also assumed responsibility for the literary magazine, *Chimes*. One summer, possibly as early as the summer of 1911,[18] he offered a cre-ative writing class to a number of novices, most of whom, like Madeleva, were completing degree requirements. He himself was a poet whose work had been published in a number of literary maga-zines. At the time he first taught Madeleva, he was writing and pub-lishing the poems that would be collected in *The Dead Musician and Other Poems*.[19]

One of Father O'Donnell's first assignments to his class of writ-ers was the composition of a sonnet. After class he called Madeleva aside. "If you can do this you must have written other verse," he said to her. "Let me see some."[20] She brought him what she had, a few lyrics, and he enthusiastically sent them off to the *Atlantic Monthly*, which was publishing at the time the work of poets such as Amy Lowell, Alice Meynell, Robert Frost, and Miss Conway's friend Louise Guiney. Madeleva was no doubt flattered by Father O'Donnell's high opinion of her poetry, even though nothing came of his first attempt to help her publish. He invited her to aim high in searching for an outlet for her verse and to desire for it the broadest possible audience.

Madeleva and Father O'Donnell began an exchange of manu-script poems that for a while also included Father O'Donnell's friend, poet Joyce Kilmer, whose *Trees and Other Poems* appeared in 1914. Prompted by their interest in her work, she found herself "isolating thoughts, husbanding moments walking to and from class, holding every fraction of quiet for milling these thoughts into lyric form."[21] What she called "the mental restlessness" of wanting to write began to pull at her. As part of her course work for the master's degree, she took a course on contemporary poetry. The study of the poetry of writers such as Elizabeth Barrett and Robert Browning and of Catholic poets such as Francis Thompson, on whom Father O'Donnell had written his Ph.D. dissertation, shaped her own desire to write.

With Father O'Donnell's encouragement and guidance, Madeleva began to write seriously. Instead of dreading the insomnia that had become chronic in the convent, she felt grateful for the extra time it gave her to write, without interruption, in the silence of the night. As early as 1912, she finished versions of many of the poems published more than ten years later in her first collection.[22] Eager for criticism, she sent these poems among others to another friend she shared with Father O'Donnell, English-born poet and essayist Theodore Maynard, with whom she had permission to correspond. (As a novice and even after her final vows, her correspondence was limited and each letter to or from her inspected by her superior.) In return, Maynard sent his poems to her for her comments.

Early in her career as a writer, then, Madeleva managed to establish a network of writers with whom to share her work. It enabled her to practice her art and develop it through mutual support and criticism. This network could have existed only with the tacit approval of her superiors, no doubt helped in their tolerance by Sister Rita's example. At this stage, most of her encouragement came from men, but she never forgot the debt she owed to Sister Rita, the woman who had sparked her initial interest in writing and who paved the way for community acceptance of nuns who not only wrote but also published. She also owed a debt of gratitude to Miss Conway, who showed her that women could take their writing talent as well as their faith into the marketplace without compromising either.

It took several years, but eventually, "A Song for a Man"—ironically, the first poem Madeleva ever wrote—was accepted by a literary journal with a national circulation, the *Bookman*, published in New York. Her poem appeared in the April 1919 issue under the initials S. M. M. Madeleva's poetry also appeared regularly, as had Sister Rita's, in *Ave Maria*, a Catholic magazine published at the University of Notre Dame.

When the United States joined the European war in 1917, Father O'Donnell volunteered as a chaplain and was sent first to France and then to Italy. He and her brother Vern, who also served in the army, brought the conflict to Madeleva's doorstep. She did what she could by contributing to the effort of the Saint Mary's community to raise $1,600 for an ambulance for Father O'Donnell's unit, the Second Illinois Infantry. She also sent him poems and letters and kept for him a small diary (which she titled "Desultory Diary") of her activities and thoughts.

In 1918, the community received word that Joyce Kilmer, their frequent visitor and lecturer, had been killed in action in France and buried there. Madeleva in particular mourned her friend and fellow poet. "Then we paused for a heart's long minute/ To grieve and pray," she wrote in "The Poet's House," which she dedicated to his memory. Father O'Donnell wrote her to say that he had visited and blessed the grave. He reflected on the omnipotence and otherworldliness of the priesthood, which he understood so much better now when he faced death daily. Madeleva wrote a gentle reply, in which she imagined a procession of Sister Death and every dying soldier in the Rainbow Division to whom he ministered.

Father O'Donnell and Madeleva wrote to each other as poets and in their letters indulged their taste for the lyrical and the romantic. From Rome, toward the end of the war, he sent her a leaf from a tree that shaded Shelley's grave and enclosed a violet from Keats's grave, both in the English cemetery there. Madeleva kept not only his letters to her, but also the envelopes in which they came. Years later, she gave specific instructions that they be preserved.[23]

Father Con Hagerty taught Madeleva philosophy in 1912, the year after his return to Notre Dame from the Catholic University in Washington, D.C., where he completed his doctorate. Like many who studied under him and thought of him as their "ideal teacher,"[24] she regarded him both then and later as "the best teacher of philosophy" she had ever had.[25] He found his young student not only brilliant but disturbingly attractive, as he confessed to her later, though he apparently kept his feelings to himself—and perhaps from himself—for several years.[26]

The young priest subdued his emotions, which he described as "irascible and concupiscible," on long and sometimes hazardous canoe trips that took him into the Great Lakes and far down the Mississippi River.[27] In 1914, he lost a college canoe lent to him by Mother Pauline because he braved the swollen Saint Joseph River just after a storm. Making his way through a flooded wood, he crashed into a tree and had to abandon the boat to make his way to dry land by moving from tree to tree. In 1916, when a young nun disappeared from the convent and was feared to have drowned, he searched for days by canoe until he found her body down river.[28] On warm summer nights, he liked to take a canoe out on the water by Saint Mary's and swim beside the empty boat.

In one of her letters to Father O'Donnell, Madeleva described with amusement an encounter with "hatless, breathless, peripatetic" Father Hagerty[29] as she crossed campus. But her mention of him, even in passing, is rare. Whereas Madeleva wrote and spoke often about Father O'Donnell and their friendship, about Father Hagerty, she was almost entirely silent. The relationship that began in his classroom and continued long afterward goes for the most part publicly unacknowledged, although she allowed clear evidence of it to remain. Among her private papers, she kept many of the letters that he wrote to her after they were separated, and several of hers to him survive.

Without consultation or warning, Madeleva received word in August 1919 that she was to be sent almost immediately to the western province, "on mission" in the language of the convent, to become principal of Sacred Heart Academy in Ogden, Utah. Not long after, Father Hagerty resigned his position at Saint Mary's. In his words, "I disagreed with the policy of sending a sister on the missions who had been specially prepared to teach at Saint Mary's."[30]

Although he did not identify the sister by name, he undoubtedly referred to Madeleva. In his opinion, she was being sent into exile, and he spoke out boldly against what he perceived to be an injustice. He knew full well that in the hierarchy of convent life, an appointment to Saint Mary's was the highest honor, reserved for the most gifted scholars and teachers. He also must have known that by speaking out, he would jeopardize his own career. Characteristically, he voiced his objection directly to Mother Pauline. Within a year he too had been sent "on mission," to Columbia University in Portland, Oregon.[31]

7

PATRINS

In Utah, Madeleva discovered one of the two great loves of her life, the mountains—the other was the sea. She had spent all of her life until now in an enveloping landscape of woods, lakes, and gently winding rivers. The Wasatch Mountains towered over Ogden, and for the first time she experienced the paradoxes of a landscape fraught with extremes—of crag and canyon, shadow and sun, barrenness and, where water flowed, bud and blossom.

Looking out the window soon after her arrival, Madeleva judged that she could run up one of the nearest peaks "in fifteen minutes after breakfast."[1] Her mountain climbing began that day; hours later she was still climbing, amazed that she had so misjudged size and distance. She took seriously Father Hagerty's advice that she should "walk and go out for birds and wild flowers" every day,[2] and soon discovered that with a deft twist of her overskirt, front and back, she could pin her habit about her waist, lace on high boots, and climb comfortably, even in her headdress.[3] Practicing the art of accommodation, she began a collection of walking sticks, which she cut, whittled, and waxed herself.

In many ways, Madeleva's adjustment to an entirely new environment was surprisingly quick and easy. She later called the three years she spent in Ogden "my happiest mission."[4] Not only was the scenery spectacular, but the convent food was excellent and the small religious community congenial. She got along well with Sister M. Celsus Hanley, a seasoned superior who had been at Sacred Heart for over twenty years when Madeleva arrived.

That fall, close to three hundred girls enrolled in the academy, of whom about half boarded. Most of the students were Mormons, sent to the convent school for the arts, in which it excelled, especially music, dance, and drama. Serving both as principal of the academy and as head of the English department as well as teaching courses in English and French, Madeleva continued her usual practice of trying to work, as she put it, "twenty-five hours out of twenty-four."[5]

Characteristically, Madeleva made time for friendship. Before long, she had gathered around her a variety of congenial young people with whom she shared a love of the arts: Gladys Rich, a recent alumna who was an accomplished musician and composer; young Phyllis McGinley, who even then was writing the witty verse that later won her a Pulitzer Prize; and Bernard de Voto, a college student at work on his first of many novels. She took an interest in their work and encouraged them as others had encouraged her.

Madeleva shared her enthusiasms with her new community. By the holiday season of her first year in Odgen, she was conducting a literary study group on the Christmas poems of Father O'Donnell. In turn, she was one by one discovering the natural wonders of the West, a discovery that even a decade and more would not exhaust: Yellowstone and the Tetons, Bryce Canyon, the Grand Canyon, and Zion. Ogden itself, although a major railroad center with its share of industry, lay at the juncture of two rivers and backed up against one of the most beautiful stretches of the Wasatch range. Mount Ben Lomond and Mount Ogden rose to the east; between them the Ogden River carved out its impressive canyon.

   This landscape inspired both Madeleva's prayers and poems; she found in it emblems of her deepest beliefs and consolation for an unsettled spirit. Early morning walks provoked the realization that even though the sun could be shining in the valley and on the Great Salt Lake miles away, it would not yet have risen above the peaks. Describing this phenomenon to a friend, she wrote: "The farther I walked up the mountain, the deeper I walked into the shadows, but at the same time the nearer I was getting to the sun."[6] She offered this image as comfort to one who, as she did then, felt overshadowed by difficulties and doubts, shut off from God's illuminating warmth.

The mountains too gave rise to the central images of some of her new poems, such as "A Snow-Capped Mountain in Summer" and "White Peace," which have as their respective and paradoxical themes sexual awakening and chaste love. Such poems reveal, perhaps more fully than she intended, the lay of her inner landscape.

Outer changes had brought interior ones, not always easy to interpret or accept. She wrote to Father Hagerty the spring after her move, "You are good to wish me back at Saint Mary's. I am still in that detached state of mind I told you of and most thankful for this year. I cannot quite find myself spiritually yet; I don't know whether it is because I am afraid to,—I think it is."[7]

The body, that vulnerable medium between outer and inner worlds, began to falter. At the close of the school year, Madeleva fell ill with what she later described as "nervous exhaustion."[8] During a visit to Wisconsin that summer, her poor health so alarmed her family that her brother Fred telegraphed the superior of the order to alert her to Madeleva's condition. Dismayed, Madeleva wrote to Mother Aquina, who was then superior general: "You know Fred can't bear to have the wind blow on me and is ready to upset a whole community if he thinks anything is wrong with me."[9] But in spite of her protests, she was far from well.

In fact, Madeleva's health had given her problems since an emergency appendectomy two years before, in the summer of 1918, just after she had completed her master's degree. Following surgery, peritonitis had set in, and she had spent seven weeks in bed. Since her arrival in Ogden, she had often pushed herself past exhaustion. Always prone to migraine headaches and to insomnia and fatigue, a few days of rest had usually restored her to good health. Now, she was not so resilient. She struggled on and off with illness through the school year of 1920 through 1921, at the close of which it was agreed that she would go to California for the summer, "to rest," as she tersely phrased it in a letter to Mother Aquina.[10] She would visit as the guest of a former superior general, Mother Perpetua, who had been a close friend of Sister Rita.

In fact, Madeleva did not rest. At Saint Agnes Convent in Los Angeles she taught three summer school classes, two in composition and one in Shakespeare, to compensate for the expenses of the trip. But she did benefit from a change of scene. For the first few weeks, she was a tourist, traveling with several sister companions to San Francisco (which "chilled and depressed her"), Berkeley (a "stimulus"), and Stanford ("an inspiration"). She stopped at San Rafael to visit her poet friend Theodore Maynard, who taught at the Dominican college there, then headed south, visiting mission churches along the way. She celebrated the Fourth of July at Carmel, where, as she put it, "I had the wonder of the Pacific Ocean at my feet."[11] An avid swimmer since her childhood on the lake in Cumberland, she now swam in the ocean for the first time,[12] and the experience thrilled her. From then on, she debated whether she liked the mountains or the ocean better.

Although Madeleva did not yet write about the ocean—she would, later—she did write other poems during that summer in California, among them "The Pepper Tree," fey, whimsical, and metrically sophisticated, like much of her verse. Her newest lyrics she added to a growing store of poetry, which she had been collecting for over ten years. As she said later, only half joking, "I have never been fortunate enough to break a leg or to have a long illness. Like Housman, who got inspiration while shaving, I have to pick my promptings at odd moments rather than by cultivating the muse."[13]

These days, however, the muse was visiting her with far greater frequency, though often the visits occurred after midnight or as she lay in a sickbed. Madeleva's delicate health, however debilitating in other ways, insured that she would have at least a modicum of time to devote to writing and reflection. She used such moments to good advantage and produced enough work to begin thinking about finding a publisher for a collection of her poetry.

During her stop at Berkeley, Madeleva had visited some classes and gathered information about the doctoral program in English. Over the previous year, she had been corresponding with Berkeley about the possibility of further graduate study. She now wrote to Mother Aquina that she could finish her Ph.D. in two years of full-time work, or in one year and several summers, if the order decided to send her to Berkeley. Or she would willingly return to Ogden in the fall, if that was to be her home in the coming year.

The decision was made that she should return to Ogden for another year. Madeleva seems not to have been discontent; in any case, she had doubts about Berkeley as the best choice for graduate study, fearing that it would be impossible for her to fulfill the year-long residency requirement. In a subsequent letter to Mother Aquina, she expressed those doubts, adding, "It would seem more sensible to come home and go to Notre Dame, and I would be very happy to do so, if you wish it."[14]

The ties to Saint Mary's and Notre Dame remained strong, and she would have welcomed the chance to return. She maintained her friendships with several of the sisters and continued her correspondence with Father O'Donnell. In addition she had started exchanging letters with Reverend Daniel Hudson, CSC, editor at Ave Maria Press, who had been a devoted friend of Sister Rita. Father Hagerty still returned to Notre Dame most summers to teach in summer school; in fact, because of her trip west, she had just missed him as he passed through Utah on his way from Oregon to Indiana.

Madeleva's health remained periodically poor during 1921 and 1922, but at least it did not deteriorate further. She wrote Mother Aquina on Palm Sunday, 1922, "I am as well as usual—more of a bear than a *Wolf* I think in that I have to go off and sleep round the clock occasionally." She was quick to add, however, that she had not missed an hour of class and in fact, had managed to get in a lot of extra work—had written a Saint Patrick's Day play, for example.[15] Soon after, Madeleva received word through Sister Celsus, her local superior, that she was to return to California to attend the summer session at Berkeley. There, she would take graduate courses in English.

Arrangements were made for Madeleva to stay with another order of nuns at the Convent of the Holy Names in Oakland, a twenty minute ride from the Berkeley campus. Ten sisters from the convent would also be attending summer classes, and Madeleva would be able to travel back and forth with them. She wrote Mother Aquina that the presence of the sisters would be, she hoped, "a very salutary leaven for the mass, 5500 strong. Quite a crowd for summer school, isn't it?" She added that she would try to make her education "a paying investment for the community."[16]

For the most part, the campus to which Madeleva commuted had been planned and built on its magnificent site on the Berkeley Hills overlooking San Francisco Bay within the previous twenty years. In the interim, it had become something of an academic watering place, attracting an array of prestigious visiting scholars from the East Coast. Although it was respected academically, it had not yet achieved the distinction it attained in the years following World War II. In the 1920s, the main emphasis of the faculty was on teaching, not on research.[17] Long-time president Benjamin Ide Wheeler had just retired, and the university was in a period of transition, with considerable unrest among faculty, who felt excluded from decision making.

With change in the air, faculty members met at teas, dinners, and sophisticated salons hosted by wealthy patrons of the arts who lived in mansions near the Berkeley campus. There they mingled with "poor poets, early Sierra clubbers, visiting countesses and pianists and Hollywood stars." According to a young faculty member of the time, Benjamin Harrison Lehman, who befriended Madeleva soon after she arrived, "Everybody came. It was never dull." The spirit of the place in those days Lehman summed up as "some ebullience, some effervescence on the surface, some creative charging underneath. There's something about the mountains, something about looking out from your windows and seeing Tamalpais, Diablo, the Coast ranges, the water, the sea climbing to Asia. There's something about what's downtown. And I think the earthquake and the fire had something to do with it. That released an enormous reconstructive energy."[18]

That first summer at Berkeley, Madeleva enrolled in two courses, the maximum allowed, one on Chaucer, taught by John Livingston Lowes, visiting for the summer from Harvard, and the other a seminar on nineteenth-century ideas, taught by Lehman, an associate professor who had recently completed his degree at Harvard, where he had

FIGURE 7.1

Benjamin H. Lehman

Reprinted courtesy of the Bancroft Library, University of California, Berkeley.

been a student of Lowes. Madeleva intended from the beginning
to study medieval literature; she had no thought of enrolling in a
nineteenth-century course—that was the one course in the schedule
she was sure she did not want—but she stumbled into it by accident
and stayed. The reason was in part the teacher, but also her own
competitive spirit and, and if the truth were known, a certain intellec-

tual vanity that most likely came from expecting to be underestimated. As a Catholic, a nun, and a woman, Madeleva anticipated that her intellectual worth would be doubted as a matter of course, especially at a place such as Berkeley—that many would regard her faith as superstition and her vocation as a sign of mental if not physical enslavement.

When Madeleva walked in, the classroom was crowded. Lehman appeared, a well-dressed, vigorous man of about her own age, and began eliminating, first auditors, then those with only bachelor's degrees, next those with master's who were not working for a Ph.D. Even though she did not yet know for certain whether she would pursue the doctorate, Madeleva found herself asserting that she would, unwilling to risk exclusion from such select company. She became one of fewer than a dozen students left in the seminar.[19]

Madeleva began Lehman's course gingerly, thinking herself on trial. The tone of class discussion was incisive and the attitude of her classmates preemptory. She felt herself among strangers, out of her element and doubtful of them and of herself. Her seminar paper, which had to be read to the class, caused her weeks of misery. Still under the influence of Father O'Donnell, she chose as her topic the prose of Francis Thompson, of whom as it turned out none of her classmates had heard; nor were they familiar with Coventry Patmore nor G. K. Chesterton, whose work she also considered in the essay. The essay might have been the disaster she feared, but Lehman's enthusiasm made converts of them all. His response transported her to delight: "This paper is practically ready for publication," he announced. "I could not have done it."[20]

In Lowes' class, Madeleva's experience was similar. The study she did of Chaucer's nuns, based on her experience of convent life, engaged her in a serious and prolonged controversy with her professor. He recognized the essay's merits, not least among them an unusually clear and vivid style, and thought the essay publishable, as it proved to be.[21] However, he cautioned her that Chaucer was not himself a nun and disagreed with her interpretation of the age of the prioress, which Madeleva contended was perhaps a decade past middle age, while he thought the text suggested she was still young. In spite of his reservations, he assured her that reading an essay at once so learned and charming was an uncommon pleasure and graciously assured her that her essay alone justified his trip across the country for the summer.[22]

Madeleva finished her courses with two "A"s—and enhanced self-esteem. She had managed to remain true to her interests and justify them to scholars who did not share her beliefs. Lehman took it upon himself to write her superior general: "Her work with us this summer was of a distinction so high and brilliant that we [he and Lowes] feel that both your order and our profession would be notably advanced by her continuing."[23]

Lehman's pleas apparently had some effect. Although she would not yet attend graduate school full-time, Madeleva's assignment was changed from Sacred Heart in Ogden to Holy Rosary Academy and Convent in Woodland, California, near Sacramento. Holy Rosary's location, three hours by train from Berkeley, would make access to the university easier. Nevertheless, during the regular school year, she was to teach high school English and French and act as principal of the academy. Mother Barbara, her former novice mistress, would be her superior in her new community.

Buoyed by renewed confidence in her work, Madeleva sent off several manuscripts to publishers in the fall of 1922: the essays written for class, including "The Prose of Francis Thompson," and also a collection of her poetry titled *Knights Errant*. The *Catholic World* accepted several of the essays, the first of which would appear in its January 1923 issue, and at the end of December 1922, she received word that Appleton-Century would like to publish *Knights Errant*. The general council of the congregation sent its approval and agreed to allow her to publish under her religious name, rather than anonymously or pseudonymously.

Mother Barbara, who had always supported Madeleva's writing, shared her pleasure. However, she seems to have taken it upon herself to chasten the younger woman, perhaps fearing that so much success would go to her head. Madeleva called her tenure at Holy Rosary under Mother Barbara "a severe tertianship."[24]

During her second summer session at Berkeley, Madeleva applied for admission to a seminar offered by another visiting professor, Henry Seidel Canby of Yale, on critical writing, submitting her recent publications and manuscripts as evidence of her writing ability. One of twelve selected, she and the other students set about reviewing the work of contemporary authors, including the poems of Eleanor Wylie and Edna St. Vincent Millay, then acted as an editorial board to select the contents of a hypothetical literary magazine from their own essays. Out of this seminar came Canby's idea for *The Saturday Review of Literature*. For the class, Madeleva submitted an essay on Millay, "Where Are You Going, My Pretty Maid?" eventually published in *Chaucer's Nuns and Other Essays* by Appleton.[25]

Madeleva wrote to Mother Aquina that Professor Canby and the class liked her essay, but added that she herself doubted its worth because "these present day writers are very thin picking and don't repay the time one spends on them." Madeleva found Canby "eminently a critic, not a creator, and hence not *inspiring*." She called him "a sure cure for effervescence."[26] His dry personality might not have appealed to her, but she admired him nonetheless. She found him unassuming, respectful of his students—she commented that he talked with them, not at them—and interested in them as individuals. She was impressed that he took the time to meet at length with each person in the seminar to discuss his or her aims and tastes. To her delight, he approved of what she called "Catholic" criticism, which approached works from a religious perspective. Still, she felt out of her element. As she told Mother Aquina, "One gets such a very lonely feeling, abroad in this world of mere knowledge (which it is for so many)."

When it first appeared that fall, *Knights Errant* surprised some who thought they knew Madeleva. Amazed by the intensity of the poems, Father Hagerty wrote to her, "I knew you were about as good as the rest of modern versifiers; but I had not taken you seriously as a poet. To be a real poet one must be a great lover. I did not think you were passionate enough to be of the family of Sappho."[27] Also betraying a note of surprise, John Livingston Lowes wrote from Harvard to congratulate her on the exquisite simplicity of the poetry,[28] and in a letter to Lehman compared her poems to those of seventeenth-century English poets George Herbert and Richard Crashaw.[29] Delighted that so eminent a critic agreed with his own judgment of her work, Lehman passed the comments on to Madeleva. Father O'Donnell, who had read most of the poems in manuscript, exclaimed over those he had not yet seen, calling "Young Moon" "matchless."[30]

Madeleva's first collection was worth taking seriously, even though many of the poems betrayed the influence of the poets she loved: Patmore, Meynell, Thompson, and Yeats. As its title suggests, *Knights Errant* is medieval in spirit, and in its spiritual approach to nature, unmistakably Franciscan. (Father O'Donnell sent her a relic from Assisi to celebrate the book's publication.) The poems depend for their meaning upon an earlier tradition: their imagery is often drawn from chivalry; their tone can be both courtly and courteous, their diction archaic, and their cadences, suggestive of the lays and ballads of the troubadours.

The collection is uneven, however, in part because it contains a large number of early poems, many of which had already been written by 1912; early versions show that Madeleva made few if any changes before including them in *Knights Errant*. Once she had finished a poem, she seems to have found further revision either difficult or distasteful, perhaps because she preferred to use the time to turn to something

new. Furthermore, she prided herself on publishing most of what she
wrote, once claiming that everything she had written since 1915 had
appeared in print,[31] implying that publication justified the time spent
and vindicated the quality of the work produced.

In spite of a pervasive air of affected refinement in the collection
as a whole, the medieval cast of *Knights Errant* supplied Madeleva
with an idiom suited to her own particular station and vision of life.
It enabled her to universalize and objectify her experience as a religious and as a woman by drawing on a tradition that belonged not
only to Catholicism but all Western culture. Other writers of the
period—for example, James Joyce, Ezra Pound, and H. D. (Hilda
Doolittle)—were using the classical tradition for a similar purpose,
and some, among them Yeats and D. H. Lawrence, were experiment-
ing with myth as a way of amplifying private experience.

At their best, Madeleva's first poems offer an intense, intimate—
and certainly, rare—glimpse of a female relationship with God. Indeed, a few go so far as to challenge the cultural view of women of
the time (although many others do not). The title poem, "Knights
Errant," radically recasts the meaning of the knightly encounter by
presenting it from the point of view of the rescued female, who sees
herself as "celestial plunder." Another, "You Sang in My Dream,"
explores the bitterness of spiritual dryness—the experience of emotional alienation from God—through the figure of an abandoned
woman. A distinctive female voice speaks in these and in many of the
other poems. Now and again, the female persona throws off her cus-
tomary submissiveness, as when she demands a divine audience for
herself—and her verse ("Read me, God!" she demands imperiously in
the dedicatory poem, "To My Favorite Author"); or when she invokes
divine authority for what she writes ("God wrote it;/ I quote it," she
says in "Red Tulips"); and when she initiates love talk with God,
demanding and receiving assurance (in "The Theme") that her "bold-
est thoughts" please him.

In response to her poetry, Father Hagerty congratulated Madeleva
on "not being afraid to love God," adding, "to be a poet it is necessary
first to have a mind, an intellect, to perceive spiritual reality; secondly,
it is necessary to have a will intensified by passion to love the vision
beheld; thirdly, it is necessary to have imagination to give beautiful
body to the purely spiritual idea."[32]

Father Hagerty and Madeleva had continued to stay in touch
during the four years since she left Saint Mary's. Not only had they
corresponded regularly, but he had visited her several times in Utah
on his trips between Portland and South Bend and, presumably, they

had met in South Bend during her periodic summer trips to the mother house. In the summer of 1923, he visited Madeleva at the convent at Woodland. He knew Mother Barbara from their prior contact at Saint Mary's, and she evidently tolerated the friendship between the priest and the nun, although she undoubtedly kept a close eye on it. Madeleva and Father Hagerty's public relationship centered on shared spiritual and intellectual interests, and the priest seems to have adopted the role of spiritual adviser as well as friend. In their letters, he characteristically assumed the stance of teacher and she of pupil.

All of Madeleva's mail passed through the hands of her superiors, and, even though it might not be read or read carefully, both she and Father Hagerty knew it could be. Nevertheless, they wrote frankly of their fondness and concern for each other, though always in the early letters in terms of Christian friendship, which Madeleva described as "a step leading up to that Mansion which is the end of [every] quest. But it must be true, without weakness, without sensuality."[33]

Father Hagerty agreed, but lamented, "We live in an age when people need to be taught the liberty and happiness of virginal love. So many think that Love is rather a wicked thing fit only for the reprobate."[34] His frequent enjoinders to Madeleva to love, and his protestations of love for her, have to be read in the context of his quite conscious attempt to integrate his sexuality into his love of God, and to move others to do the same. He hoped for a disciple in Madeleva, so that she would teach sisters through her poetry to "use their sexual gifts in their prayer with Christ."[35] Both believed it to be possible through their love for Christ to love each other, humanly but chastely.

But as the two friends discuss spiritual topics, the sexual energy between them crackles on the page. Madeleva writes to Father Hagerty, in response to something he has written, since lost, "Your letters would be strange—from anyone but you. All that you tell me—or much of it—I saw in your face years ago as I watched you day after day, in and out of class." Later in the same letter, she writes, "I know you as another precursor of my Lord, a friend of the Bridegroom. . . . You are always an 'alter-Christus' to me, who every morning makes divine my daily Bread, and is for one infinite moment identified with the God of my heart."[36] He writes to her, "I suspect that you have been 'naked with God' and were not ashamed," and encourages her to love God with "the wisdom of Athena, the passion of Venus, and the chastity of Diana. Most sisters," he continues, "fear to love lest they become unchaste. In loving God you must have all the passion of the wildest woman with none of her viciousness."[37]

From the fall of 1923 through the following summer, Madeleva juggled full-time teaching and what amounted to full-time study. Bi-weekly, she traveled the three hours each way to the Berkeley campus from Woodland, where she continued to teach and run the English department. In spite of the perennial problem of too much to do, her work continued to go well. Personally, however, she was increasingly miserable. Over her time at Holy Rosary, her relationship with Mother Barbara deteriorated, so that it became almost intolerable. In her correspondence with Mother Aquina, the superior of the congregation, Madeleva frankly discussed her difficulties. She had no doubt already spoken privately with her on one of the superior's biannual visits to the houses of the order. "[Mother Barbara] has undertaken to dominate me completely. [She] suffocates and flays alive"—her way, Madeleva commented sardonically, of "showing an interest in people."[38] In another letter to Mother Aquina, she wrote: "These two years have been desperately hard as I am sure you realize. . . . Altogether you have been one of the stablest and most reliable influences in my community life, although you may not be conscious of it."[39]

Weary and depressed, Madeleva wrote Father O'Donnell in general terms about her growing sense of darkness, and in response he comforted her gently, recounting his own sense of desolation at the recent death of his mother.[40] Probably because she had spoken to Father Hagerty about her problems on one of his visits, he wrote to defend Mother Barbara, praising what she had done to encourage intellectual life among the young nuns. In his role as teacher, he scolded Madeleva roundly: "Both of you are intelligent; it is a shame and a scandal that a mother and daughter in the supernatural order should not get along harmoniously." Then, betraying his characteristic combativeness, he advised her, "If Mother is tyrannical fight for your rights in open, honest warfare."[41]

Alienated from her local superior and, it would seem, from the community at Holy Rosary, Madeleva rejoiced when she received word from Mother Aquina that she would be given a semester's leave from her teaching duties to study full-time. To make commuting easier, she would live in San Francisco, at the Holy Cross convent connected with Saint Charles' School, and commute by ferry to Berkeley.

As the new semester began, Madeleva wrote a long, thankful letter to Mother Aquina in which she described her courses and her professors, and concluded, "I love the work and I love to work. I am feeling splendidly, I can eat with the appetite of a small boy and sleep like a baby."[42] She was, she said, studying Old English literature, philology, and French as well as auditing a second French course.

Madeleva had decided to write her dissertation on the medieval poem *Pearl* as a study in spiritual dryness. Her interpretation of the poem differed radically from that of other scholars, but as she told Mother Aquina, "All the professors here as well as the most eminent critic on the subject, who visited here some weeks ago, agree that I am right and all of them are wrong. It is good to have beat them at their own game with the simple weapons of Catholic love, the *Imitation of Christ*, the *Rule* of Saint Benedict, and the like."

This was one of her last letters to Mother Aquina, whose term as superior general ended in 1925. Word of Madeleva's growing reputation at Berkeley soon reached the mother house in Indiana. One of the Holy Cross sisters wrote that she had just spoken to Dean Lipman of the university and that "he spoke in the highest terms of Sister's work, and said the three best minds at Berkeley were women and two of them nuns, one of course Sister Madeleva. . . . Sister works so hard and is not strong. She certainly deserves a little encouragement."[43]

With or without encouragement, Madeleva read for and researched her dissertation while she continued taking classes. She set about reinterpreting *Pearl*, at the time generally regarded as an elegiac lament of a father for his dead infant daughter, as the spiritual autobiography of a religious, writing allegorically of his sense of separation from God. In the poem, she apparently recognized her own descent into darkness. Indeed, her own interior state at the time may very likely have influenced the way in which she read the poem and motivated her to choose it as her special topic. In retrospect, Madeleva admitted: "All my poems reflect my life and myself."[44] In fact, all of her writing reflects herself and her experience.

Reading the accounts written by other religious of the experience of spiritual dryness must have salved Madeleva's hurt spirit. She read, and quoted in her work, Saint Teresa's account of "the restlessness and discomfort with which it [spiritual dryness] begins, and the trouble it causes the soul while it lasts."[45] She read in the *Institutes* of Cassian of "the pangs of gnawing dejection" that "depress the mind" and will not allow it "to say its prayers with its usual gladness of heart, nor permit it to rely on the comfort of reading the sacred writings, nor suffer it to be quiet and gentle with the brethren; it makes it impatient and rough in all the duties of work and devotion."[46] Madeleva found solace in the *Revelations of Divine Love* of Julian of Norwich, written to comfort believers in such times; she often quoted from the book in her study and continued to return to it in later years.

Living closer to Berkeley and relieved for the time of her teaching responsibilities, Madeleva was able to see more of the friends she had made over the previous few years. Ben Lehman, her early mentor at Berkeley, continued to take a special interest in her and, as chairman of her dissertation committee, met with her often. Their conversations expanded to personal concerns: to their respective childhoods and families, his spent in an Idaho mining town as raw as Cumberland ever was; to his mother, born in Germany as her father had been; and eventually to their religious views, he a nonpracticing Jew who regarded her Catholicism with puzzled fascination.

Madeleva invited Lehman to Woodland and introduced him to her community; later, he often came to Saint Charles, where they met in the convent parlor. He introduced her to his young son, Hal, who according to his amused father was intrigued by her peculiar hat and by her eyes; and he arranged for her to meet his wife, Gladys Collins, a Hollywood screenwriter, who had been his student before he returned to Harvard for his doctoral studies. He saw to it that Madeleva met his mother when she visited Berkeley, and also one of his nieces, and he took her at different times to meet the poet Robinson Jeffers at his home at Big Sur and to visit Hollow Hills, the Carmel estate of his eccentric Catholic friend, millionaire Noel Sullivan, with whom Madeleva began a long if sporadic correspondence.[47]

They were unlikely friends, this soft-spoken and, to all appearances, simple nun and the suave man of the world, so carefully and elegantly dressed that Mrs. William Randolph Hearst was said to have invited him to San Simeon because of his spats.[48] They made a pair that Hollywood film makers of the next decade or two might have delighted in juxtaposing. In spite of obvious differences between them, their minds and similar tastes drew them together; and, as if they sensed it in each other, their uneasy spirits. At the moment, their personal worlds were shaken and splitting. As Lehman later described that fall of 1924, he was "trying to hold [his] cracking private heavens up," much as she was.[49] His marriage was breaking apart and would finally end in divorce in a few years' time. They did not speak of that until later, and she probably never spoke to him of her difficult community life, but they found temporary respite in each other's company. They talked to each other by day and sometimes wrote notes to each other afterwards, to continue the discussion, all through that year. Yet they observed the strictest formality in their exchanges; she never addressed him as anything other than "Professor Lehman," and to him she was always "Sister Madeleva."

"This afternoon and once before you spoke to me of Faith in terms of a spring-board; had you ever thought of it under the figure of swimming?" So begins one of Madeleva's postscripts to a conversation with Lehman. They had been talking about religion again, and afterwards, she may have remembered her experience of swimming in the sea at Carmel. "I feel it is always so, and in it know by experience that 'underneath are the everlasting Arms.' It was as if you touched the very Support of my being when you quoted that [phrase] . . . you know that the one thing a person *must* do in order to swim is to let go. His strokes only propel, they do not sustain him. His abandonment is all. The water must support him by all the natural laws involved. . . . [His] supreme act of faith was made when [he] plunged in. Think of the immense relief of finding that the thing one fears the most is the Thing and the only Thing which can hold one up, the only Thing big enough, omnipotent enough to buoy up a human soul."[50]

In her poem "The Swimmer," written about the same time as this passage, Madeleva expressed a similar idea, and even referred specifically to the everlasting arms in both:

Afraid? Of you, strong proxy lover, you, God's sea?
I give you my small self ecstatically,
To be caught, held, or buffeted; to rest
Heart to your heart, and breast to breathing breast;
To know on arms and cheeks, on brow and lips the bliss,
The stinging madness of one infinite kiss;
Daring your most exquisite, sweet alarms
In the safe compass of the everlasting arms.

Meditation most likely forged the link between the letter and the poem, though it is not certain which came first. A few years later, Madeleva wrote to a superior about the connection between her writing and praying: "You know that I write honestly and sincerely and that it is as much a means of sanctification for me as my prayers. Indeed, much of it is prayer to me."[51] As she had written of Chaucer's nuns, "What their interior life must have been we can guess from the spirituality of their own prologues and stories proper, unconscious as their breathing and quite as natural."[52] In a similar way, Madeleva's writing revealed her own interior state.

Madeleva has described how she came to write "The Swimmer," the circumstances of which she recalled vividly.[53] As she was running to the water on the beach at Carmel, she slipped and turned an ankle. She swam anyway, finding the ocean irresistible. That night, she awoke in pain and, as she often did when she could not get back to sleep, she wrote a poem. In it, she recreated her personal encounter with the God whom Saint Catherine of Siena called the "Sea Pacific."[54]

Whether or not her conversation with and subsequent letter to Lehman played a part in the poetic process or merely benefitted from it, Madeleva does not say. She was, however, regularly transforming life into art and art into prayer. Some of her new poems she gave to Lehman as she wrote them, and several she dedicated privately to him (as in the case of "Penelope," when she inscribed "For you" on the typescript copy she sent him).[55]

Madeleva offered Lehman spiritual counsel as he offered her intellectual guidance, and for a brief moment now and then lifted for him the veil on her own inner life. In different ways, they both feared failure and set themselves the task of heartening each other to see past it. Early in 1925, she wrote him, "You spoke of changing your field of activities next year [he considered for a time changing from college to high school teaching]; the enclosed letters and compositions I brought down from Woodland to show you—they may suggest possibilities. Sometimes I think the object of your quest is nearer than you know; have you ever thought that it might be in yourself rather than in your occupation?" She referred him to Louise Guiney's *Patrins* and her concepts of holy indifference and the relaxed grasp.[56]

About herself, Madeleva told Lehman, apparently in answer to a question as to why she had entered religious life:

> It was the quest for peace that sent me to the convent, humanly speaking. I found what I sought,—and that Possession transfigures all of life for me. I think that becoming a Religious involved almost as radical change in my life as becoming a Catholic would in yours. Yet so complete is the mental, intellectual, as well as spiritual security that I feel that, were I free now to choose again—knowing all that I do of religious life—I should choose it without an instant of hesitation. I should desire more rather than less austerity, however. Only when one has given not only all his actual self, but all his potential self, is he free. I think perhaps this answers your question more directly than my irrelevant and unnecessary autobiography this afternoon may have done.[57]

Lehman wrote the introduction to *Chaucer's Nuns and Other Essays*, which came out early in 1925. Madeleva sent him a copy, with the words, "Isn't this foreword too beautiful. . . . It is the one thing in the book of which I am abnormally proud."[58] He also saw her through the completion and the defense of her dissertation, which was accepted for publication by both Appleton and the University of California Press (she chose Appleton because of financial considerations).

"It has been a strenuous year; knowing it now from the other side I do not think that I would have the courage to go through it again," she wrote her superiors as it came to a close. She added that the most senior of her professors was asking the graduate council to require the study of the Catholic religion for all graduate students in English. "One does not lose her Faith necessarily in these places," she concluded, still distinguishing the secular from the sacred, an attitude she later revised. "Teachers and students alike have taken us [sisters] into their hearts as they never do their secular associates . . . but I shall be glad to subside into utter obscurity for the rest of my days and expend just half as much energy in learning to know God as I have put on secular subjects this year. If one can work so unremittingly for a degree, one can surely do the same for one's sanctity."[59]

The process culminated in the defense of her dissertation on April 23, 1925, the Feast of Saint George in the church calendar. It was a day for dragon slaying, even though in the final moments before the defense, Madeleva had her doubts. If she passed the three-hour, public oral examination, which she dreaded, she would be the first nun to qualify for the doctorate at Berkeley (although another would follow shortly and officially receive her degree when Madeleva did). Lehman gave her a pep talk, and she encouraged him in turn. Following her examination, he would be leaving for six months in Europe—a step toward becoming the novelist he hoped, and feared, to be.[60]

A crowd of observers had assembled to watch, so that the room was filled to capacity. One of those who had come out of curiosity, because he had seen her "going and coming so serenely on campus," was an undergraduate named Vernon Patterson. Many years afterward, he wrote her that he remembered especially her "evident dignity and self-possession" in a situation where she might have been "in turmoil," as he suspected he would have been. "You were like a gentle fox surrounded with hounds, and you were mysteriously unafraid," he told her.[61] His perception matched that of her professors, one of whom congratulated her with the words, "The thing that came through to all of us most clearly was that you were sustained by something beyond mere academic competence."[62] Madeleva's fears of academic failure quelled once and for all, she intended to go back to the convent and "save her soul."[63]

Afterwards, Lehman wrote her, "It fills me with despair, the way you do a day's work at school, write up-holding letters to us needy, make beautiful books, snatch up a degree of the formal sort by the way! But it inspirits me, too, the while."[64] As a parting gift, she sent him a handwritten copy of her sonnet "Patrins," which she wrote

crossing the bay for the last time—wrote for him, presumably to say
goodbye but also to remind him to "dare/ To follow dreams":

> Yes, I shall leave these patrins as I go:
> Plucked grasses here, a few blown blossoms there,
> To tell you, though I've gone, how much I care;
> To tell you, also, should you want to know,
> The way I've taken, my beloved, so
> That you can find me, find me anywhere.
> Be still, my heart! You know he does not dare
> To follow dreams; have you no signs to show?
>
> Only the wide, white comfort of the stars,
> And strange, lone rest within the arms of dawn,
> And Love that binds, and Truth that sets me free.
> Why should you fear such infinite prison bars?
> The wild and wistful way that I have gone
> Leads but to peace. Beloved, follow me.

8

PENELOPE

Is it naught that I pause in my web as yon suitor woos me;
That I ravel at night with regret the design of day;
That loneliness sickens, grief dazes, and doubt pursues me
With You away?

—Sr. Madeleva, "Penelope"

"Woodland is not far from Berkeley, but Ogden is, for conversational possibilities, and while we were anticipating those, I am here." Thus Madeleva informed Ben Lehman, just back from Europe, of her whereabouts. It was the end of January 1926, and she was back in Utah after a final autumn in Woodland, California, spent teaching at Holy Rosary.

Madeleva would miss most, she told him, "the stimulus, the incandescence of your mind, now indefinitely denied." Solicitously, she cautioned him, if he had not done so during his travels, "to blow out the candle at one end." For her part, she wrote, she had resumed her former life at Sacred Heart with "great happiness. On three sides I can look out at the mountains almost a mile high. Do you know the feeling of beginning every day by being caught out of yourself by the sight of something unattainable? It becomes both a craving and a satisfaction, an unrest and a consummate peace. . . . I find the snow here more soothing and restful than a long and dreamless sleep. It is falling now, profound white peace, deliberate and untroubled as eternity. Can't you participate vicariously in the benediction of such tranquility?"[1]

Such peaceful moments, though real, were rare. Ironically, those who observed Madeleva from a distance saw her as radiantly serene—beyond the hurry and distractions of the ordinary world, as John Livingston Lowes described her.[2] Almost thirty-nine, she looked younger; her face was still fresh and her manner ingenuous. She had about her an air of quiet composure, and when she spoke, her words, uttered in a soft, slow voice, calmed and reassured others. Even her

prose style, spare and simple, suggested balance and thoughtful restraint. Everything about her perpetuated the image of the tranquil
nun. The reality, however, could be intensely different as she wrestled
with her own inner angels, and demons.

During the previous three years, Madeleva had spent her talents
freely and fully. Exercised to the extent of her powers, she had in fact
demonstrated both her ability and her stamina. She returned to Utah
with the prizes of victory: a doctoral degree and several published
books. She had won the regard and often the friendship of brilliant
and influential people. Back in her religious community, once again a
high school principal and teacher, Madeleva experienced the letdown
that often follows a demanding and exhilarating time. While at Berkeley, she had often expressed her desire to return to a more prayerful
environment. Returned to the convent, she found herself busier than
ever with little time for the solitude and reflection for which she longed.
Her hope that a stable community life would offer the peace she desired was dashed, and her spirits with it.

Madeleva felt spiritually bereft, like a contemporary Penelope
yearning for a long and far distant husband and lover. In God's absence, daily activity seemed futile. Madeleva wrote to Father O'Donnell
about her disquiet, fearful that even her poetry was failing her. The
priest did his best to calm and hearten her in his gentle, wise way.
"Hush, my child," he had written her the previous November, "your
best songs are coming. Everybody has those times of dark uncertainty.
And you can't lose your Dream in any other way than the way one
loses one's soul—through one's own doing, which is, of course,
misdoing. No, no, be quiet for years, if He wishes it, as He might
royally wish it."[3] His advice to her as she continued to fret over the
vicissitudes of recent years, was simply, "Go up in the cañon and
whoop!"[4]

Longing to sustain the rich intellectual and creative life she had
achieved at Berkeley, Madeleva struggled to read, think, and write in
spite of numerous obstacles, both interior and exterior. By Easter of
1926, she had about two-thirds of a second book of poetry completed,
although she regarded the poems as woefully uneven. She hoped to
have it ready for publication in the fall, though in fact it would not be
completed for another year. During Holy Week, she translated "Dream
of the Rood" for inclusion in an anthology of Old English poems. She
continued to read the writings of the mystics, a taste she had indulged
while she researched her dissertation. She began work on a scholarly
project that she referred to as "The Life and Writings of Dame Gertrude
More" and hoped to find time to begin another that she had discussed

with Ben Lehman before she left Berkeley: to trace the continuity of the religious theme throughout English literature.[5]

Through the spring and summer of 1926, Madeleva and Lehman wrote long letters to each other. In them, they traced the pattern of their daily lives, discussed books and ideas, and continued their discussion of religious matters. Thus, they sustained the friendship that offered both of them a crucial emotional outlet.

During this time, Lehman sent Madeleva the news that he and his wife were divorcing and that he would raise their son, Hal. She grieved for him, prayed for him, and tried to convince him to seek spiritual guidance. She went so far as to send him a brochure of a retreat house near San Francisco. "I come to you along all the high and holy paths of friendship that I know," she wrote him. "Is there more that I can do?"[6] She invited him to confide in her. To her own spiritual difficulties, she referred only obliquely, enclosing a copy of a new poem, "Penelope," which she inscribed, "For you."

Ben Lehman was not the only friend for whom Madeleva felt concern. Soon after her transfer to Ogden, Father Hagerty wrote her two letters about his poor health and depressed spirits that alarmed her. When a month later he still had not responded to her queries, she wrote again, fearful that he was worse and that she would hear nothing through Lent, when all correspondence customarily ceased. She recalled bitterly a long silence he had imposed on her the year before, while she was still in San Francisco—"with disciplinary intent"—and worried that he was once again resorting to such extreme measures. She longed for even a word from him to put her mind at rest.[7]

At the close of the school year, his health apparently restored, Father Hagerty traveled north to Minnesota and Wisconsin, visiting various members of the Wolff family along the way and stopping at Fred's home in Duluth.[8] Fred's daughter, Mary Lucia Stevenson, recalls many such visits, during which Father Hagerty held her on his knee and played with her and her brothers.[9] In the fall, he would begin a new assignment as professor of philosophy at Saint Edward's University in Austin, Texas. After three years in Portland, he had spent the previous two at Notre Dame. The transfer to Saint Edward's was his third in five years.

The culmination of Madeleva's school year was an outdoor production of *A Midsummer Night's Dream*, which she directed. She spent hours in rehearsals after teaching all day and designed, bought fabric for, and made the costumes herself. She oversaw the music for the play, set up "truckloads of canyon vegetation on the grounds for 'hawthorne breaks,'" applied grease paint to her young actors, and manipulated the lights for the show. Puck and Bottom, she thought, were "genuinely commendable" and the dances charming.[10]

Madeleva then went on her annual retreat, spending a week in much-needed solitude. Afterwards, she resumed her usual hurried pace. She attended a series of lectures at the University of Utah given by a visiting professor from England; taught summer courses in philosophy, the essay, and a survey of English literature to young nuns completing their degrees; and between times taught a young girl who worked in the convent kitchen to spell. She worked in a little flower garden she kept and, as she had when a child, weeded a strawberry patch she had planted.

After the close of the summer session, Madeleva, another nun from Ogden, and two of her closest friends from the convent in Indiana met at Rawlins, Wyoming, at a ranch owned by the parents of one of the nuns. The four friends—a philosopher, a political scientist, a musician, and a poet—spent their vacation "fifty miles from a railroad, in log-ranch houses equally supplied with the modern conveniences as emancipated from the modern inconveniences of life"—with "*real* magazines, *real* books,—cars, radio,—*no* telephones, no doorbells, no rush, no people—but oh, such persons!"[11]

Just as Madeleva settled once more into the familiar cycle of convent and academy life in Ogden, she received word of yet another transfer, this time to Salt Lake City. Her assignment, she discovered with understandable trepidation, was to found a college, which would be the only one for women between Omaha and San Francisco. As she explained to Ben Lehman, "In communities, we leave ourselves utterly at the disposition of our Superiors. We do not express a choice of work or locality, nor scarcely a preference. Any difficulties arising in any particular place or employment we are expected to make known. Beyond that we are indifferent."[12] Madeleva regarded such self-abnegation as an opening through which God's will moved. Nevertheless, as her experience with Mother Barbara showed, she knew when and how to make difficulties known.

Madeleva squared her shoulders for what lay ahead. The college, to be called "Saint Mary's-of-the-Wasatch," was established on September 9, 1926, the day following the consecration of the new bishop of Salt Lake, John J. Mitty. Two days later, the sisters moved the old Saint Mary's Academy into new buildings two miles east of the city, which had just been completed to house both the high school and the new college. Two days after that, classes began with more than one hundred students in attendance. Most were enrolled in the academy and only a few, by and large transfers from other schools, were in the college department.

The buildings, Gothic in style, were spectacularly located on four hundred acres along the east bench of the Wasatch Range. Madeleva described the view from her new office: "I have a west room and from my wall of windows I can look down on all of Salt Lake and the far south valley, across the Salt Lake to a magic horizon of mountains and the sunset."[13] As dean, she was the chief administrator of the college and bore responsibility for its eventual certification. The decision had been made to offer only first- and second-year classes in the college department and to add upper-division courses within the following two years. Degrees would be offered in English, philosophy, science, art, and music.

This was Madeleva's opportunity, given few educators, to embody her own "idea of a university." Convinced that the study of theology should hold pride of place in a Catholic institution, she mandated that the "first and best hour of the day"[14] be devoted to the study of religion. As her educational idea took shape, it evinced its origin in her knowledge and love of Christian culture, and of medieval culture, in particular.

During this time, Madeleva wrote several of her friends about her desire to turn Saint Mary's-of-the-Wasatch into "another Whitby."[15] Her paradigm of education was the seventh-century Northumbrian monastery school headed by the Abbess Hilda. There the arts flourished—Caedmon the poet sang his lays at Whitby and there, the chants of sacred music were heard for the first time in England—along with sacred and secular learning. Hilda presided over a double foundation of monks and nuns, "sustaining the high and holy spirit of the group."[16] In her student days at Saint Mary's, Madeleva had become aware of Whitby, held up as an ideal by Mother Pauline as well as by several of her teachers.

As dean of the Wasatch, Madeleva found herself in a position to give substance to her dream. She put scholarship and poetry aside to devote all her energy to building the new college. With a small faculty composed for the most part of sisters chosen for her by their superiors, Madeleva decided that her most pressing need was to build a strong library collection, which she did by hiring the best librarian she could find and by contacting friends for contributions. Ben Lehman and his wealthy friend Noel Sullivan joined forces to send her boxes of books for what she referred to as "my child."[17]

Recalling Mother Pauline's distinguished schedule of lectures and cultural events at Saint Mary's, Madeleva set about establishing links with the University of Utah that would give her access to visiting speakers and performers, some of whom she hoped to entice to visit the Wasatch. Furthermore, she obtained for the college a gift of fifty

FIGURE 8.1

Saint Mary's-of-the-Wasatch, Salt Lake City

Courtesy Saint Mary's College Archives.

paintings, both copies and originals, all very old and brought from Europe by the former bishop of Salt Lake. Thus, she set about creating a rich environment both for faculty and for students.

To this end, Madeleva subdued requirements and formalities in the interests of broader educational aims. Refusing to be bound by convention, she demonstrated her ingenuity in a number of educational innovations. For example, she saw to it that faculty met with residential students for conversation each morning after breakfast and each evening after dinner. Together, they read from and discussed the *London Times* and other newspapers and periodicals and read aloud to each other from recent books. On fine moonlit nights, she and other faculty joined the students as they hiked up the canyon, and when the snows came, sledded with them down the steep hill outside the gate.[18] Occasionally, she would declare a "holiday" to be devoted to lectures or trips. One such was the feast of Saint Thomas Aquinas, when she called off regular classes and organized talks and presentations on the life and works of the premier Catholic philosopher. She saw to it that the students were introduced to his time and his contemporaries. They even sang, in Gregorian chant, thirteenth-century hymns and sequences.

Although the student body was tiny, Madeleva made provisions to allow for a system of student government. She involved students in planning their own programs and activities. By March of its first year in existence, the college orchestra broadcast a program on station KDYS from the campus. Soon students were gaining recognition for the college by writing and producing their own musicals, by winning prizes in state competitions for science, and by earning top scores on examinations held by the State Board of Public Instruction.

At the end of Madeleva's first two years as dean, the college received high commendation in its review for accreditation (full accreditation as a junior college was granted in 1933 and as a four-year institution in 1935), with most of the credit going to the dean. Shortly afterwards, Madeleva was invited to represent the private schools of Utah on a committee to draft legislation to strengthen junior and teacher college training in the state.

Such recognition highlighted Madeleva's achievements as an administrator. With increasing frequency, however, physical illness shadowed her successes. Concerned, Father Hagerty warned, "I think you work too hard to build up a famous school."[19] She attributed the cause of her frequent collapses only indirectly to overwork. "Last weekend I spent at our hospital here," she wrote Ben Lehman, who also suffered from chronic fatigue. "Just the ascetic and aesthetic practice of living is what blows out our fuses, don't you think? Moderation is a colorless, insipid thing to counsel. I know its practice to be well-nigh impossible. To live less would not be living."[20]

The spring of 1928 passed in what Madeleva called "a grim procession of sick days."[21] So frequent were her spells of ill health that her superiors decided to send her home to Cumberland for the summer to recuperate. She had spent several weeks in Wisconsin the previous summer and in regular two-year intervals before that, as stipulated by the *Rules* of the congregation; but now she stayed from June until August.

"My four weeks at home have been tonic to body and spirit," she wrote Lehman in late July. She would spend most of August at Saint Mary's, at the mother house (as most of the sisters did from time to time), and she hoped to meet him there as he passed through South Bend on his way back to California from the East Coast. "You will laugh at my round face when you see me. . . . Tensions relax and nerves stop driving and insisting. And of course the profound monopoly of sleep is best of all. So you see I have stopped riding poor Brother Body to death, and the reaction is cheering."[22]

Madeleva anticipated at last introducing her friend and mentor Professor Lehman to his counterpart Father O'Donnell, who had just been appointed president of the University of Notre Dame. Of all her friends, they could most appreciate each other, she felt. But Lehman's poor health delayed, then aborted the anticipated visit as he in turn was hospitalized.

At Saint Mary's, Madeleva spent most of her time in her annual retreat. She spent several evenings with Father Hudson, the editor of *Ave Maria*, whom she called her little "white saint." They had corresponded regularly during her decade in the west, and he delighted in the long talks they always shared when she returned to her mother house. He idolized Madeleva as he had idolized Sister Rita and saw in her a worthy successor. His perpetual lament was that Madeleva belonged at Saint Mary's, and he yearned for her permanent return.

Also during her stay, Madeleva "distinguished herself," as she playfully put it, by a visit with Father O'Donnell, although without Lehman as an added fillip.[23] She no doubt also saw Father Hagerty, who continued to return to Notre Dame every summer to teach in the summer school.[24] And possibly for the first time since she left California, she saw Mother Barbara, who had been transferred back to Saint Mary's. Any visit to the mother house meant reunions—some more welcome than others—with the many sisters she knew intimately from various assignments. In some ways, a visit to Saint Mary's was like a visit to Cumberland; both involved a return to familiar places and a renewal of old relationships.

Trips home or to the mother house also meant a bit more time for poetry, which Madeleva had been forced to neglect in the past few years. In her first six months in Salt Lake, she had written only "a couple of sonnets and a little play for children."[25] Although a new collection, *Penelope and Other Poems*, appeared in 1927, she had written many of those poems during her time in California or even earlier, with the later ones being hastily composed in time snatched from other, more pressing duties. When she sent a copy of *Penelope* to Ben Lehman, she apologized for its uneven quality, predicting he would like the first two parts of the collection, "Penelope" and "The King's Secret," but dismissing the other two sections as inferior.

Nevertheless, Madeleva knew that *Penelope* contained some of her strongest work to date: "The Black Knight," "The Swimmer,"

"Concerning Certain Manners of Dress," and the title poem, "Penelope," among others. Prior to their publication in *Penelope*, she had sent several of the poems she considered best to Harriet Monroe, editor of *Poetry* magazine, a shrewd critic and good judge of contemporary verse. In her reply, Miss Monroe expressed strong interest in Madeleva's poetry and consequently took the time to critique it thoroughly. She found most of the poems confusing because the speaker or context was unclear (as in "The Black Knight," which she nevertheless considered the best of the poems Madeleva sent). She also found the technique of others (such as "Questions," which became "Questions on a Nun's Habit") prosy. She ended by inviting Madeleva to rewrite, and to submit other poems.[26] Apparently, Madeleva decided to do neither. Appleton was eager to print more of her work and pressed her for the second collection she had promised them. As it was, she had to scramble to gather enough poems, resurrecting even poems that she had written years before, at Saint Mary's, and had for one reason or another left out of *Knights Errant*. At least two of these, "To Swing You" and "To a Young Girl," she had published close to a decade earlier in *Chimes*, the Saint Mary's literary magazine. And so, at a crucial juncture in her career as a poet, Madeleva found herself with almost no time to write and even less to revise.

Madeleva and Father O'Donnell still exchanged their poems by mail and talked about poetry when they met, although both had less time to write as they assumed positions of greater responsibility in their respective congregations. In response to her comments on some of his recent poems, which he admitted were not his best, he wrote her, quoting poet Conrad Aiken, "'Music I heard with you was more than music,/ and bread I broke with you was more than bread.' Well, praise that comes from you is more than praise, while criticism from the same source is very excellent criticism."[27]

The pair shared their amusement over their mutual friend Theodore Maynard's comment in a recent article that they were the best Catholic poets then writing. Father O'Donnell found the distinction "amusingly absurd," akin to singling out the best Catholic editor or floor walker.[28] Yet his objection to many of the poems that appeared in *Penelope* was nothing if not Catholic; even though he admired the verse, he criticized the theological content in some of the poems, which he characterized as spiritually "astray."[29]

In her later years, Madeleva was fond of quoting philosopher Jacques Maritain's definition of poetry: "The divination of the spiritual in the things of sense."[30] In many of the poems in *Penelope*, sensual and spiritual, natural and supernatural merge. Madeleva adopted the sensual, sexual language of the Canticle of Canticles and of mystical poets to write of God's relationship to the soul. The extent to which this language was mere literary convention and how much it reflected her own intimate relationship with God, she alone knew. As an old woman looking back, she spoke indirectly of her vow of celibacy as a sign of "the complete surrender of the Body and Soul to the love of God. . . . As we grow in the experience of acceptance we become more and more acquainted with the contents of acceptance. That's true in marriage."[31]

The participation of the physical body in spiritual love was a theme that appeared more and more often in the poetry of these years. As Madeleva's physical ailments surely reminded her, her youth was evaporating. She was now, just turned forty, a mature woman moving into middle age. The poetry speaks of passion, with passion. In what she was writing, she neither ignored nor concealed her sexuality but explored it frankly and boldly. God was her sexual partner, imperious, rough, and demanding. She responded with appetite and abandon. Let anyone blanch who might; the mystical love poetry of the Old Testament had shown her the way.

Father O'Donnell was not the only one who found Madeleva's recent poems objectionable on certain counts. The pervasive sensuality of the poetry, not all of which could be read allegorically, was beginning to attract the attention of others, including her own superiors. Certain poems in *Penelope* referred unmistakably to human love and desire: "If You Would Hold Me," "On This Condition," "Tribute," "Ultimates," and "Futility," all of which appeared to be addressed to a human lover.

Whom, for example, does the speaker of "Futility" address with the following words?

> I have to dress you in your shroud
> (A crude device by no means new)
> And look on you who are so proud
> To worms consigned, to ashes bowed,
> To keep my heart from loving you.
>
> I have to call your faults by roll
> (Who once had sought to find them few)
> To scrutinize your flaws of soul,
> Then memorize and cite the whole
> To keep myself from wanting you.

And when I painfully have taught
My mind to scorn you and forget,
I look upon the thing I've wrought
So futilely. It comes to naught.
I love you and I want you yet.

Madeleva had privately dedicated several of the poems in *Penelope* to Ben Lehman, and told him, "Whatever I write that seems of worth at all, I always submit in desire to you."[32] Upon receiving a copy of the volume, he wrote her that he felt "a special vested interest" in it.[33] However, most of the poems dedicated to the man she continued to address as "Professor Lehman" centered on religious themes and not on human love.

It was Father Hagerty who had tutored Madeleva in the philosophy of love expressed in the poems, and one by one, Madeleva's superiors took him to task for his influence over her. Father Hagerty wrote Madeleva about a conversation he had with her superior general: "Mother Francis Clare told me I *got some of the blame for your poems* [italics his]. I knew this was inevitable.—But let it pass!"[34] In a subsequent letter, he told her, "Every time I meet Mother Barbara she seems to say, 'I told you so'—never reflecting that her community should have had a *censor librorum*. She told me last summer [1928] that you should have been confined to good honest prose."[35]

Ironically, what galled Father Hagerty most about these reprimands was that he felt Madeleva had not gone far enough in her poetry to express the power of "virgin" love. "Either you did not see my idea or it did not interest you," he wrote her. In the same letter, he did his best to exert the influence for which he was being blamed. "Do you want me to love you?" he asked. "If you do, invent a code so that everyone will not know what I am saying to you." Apparently, however, his influence was not as absolute as her superiors feared. His continued "assistance," he cautioned her, depended upon her attitude; he warned her against "feigning submission while not yielding it," which he condemned as a characteristic of most nuns.[36]

During the winter of 1928 and the spring of 1929, the relationship reached a crisis. In spite of the warnings from her superiors, Father Hagerty decided that to mold Madeleva properly and shape her into the poet and mystic he desired, and thought God also desired, he must spend more time with her. To that end, he offered to come to Salt Lake City during the summer, to teach philosophy in the general summer session for the nuns and to offer a special, postgraduate course to Madeleva and a few other carefully selected sisters. He asked her to arrange an invitation from Mother Francis Clare if she wanted him to come.

Madeleva replied to this proposal in a way that pleased Father Hagerty. He wrote her, "My heart rejoiced to have you for my own again, humble, reverent and ardent." He went on to tell her that he had written to her mother, Lucy, for guidance. "I told her I was very fond of you and asked her whether I ought to try to influence you any further. She wrote me a beautiful letter full of motherly affection in which she banished my fears and told me it would do us both good to be together."[37]

Over the course of the following two months, both Madeleva and Father Hagerty were subjected to what in a letter to her at the beginning of June, he referred to as "a lesson that cost us both so dear, and also the cause of mysticism within your community."[38] As Father Hagerty construed his position, he was struggling against Madeleva's superiors, bolstered by his priestly authority, to help her achieve union with God, which would in turn intensify and deepen both her spiritual life and her poetry.

In answer to his request for permission to spend the summer at the Wasatch, Father Hagerty received a curt reply from Madeleva's superior general: "I beg to inform you that I cannot approve of the chaplaincy for St. Mary's-of-the-Wasatch, not even for the period of summer-school." He commented sarcastically: "Mother has spoken from her throne of high authority."[39] After reflecting for a day on the current state of affairs, he wrote Madeleva to say that he still wished to come west, and to stop for a few days to see her. "There is something about you and the high-spirited struggle you are waging to be somebody that rouses my chivalry. If you would only be respectful and 'trust my literary judgment' [quotation marks his] I could love you with great devotion."[40] In large part, he blamed Mother Barbara for the rejection of his request to teach at the Wasatch and fulminated against her "disrespect" for him, a priest.

Referring sarcastically to Mother Barbara, he wrote, "I suppose she thought if I spent the summer at Saint Mary's-of-the-Wasatch more poems might be born. You gave yourself away more completely than you realize as yet and you told on me more than you yet comprehend. Even poets cannot think about nothing and nobody."

Throwing caution to the wind, Father Hagerty concluded: "This is meant to be a love letter with lots of kisses and hugging and tears of joyful reconciliation. I love you as a sister and a wife. I am not strictly a monogamist; but out of the fury of my very passionate life of love while a teacher at Saint Mary's you emerge as one of those on whom I should be glad to spend my manhood. I require obedience, docility, reverence, loyalty, but in return I hope to give my best devotion."[41] As in this letter, his passionate language often suggests the conventions of courtly love; he assumes the role of knight errant, and she is cast as the distressed damsel who must be saved and served, albeit on his terms.

Father Hagerty's next plan was to spend the summer teaching a theology course at Saint Mary's, Notre Dame ("I do not know if I will be wanted," he wrote. "I may be further humiliated by Mother General. But this is my play, so far as I understand the game"), then return to Texas by way of Salt Lake City. "I want to see you, to talk to you, to be with you. Pray that I shall be able to carry out this resolution and that you will want to see me with as much desire as I have for you. . . . If it is God's will that I should see you, pray that I will not foil God and you. My little sweetheart. What shall I do to you to show you my love? Tell me, girl, not with your prosaic words but with your poetic eyes."[42]

Throughout their correspondence, both Madeleva and Father Hagerty continued to speak of their relationship as "friendship in Christ" and as "virgin love" and eschewed sensuality while praising love incarnate. But in practice, as their letters show, the distinction could be hard to make. The content of even their earliest letters—and certainly, of the later ones—was often both intimate and erotic. That they felt emotionally drawn to each other seems plain, and he admitted to a strong physical attraction, which her poems suggest she too experienced.

"Whether I am a villain or a holy man I do not know," Father Hagerty confessed to Madeleva in the midst of one of his most passionate outpourings.[43] Both no doubt found their feelings hard to deal with in lives vowed to celibacy; the line between openness to the new and fidelity to the established is usually walked unsteadily. Still, they had strong reasons for curbing both feelings and actions and a sturdy support for doing so in the community life they lived. They met, as it were, face to face in a doorway through which neither passed but from which each could see into unentered rooms beyond.

Although no record remains of his visit to the Wasatch that summer, Father Hagerty came as planned. Afterwards, in his letters, he sent greetings to various members of the community by name, including the local superior. However, Madeleva's "prosaic words" appear to have prevailed. He wrote later of his consciousness of having "made a mistake once that cost me dear in my influence over you." What the "mistake" was and when it occurred are unclear, but in his opinion Madeleva "played into the hands of our enemy"—that is, her superiors.[44] What she probably did was talk honestly to them about her relationship with him and her feelings for him.

After all, as Madeleva must have realized, her superiors were in a difficult position, wishing to recognize her as an adult but also feeling a heavy responsibility to help her remain faithful to the vows by which she had chosen to live. From their perspective, Father Hagerty deserved special reverence and deference as a priest, but as a still young and vigorous man, he required watching.

With a certain chagrin and an honesty characteristic of him, Father Hagerty admitted several years later, when the crisis had passed, that he was aware that he played "a dangerous game" in practicing his theory that to love God one must begin by loving people. He questioned whether he could be considered any safer as a friend for her, admitting, "I still tend in the same direction, as far as the part the body plays in love is concerned," but protested that he felt he had "made progress in continence."[45]

What Madeleva felt and how she evaluated the relationship is difficult to discern. Few of her letters to Father Hagerty remain, and those few were written early in the friendship; she almost never mentioned him in her letters to others; and he is absent from the pages of her autobiography. Indeed, the only glimpse we have of her response is through his allusions to her correspondence and through the poetry for which he received his share of blame.

The only other relationship on which Madeleva maintained as profound a silence is her relationship with God. She once wrote to Father Hagerty, as his reply reveals, that she loved God but did not want anyone to know it. "You want to keep it a secret," he wrote. "It is only an illicit relation men try to conceal."[46] Does her silence concerning Father Hagerty suggest shame, then? More likely, it connotes the importance of the relationship to her. In the preface to her autobiography, she wrote, "Our thought we can share freely and happily. We have words for much of what we think. Our profoundest feelings we need not try to explain even to ourselves. They simply are. The silence of my text is all that I can tell you of these."[47]

Whatever she felt for Father Hagerty, Madeleva seems to have had no real doubts as to her vocation. Her main question was whether she should have chosen a contemplative order. As she wrote to Ben Lehman more than once, she thought that if she could choose again, she would enter a Carmelite monastery. Her desire for a life devoted to prayer—like her attachment to Father Hagerty—was inextricably bound up with her mystical aspirations, which her poems suggest were fueled by sexual energy even though they required its sublimation. As a priest, a philosopher, and a spiritual director, Father Hagerty guided her search for union with God, a dangerous and perhaps foolhardy undertaking for both of them, but a brave one. That search occurred as Madeleva entered middle age, at a time when God seemed far off and the body, always a noisy companion, clamored for satisfaction. In her vocation as a nun, Madeleva's spiritual search assumed many manifestations, including a longing for a cloistered existence (in many ways antithetical to her outgoing nature) and a passion (if that is what it was) for Father Hagerty.

Nor did Father Hagerty doubt his priestly vocation, but he fought hard all his life to embrace God without cutting himself off from his physical nature and bodily appetites. In Madeleva, he thought he recognized a sister soul, "one to whom God gave . . . exquisite faculties for enjoying all the subtleties of sense"[48]—and, one presumes, for directing them to spiritual ends. Neither wanted sex nor marriage in itself; but each desired intimacy—someone (to borrow a figure from the New Testament, one that Madeleva used in the poetry she was writing at the time) with whom to walk the road to Emmaus until the Lord joined them, alive and clothed in glorious flesh. "To the Initiate" describes such desire:

> My kiss upon your brow,
> Subtle and cool and continent,
> Is two parts vow
> And two parts sacrament.
>
> But to your lips I press
> Only the white flame of desire;
> If two parts are caress,
> Two parts are cleansing fire.

In the poems collected in *Penelope* and in a subsequent volume, *A Question of Lovers*, many of which were written during this time, Madeleva identified her own voice with that of legendary women who, tormented and often tempted, nevertheless found within themselves strength to remain faithful to their true loves.

"Mary of Magdala: Autobiography" describes an anguish that Madeleva apparently knew firsthand as she struggled to resist temptation:

Seven expert and competent devils have harassed me all the day!
They have knotted so deftly my hair I can scarce unbind it;
They have hidden my most subtle perfume; I cannot find it.
My lips they have reft of their kisses, my eyes of their tears;
My heart they have stricken with hardness; my soul they have
    shaken with fears;
And the end is not yet, possessing what power they do over
    past, over possible years.

Like her persona, also her patron and namesake, Madeleva determined to withstand every device her personal demons might "know
or possess or discover" to cause her to betray her lover Christ. Somewhere inside herself she, like her namesake, would find a place of
"sure peace" in the midst of conflicting desires. The speaker of the
poem explains, "I have one foolish weapon of love. I have Christ for
a lover." As a later poem, "A Question of Lovers," makes clear, no
other lover can compare with him.

9

'Procrustes' 'Bed

The bed's dimensions are precise;
One simply must be made to fit;
The methods it employs are nice,
Exact, and there's an end of it.

Once I was stretched to fit its length—
I bear about me yet the scars—

—Sr. Madeleva, "To One Procrustes"

Madeleva's health continued to give way. A visit from her parents early in 1929 temporarily cheered her—she loved showing them the Wasatch—but she was back in the hospital for two weeks at the end of Lent, suffering from nerves and exhaustion. In spite of illness, she continued to teach as well as to bear full responsibility for the administration of the college. She even taught English and Scripture classes to the young nuns who attended summer school. She tried her best to relax, hiking with the convent dog, Caesar, doing a bit of gardening, playing tennis or softball with the other nuns, or listening to the radio in the evenings. But in August, she once again was "miserably ill."

Even though the Wasatch was beginning its third year of existence, enrollment was still worrisomely small. In the fall of 1929, thirty-one students registered for college classes; another seventeen enrolled under "special" status, which meant that they were taking classes without working for a degree. The college still depended upon the academy, which had three times as many students, to subsidize its operation.

Haunted by financial worries, harried by the need to obtain full certification for the college, and burdened by her own personal difficulties, Madeleva was not at her best physically, emotionally, or spiritually during her last four years at the Wasatch. Lucy Lockwood

Hazard, who had been a fellow student and friend of Madeleva at Berkeley, spent a year teaching at the Wasatch during this time and was appalled by the changes she found in the woman she had once idolized.

The two women had first met in Ben Lehman's nineteenth-century seminar at Berkeley and had kept in touch since then, Mrs. Hazard writing long, soulful letters to Madeleva. "The very sight of you tormented and fascinated me," she wrote Madeleva.[1] She credited to the nun's influence her subsequent conversion to Catholicism. After completing her doctorate, she returned to a teaching position at Mills College in Oakland, but in 1929 she requested and received an indefinite leave of absence to pursue her desire to live some form of committed religious life. She wished to live in a convent atmosphere for a time and to be near Madeleva while she explored the possibility of joining Maryknoll or some other order as a lay associate. Hers was a complicated history; she had two children to consider, a son from a former marriage and a daughter whom Madeleva had helped her to adopt from one of the Holy Cross orphanages.

Madeleva told Lehman that the prospect of having Mrs. Hazard at the Wasatch was like "the promise of a fairy godmother. I am afraid to believe it for fear of miscarriage of some plan."[2] Madeleva looked forward to the addition of such a well-qualified teacher and scholar to her tiny faculty. However, Lucy Hazard came to the Wasatch for personal rather than professional reasons; she expected both intimate friendship and spiritual guidance from the nun who would in fact now be her boss.

Although the events of their year together remain vague, at its end Mrs. Hazard found herself disappointed and disillusioned. She wrote Madeleva: "During this bewildering year of disappointments and anxieties the best that has seemed possible to do was to do my work conscientiously and keep things civil on the surface. But our relations have not always been on the surface; and however much they have altered during the past year, I do not like to leave you, taking no farewell. . . . I cannot reconcile what I have seen of your conduct, not only to me, but to many others, with the exquisite spirituality which first drew me to you." What particularly upset her, she wrote, were Madeleva's coldness and her many "inconsistencies."[3]

If Madeleva offered her perspective on Mrs. Hazard or her stay, no record of it remains. However, shortly after Mrs. Hazard left the Wasatch, Madeleva wrote to Father O'Donnell about her own sense of herself: "This year [1930] has been better than three novitiates for me. As you say—much of it one can never tell anyone about. To be alone, to be detached, to be childishly dependent on God become the rule of one's life."[4]

Although Mrs. Hazard's perceptions of Madeleva may very well have been distorted, they offer an external view, however subjective and partial, of the way Madeleva could appear to others. Through Mrs. Hazard's eyes we catch sight of the dark side of a woman known for her empathy and charm.

Madeleva frankly accused herself of a tendency to perfectionism combined with a "propensity to be Atlas and take the world on [her] shoulders"[5] Those traits would have made her difficult to live and work with even at the best of times. In the circumstances then prevailing at the Wasatch, which required her to build a college with limited resources, she could become irritable, severe, and remote. Madeleva demanded the sort of dedication and effort from others that she herself devoted to her work, and when they disappointed her, she let them know. Because her superiors decided the appointments of the sisters who filled most of the positions in the college, Madeleva had little say about whom she employed, nor could she fire those she regarded as incompetent. She often ended up doing their work as well as her own.

Although her relationships with some of the sisters in the college and the convent were undeniably strained, Madeleva got along well with Mother Vincentia Fannon, who acted as her local superior from 1929 through the summer of 1931. So long as Mother Vincentia remained at the Wasatch, Madeleva felt supported and appreciated. She trusted the judicious older nun, whom most regarded with a respect that bordered on fear, and confided freely in her.

Mother Vincentia valued and encouraged not only Madeleva's talents as an administrator but also as a poet. When *Penelope* was under fire from critics both within and outside the congregation, Mother Vincentia was one of the few who came to her defense. "Your approval of what I write has always meant much more to me than I have ever tried to tell you," Madeleva wrote shortly after Mother Vincentia left the Wasatch. "It is almost the only sustained appreciation that I have had from the community and touches me very deeply."[6]

After Mother Vincentia was elected superior general of the Holy Cross congregation in 1931 and left for the mother house in Indiana, Madeleva became increasingly alienated from those with whom she lived and worked. Sister M. Lucretia Kearns, who replaced Mother Vincentia as local superior, had for the previous ten years headed the department of science at Saint Mary's, Notre Dame. At first, Madeleva expressed delight at the addition of so distinguished a teacher to the staff of the Wasatch (she seems not to have anticipated a conflict of interest in her superior's also acting as a member of her faculty, probably because such dual appointments were the rule). She also welcomed the arrival of five other sisters from Indiana whom she considered to be among the best teachers in the order.[7] However, she soon began to suspect that Sister Lucretia and some of the other new arrivals resented their transfer. Nursing their hurt pride and satisfying their sense of superiority, they formed a formidable clique within a community of only thirty members.

Both the college and the convent suffered from the negative influence of the faction, who set themselves against Madeleva and her supporters. Madeleva indignantly wrote to Mother Vincentia, "The members of that vicious crowd at Saint Mary's who are here now are doing the same thing here that they did at the Mother House. And they are every whit as righteous here as they were there. I want to give up the whole thing at times for the spirit is so insidious and hopeless to combat."[8]

As head of the college, Madeleva perceived herself to be in an intolerable position, unable to assert her authority over uncooperative subordinates. At the time of Vincentia's leaving, the administration of the college had been reorganized and Madeleva's position redefined in response to increased responsibilities. Her title had been changed to "president" as distinguished from "dean," and the latter position filled by one of the nuns transferred from Saint Mary's. From the start, the new dean bluntly refused to perform certain tasks, complaining that she was overloaded. To keep the peace, Madeleva once again took on some of the work of the dean, although reluctantly.

In spite of multiple problems within the convent and the college, Madeleva managed to present a benign, untroubled face to the many distinguished visitors who passed through the Wasatch during these years. Thanks in large part to her gracious demeanor, officials at the University of Utah often shared speakers and faculty members with the Wasatch at no cost to the college. In return, Madeleva occasionally gave talks and conducted seminars at the University.

Madeleva seems to have delighted in such encounters; she cultivated them, perhaps in imitation of Abbess Hilda, as part of her attempt to build a "famous school." A sense of their importance to her students may also have motivated her, and most likely a personal need as well. All who came felt her charm, and those who spent an hour with her seldom forgot it.

Lew Sarett, a novelist and a professor of speech at Northwestern University, wrote her after one such visit to tell her of the impression she had made on him, confessing that he often spoke of her to others, using her as an example of how spirit can tranform flesh.[9] Poet Louis Untermeyer also wrote to say he had enjoyed the time they spent together as much as any he could remember,[10] and his wife, Jean, elaborated in a separate letter, describing her husband's enthusiastic account of their meeting and quoting his assertion that Madeleva was one of the most attractive persons he had ever met: full of wit, wisdom, and kindness.[11]

Best of all was the long-hoped-for visit from Ben Lehman in the spring of 1931. He would lecture at the university but stay at the Wasatch, meeting with the students there and staying on for several days to be with Madeleva. She now felt, she told him, that they could for the first time talk "as persons, not as a real and a possible Ph.D."[12] Anticipating his arrival, she imagined the coming visit: "Here, after we have told one another how well we look and how glad we are to be so met, you shall be put to bed with hot malted milk or cold ginger-ale and cream or egg-nog of any temperature. . . . Lunch can be served when you will; there will be time for rest and talk before or after as you wish. As for dressing, you cannot imagine a boarding school without mirrors and a bevy of very simple nuns to see and to tell you that your tie is quite right and that you look charming."[13] After his departure, Lehman wrote her, "Something has been added to living."[14]

In those impervious to its spell, charm like Madeleva's may rouse a certain suspicion and even cynicism. Some of her detractors in the community looked askance at her company manners, which could contrast sharply with her behavior toward those with whom she lived and worked. The scorn with which they regarded Madeleva was probably tinged with envy, and it quite likely mirrored her scorn for them. It is also possible that her social grace struck some as incongruous in one vowed to detachment from the world.

Did Madeleva, consciously or unconsciously, use religion to captivate others? Surely, she recognized its allure, its glamour even, for those who, as Lehman did, viewed it from afar. Like Chaucer's prioress, for whose piety she argued vehemently while at Berkeley, Madeleva's ambiguities defy definitive interpretation. Behavior that some might consider worldly, she justified as part of her religious and professional mission. By reaching out to others of different faiths, or of no faith at all, she acted as an ambassador for Catholicism as well as for the college. That is not to deny that she personally enjoyed the company of distinguished people. She came alive in the presence of intelligence, beauty, and goodness and made no secret of her respect for talent and achievement.

Admittedly, Madeleva was flattered and gratified by the respect men and women of the secular world showed her and others in religious life, and she wished to return their courtesy. With irony, she noted the difference between their deference and the disdainful and at times dismissive attitude of many Catholics, especially the clergy, toward women religious. She remarked to Mother Vincentia, "I feel about my experience with university professors as you do about the Mormons; they always distinguished themselves in their relations with the Sisters by much more respect and reverence than Catholics or priests regularly show us."[15]

To illustrate her point, Madeleva might have offered her ongoing difficulties with Bishop John J. Mitty and his staff. Neither charm nor reason convinced the bishop of Salt Lake City to help the Wasatch, in dire financial straits. Even though the college had been founded at the request of his predecessor, he expected the Holy Cross congregation to shoulder the entire debt, which amounted to more than a million dollars. When the college experienced tax problems on the new property, he offered little support, financial or otherwise. In April 1931, shortly after Lehman's visit, Madeleva again appealed for help after violent winds blew off part of the roof; the following July a big rain storm damaged the water supply. The bishop grudgingly contributed a thousand dollars toward repairs.

Bishop Mitty again angered Madeleva when, in return for a chaplain and a priest to teach theology and philosophy at the Wasatch, he demanded a supply of nuns to teach in the diocesan high school. She refused with the explanation that the Holy Cross order had barely enough sisters to meet the needs of its own institutions. He insisted, and Madeleva turned to her superior general, who presumably settled the matter. When the bishop expressed dissatisfaction with the way the college was setting up its social science department, Madeleva sardonically offered to appoint him chairman so that he could shape it as he liked. He turned the offer down, apparently missing her sarcasm.

When the bishop began to discuss founding a Catholic teachers training school in Salt Lake, Madeleva once again resisted, writing him: "It seems to me we are greatly overbuilding in Catholic colleges. I know that we religious are pouring our vitality into a competitive scheme of education in which we have not only the state but also other Catholic schools as rivals. And we are bleeding our Catholic laity to support financially this extravagant system. Don't you think that we should concentrate and combine rather than multiply and weaken?" She went on to propose regional Catholic colleges with travel scholarships for students from the periphery of the regions.[16]

Bishop Mitty's sudden death in 1932 put an end to the plans for another college, but the financial situation at the Wasatch did not improve; in fact, it deteriorated when enrollment in the high school as well as the college dropped precipitously as the national economy worsened. By the beginning of the 1932 through 1933 academic year, there were only thirty-seven students left in the high school, down from sixty-two the previous year (six years earlier, when the college was founded, there had been well over a hundred students in the academy). There was exactly the same number, thirty-seven, in the college, down from forty-five the previous year.

Madeleva wrote her superior general: "Personally, I am beginning to question the wisdom of trying to continue the school here with its terrible debt. I know that the college can be built up, but meanwhile we are bleeding the entire western province to finance it. Is it worth that cost?"[17]

Madeleva consoled herself with small successes. One of the most personally satisfying of her achievements at the Wasatch was the summer program she instituted for sisters from the congregation. Holy Cross sisters from all over the country enrolled in summer courses at the Wasatch, putting Madeleva in touch with many of the younger members of the congregation.

In some of these young nuns, Madeleva took a personal interest, and saw to it that the most talented received the educations they deserved. As others had done for her, she interceded on behalf of numerous sisters, helping them obtain admission to the University of California and permission from their superiors to attend. A few times she shepherded groups to Berkeley to get them settled and to introduce them to her former teachers.

Madeleva spent several years planning for a special summer session based on the principle of the academic sabbatical year, but aimed at spiritual renewal. She designed the program herself, submitting it to Father O'Donnell for his criticism and suggestions. Her ultimate goal was to offer such a sabbatical session every seventh summer and give it over exclusively to a consideration of the spiritual life, with a curriculum designed to that end. Her tentative curriculum she divided into seven parts: prayer, the Liturgy, Scripture, dogma, philosophy, religious literature, and church music.

Father O'Donnell advised her to keep the program flexible. "There should be the widest liberty and the least formality conceivable," he suggested. "The ideal thing would be a desert island with no staff of teachers and only a few books, but with dispositions. By dispositions I mean, as you may guess, a hunger and thirst for the opportunity offered."[18]

Over one hundred sisters attended the special sabbatical session offered in the summer of 1932. *The Journal of Religious Instruction* reported on it in glowing terms in its November issue. Madeleva's assessment: there was only one problem—a "plague of great rattle snakes" on the grounds of the Wasatch that summer.[19]

In their letters, Madeleva and Father O'Donnell not only advised but also commiserated with one another, speaking often of their utter weariness, which with increasing regularity was sending each of them into the hospital for extended periods, and their shared sense of distance from the things they loved best, especially poetry. He joked, "I am doing no writing except in brick and mortar. I think you may find our new Law Building a lyric, and the Stadium a good limerick." More poignantly, he confessed, "In this mood, I want to do nothing so much as join the ranks of the blind old men at the Community House who have nothing to do all day long but say the Beads. None the less, I am planning a fishing trip for Sunday and hope to land a muskellunge."[20]

Madeleva had written little poetry since coming to Salt Lake. Incensed, her friend Theodore Maynard wrote her in 1931 from Georgetown University, where he was then teaching, that he wished "the authorities could understand that it would be of benefit to the church to distinguish between the fire of genius and administrative competence."[21]

During a ten-day stay in the hospital, Madeleva began writing again. She composed "Details for My Burial," which she cavalierly handed to her doctor, and several other poems in rapid succession. After so long, it was sweet relief to know she could still write. She found herself full of new ideas, eagerly planning a series of poems on Old Testament women, whom in her opinion everyone ignored but whose "unflinching courage," as she put it, "makes the rest of us look aenemic."[22]

Madeleva sent her new poems to Father Hagerty for his response. Although he approved of "A Question of Lovers," which celebrates God's superiority as a lover, and "I Will Remember Rahab," about the courage of an Old Testament harlot, he grieved over poems such as "Details for My Burial," with its desire for "the quick, close earth" and "the consecrate cell" of the grave. "I wish I had you as my Rahab for a season so I could love you back to your old joy of living and the passionate delight of living in a body," he wrote her. "I think your poem on your burial is the negation of all your former theory of living. When you wrote 'The Swimmer' you were a woman then, not a disembodied soul nor a mere body delighting in the companionship of worms."[23]

Others also disapproved of some of the new poems, although for reasons different from Father Hagerty's. After a sequence of poems called "Personalities" first appeared in *America*, several readers wrote Madeleva's superiors to complain about the immodesty of the verse. One, a priest, singled out "Virgins" as particularly reprehensible:

Though they be lovers, this lithe wind and his clean maid, the
     snow,
She has no thought to hold him, nor will he
Touch with his innocent importunities the whiteness of herself.

Still upset by *Penelope*, her superiors took such complaints seriously.

In response, Madeleva wrote Mother Vincentia, who was then superior general, defending her theme and its treatment. "The theme of 'Virgins' is the integrity of virginal love, which can be shared without violating the integrity of the lovers," she explained. "Our Lady and Saint John knew such love: Christ and the Magdalen. It is the one perfect love in the world, and I think that the innocent intimacy of wind and snow, all vitality and all purity, illustrate it. Many of us seem to be Manicheans, really, assuming that the body is all evil." She took her parting shot: "It is unfortunate that Holy Orders doesn't make literary critics, isn't it?"[24]

Reassurance once again came from Father O'Donnell, who wrote Madeleva that during a recent visit with William Butler Yeats, he had given the Irish poet her poem "Penelope" to read. According to Father O'Donnell, after he had read it carefully twice through, he commented that it had what "most recent American poetry lacked, namely, 'passion.'"[25] Through Father O'Donnell, Yeats sent Madeleva an autographed copy of "The Lake Isle of Innisfree." She responded to her friend that his letter and the enclosure made her "tremulous with happiness." She wrote, "There have been so many hard, almost unbelievable things to face these past years that the advent of pure joy is almost terrifying. . . . 'The Lake Isle of Innisfree' will be only less precious to me than the manuscript copies of some of your own poems which I keep carefully."[26]

Within the convent, Madeleva's situation grew desperate as Sister Lucretia refused to bend any of the convent rules, no matter how ill Madeleva might be. Her superior apparently interpreted her poor health as an excuse for self-indulgence—one that revealed a dangerous spiritual laxity. Madeleva wrote Mother Vincentia, "I am hopelessly tired in body and soul which is a condition outside Sister Lucretia's experience and consequently beyond her belief or understanding. Disregarding Dr. Curtis' directions and refusing to make any inquiries from him, she insists that the two places I must be always are at meditation and night prayer, whether I am able to teach or not, or regardless of consequences. But I mustn't go into the situation to bother you. We are living by the letter of the law which certainly killeth. You see I am beset with bitterness."[27]

Madeleva attributed her poor health to the effects of stress and overwork on a frangible constitution. Her frequent illness discouraged, exasperated, and deeply mortified her. No longer able to deny or disregard it, as she had when she was younger, she sought to adjust her expectations to its demands, tacitly acknowledging it as endemic to her way of life. She had not yet come, as she did later, to regard her recurring prostration as a posture appropriate not only to abjection but also to adoration. By means of the poetry and prayer that illness— and solitude—made possible, she eventually learned to move from humility to praise and to accept the condition that compelled such motion. Always painfully aware of the limitations her illness imposed, Madeleva resented Sister Lucretia's lack of sympathy, betraying as it did a deficiency of the good will and concern as well as the trust and respect that she expected from a religious superior. An unfortunate although predictable consequence of her superior's unyielding attitude was to exacerbate the condition it was meant to remedy. As Madeleva struggled to live by the letter of Sister Lucretia's law, she became even more unwell, even more spiritually bereft.

During what proved to be her last year at the Wasatch, Madeleva fought one battle after another with her superior. Perhaps the one that exasperated her most involved the censorship of her mail. Sister Lucretia insisted on stamping and sealing all of Madeleva's letters, which then backed up. Pleading the "dignity of her office"—such a bottleneck was intolerable for a college president—she went over her superior's head to Mother Vincentia, asking to be trusted with "a few stamps and permission to use them."[28] When Sister Lucretia discovered that Madeleva had challenged her authority, she was angry and hurt.

By the spring of 1933, Madeleva's relationship with Sister Lucretia and some of the other sisters had deteriorated to such an extent that she wrote Mother Vincentia: "I am practically a stranger in the house and am opposed or refused on principle. So for the whole year I have been passive while the program of absolutism and secrecy has prevailed."[29]

Unable any longer even to pretend indifference, holy or otherwise, Madeleva implored Mother Vincentia not to reappoint her to the presidency of the college. Because the convent and college administration were inseparably connected, neither community could function well with the superior of the convent and president of the college at loggerheads. The grievances of one group inevitably invaded the other, with devastating professional and personal consequences.

With Madeleva's spirits at their lowest, word came from her superior general that in spite of the desperate state of the finances of the congregation (the deficit in the western province alone that year was over five thousand dollars), money had been found to send Sister Madeleva and a companion abroad. She was instructed to explore various possibilities for the summer, and possibly for the year, but cautioned to keep the matter quiet. "Simply give it out," she was told, "that a friend of yours will meet your expenses if you go and that no community money will be used." In a penciled note, Mother Vincentia added, perhaps justifying her unorthodox decision as much to herself as to Madeleva: "I have the promise of the money, close to enough. I am doing this for the community—not for favoritism."[30]

Madeleva prepared to leave the Wasatch at the end of the school year, packing most of her belongings in a small trunk and her books in a separate box. All she had in the world she would carry with her. She later wrote,"For seven years Saint Mary's-of-the-Wasatch had been more than a school, more than a convent, more than a home to me. It was my self."[31] She must walk away from all that she had struggled so hard to achieve, knowing others were glad to see her go. Hardest of all, she would leave feeling like a failure. The college into which she had transfused her life's blood was foundering. Once again, as in California, she had been unable to live peacefully with a superior. Her spirit languished, waiting for God.

Through the spring of 1933, plans for the European trip changed almost weekly as new crises arose in the finances of the community. At first it was proposed that Madeleva should spend four months in Europe visiting schools in order to determine which might be appropriate for the further education of Holy Cross nuns. Then it was thought perhaps she should travel to Oxford for a summer session, as a sabbatical. Upon further consideration, Mother Vincentia informed her, the trip abroad might be delayed for a year, until the consecration of the Church of Holy Cross in Rome, at which she could represent the mother house. In the meantime, she should plan to return to Indiana.

On May 29, Madeleva "pulled herself up by the roots," as she put it,[32] to leave the mountains she loved, the college she had created, and the person she had been. Nor were those sacrifices all that would be asked of her. She returned to South Bend in time for commencement at Notre Dame. Horrified, she saw for herself the precipitous decline in Father O'Donnell's health. He sat on the stage for the graduation ceremonies, hardly able to move. She knew then that her friend was dying.

The "fatigue" to which Father O'Donnell had referred in recent letters had been diagnosed as successive staphylococcal infections, first of the throat and then of the lungs. He had spent most of the spring in the infirmary. Madeleva took some comfort from the knowledge that he would spend the summer convalescing. Soon after graduation, he left on a fishing trip to northern Michigan, too ill to accept the trip to Europe that his superiors offered him.

For the next few months, Madeleva lived from a suitcase, unsure of her ultimate destination. She traveled to Saint Paul for an educational convention. She visited the World's Fair. She spent two weeks in Wisconsin with her family, during which they celebrated the fiftieth wedding anniversary of Lucy and August, delayed so that Madeleva could attend. Mother Vincentia joined the Wolffs for the celebration, a public show of support that salved the raw memory of her final days at the Wasatch. Afterwards, Madeleva headed east for three weeks to deliver a series of lectures on Chaucer to the Newman Center at Columbia University in New York and at the Catholic University in Washington, D.C. To her amazement, over five hundred people attended the Washington lecture. She received an invitation to the Roosevelt White House, where she, a staunch Republican, nevertheless drank lemonade with pleasure.

During the visit to Washington, Madeleva spent time with a former student, now a Holy Cross nun, Sister Rose Elizabeth Havican. They had become to each other what she and Sister Rita might have been, had her mentor lived. Five years younger than Madeleva, Rose Elizabeth had already begun her rise to positions of leadership in the community; she had been recently appointed as superior and principal of the Academy of the Holy Cross in Washington D.C. A gracious, cultivated woman, she shared Madeleva's tastes for the asthetic and the intellectual, and her diverse talents paralleled those of her teacher.

Madeleva called her stay in Washington "the most wonderful ten days of my life."[33] Before her return to Indiana, she and Rose Elizabeth traveled together to a convent at Ocean View, Virginia, where they walked along the beach, swam in the Atlantic, and turned "lobster red" from too much sun.

When Madeleva returned to the mother house late in August, Mother Vincentia handed her a passport and told her to make arrangements to leave for Europe as soon as possible. She and a companion, Sister Verda Clare Doran, would travel to Europe together.

They would explore various possibilities abroad for the education of Holy Cross nuns and at the same time take graduate courses themselves, Verda Clare at the Sorbonne and Madeleva at Oxford. The congregation would allow them one year's leave and one thousand dollars each for expenses. They could stay until the time or the money ran out.

Madeleva wrote Ben Lehman that she felt herself somewhere between "heaven and earth and Europe."[34] On her way to the train, she stopped for a last visit with Father O'Donnell, who had been admitted to a South Bend hospital with an infection of the intestines. They spent a quiet hour together, and then the friends said goodbye. With his blessing, she set off for Canada to board the passenger liner *Aurania*.

10

This Other Eden

This royal throne of kings, this scepter'd isle,
This earth of majesty, this seat of Mars,
This other Eden, demi-paradise . . .
This blessed plot, this earth, this realm, this England.

—Shakespeare, *Richard II*

To Madeleva, Europe did indeed lie somewhere between heaven
and earth. If not exactly sacred ground, it was for her the primal place,
a cultural, religious, and personal Eden often pictured yet tantaliz-
ingly remote. Since childhood, she had heard about Europe from her
father and her grandparents; she had read about it in the books she
loved, and she had devoted her energies to the study of its literature
and languages. She looked to Holland and Germany as her ancestral
homeland, to Rome as her religious mecca, and to France as the birthplace of her congregation. Her delight in things medieval, which
stretched back as far as she could remember, sustained and was in
turn nourished by her enthusiasm for all things European. Now, at
forty-six, she would set foot in this imagined world, inhabit it, and
claim it for herself.

Madeleva intended to make the most of her year abroad and to
savor every moment of it. She collected letters of introduction to writers and scholars she wanted to meet and wrote to friends for advice
on what to see, where to go, and how to get the most for her money.
She also kept a journal of her travels in a small black notebook. On
August 27, 1933, she made her first entry as she recorded that she and
her companion, Sister Verda Clare, departed from South Bend for
Toronto via the Grand Trunk Railway at 8:45 in the evening.

The two nuns had one day in Toronto, most of which they spent
at the University of Toronto. They visited the Medieval Institute, where
two luminaries of Catholic philosophy, Jacques Maritain and Étienne
Gilson, were in residence. Professor Maritain spent five hours a day in

prayer before the Blessed Sacrament. Madeleva marveled at his sanctity and called him "the greatest man in the world."[1] During their visit, the nuns dutifully collected information about the costs of sending Holy Cross sisters to Toronto for graduate education and sent home the information that tuition would only be about twenty-five dollars a year.

In Montreal, where they were to board their ship for England, Madeleva and Verda Clare stayed at the Convent of Saint Laurent, the mother house of the Canadian Sisters of the Holy Cross. The old-world charm of its gray stone buildings and formal parlors gave the travelers a foretaste of Europe. Unable to contain their ebullient spirits, they stole into one of the empty parlors and, Madeleva confessed in a letter to Mother Vincentia, sat in straight-backed chairs opposite each other "to see how it would be." She added, "This is a place to write stories about."[2]

Madeleva repaid the hospitality of the sisters by giving a talk on poetry. During their stay, Verda Clare impressed everyone, including Madeleva, with the fluency of her French. By contrast, Madeleva spoke French haltingly, although she had studied and taught it for years.

In spite of a disparity in age and temperament, the two women seem to have warmed to each other's company as they traveled together. Madeleva soon described Verda Clare as "the perfect companion."[3] Just past thirty, she was not only physically attractive but also lively and intelligent. She was also young enough to defer to her older companion, who was to act as her informal superior during their year abroad. Moreover, Verda Clare may have been eager to impress Madeleva, who had achieved a certain stature in the community in the past decade. In any case, she made herself especially agreeable. They enjoyed sharing their impressions as they traveled and even began telling each other their dreams every morning.

Madeleva did not expect much of the crossing; for one thing, they had been forced to change their reservations from a better ship to the *Aurania* at the last minute. But a full moon worked its magic. Entranced, they saw Quebec by moonlight as they headed out to sea.

On board Madeleva was surprised to find another group of sisters bound for study in Europe. She befriended the four young religious of the Sacred Heart, for each of whom she wrote a poem to commemorate their shared journey. She also met a pleasant young Canadian, Madge Vaison, who sought her out and introduced herself.

After a visit home, Madge was returning to France, to her position as the secretary of French intellectual Charles Du Bos. Madeleva knew and admired the work of the celebrated convert, and her admiration forged a link between the two women that daily walks on deck, long conversations, and shared prayer deepened into friendship. Madge regarded her meeting with Madeleva, which occurred on her birthday, as the "loveliest of birthday gifts."[4] They made plans to meet again in a few weeks, when Madeleva visited Paris; Madge looked forward to introducing her to the Du Bos family, with whom she lived.

Madeleva and Verda Clare planned a month-long trip together through the south of England, Belgium, Germany, and eastern France; they intended to arrive in Paris in late September. Officially, they would be investigating the educational opportunities for sisters at a number of universities in northern Europe, most specifically at Louvain, and had arranged to stay at convents along their route. But they definitely intended to sightsee and soak up culture before Verda Clare began her studies at the Sorbonne and Madeleva returned to Oxford for the beginning of Michaelmas term in early October.

The gardens of England thrilled Madeleva. She had always gardened, even as a child, when she helped in her mother's garden. In her first days in the convent, her father had sent her and her band of postulants gardening tools and seeds for recreation. At the Wasatch, she had taken a special interest in landscaping the new property and had reserved a plot of land for herself, to raise flowers and vegetables. With the "imminence of autumn upon it," Madeleva noted, the English landscape was strangely beautiful and moving. In the soft air and mist, the red holly and thorn berries glowed within the shining green of trees and hedges. After years in the arid Utah mountains, Madeleva marveled at the lushness of England. She rode contentedly through miles of countryside, distinguishing types of hedges, trees, grasses, and plants. The farms too delighted her, although she wondered at the absence of barns.

At Exeter Cathedral, Madeleva the medievalist took notes on the iconography of the statues she saw: if a knight had his legs crossed at the ankles, he had fought in the first crusade; if they crossed at the knee, he had fought in the second; if they crossed above, in the third. Those with their sword crossing their legs had perished; those with their sword by their side had returned. She studied the architecture of the ancient buildings with interest and made tiny sketches to remind herself of the most interesting features: a vault or a buttress or a rose window that impressed her. She drew maps of where she had been and jotted down the quaint names of inns along the way, delighted by the connotations of the likes of "The Shepherd and Flock." She stopped at every antique and book shop she came across and found it hard to leave any toy store. The dolls bewitched her. "I have just about decided to discontinue culture for childhood," she wrote Mother Vincentia.[5]

Madeleva celebrated the twenty-fifth anniversary of her entrance into the convent by visiting Chaucer's tomb at Westminster Abbey. Four days later, she and Verda Clare made their own pilgrimage to Canterbury, and the next day left for the continent. They had visited as many religious and literary shrines as they could in the ten days since they had arrived in England. They saw more in a few hours, Madeleva wrote, than many of the sisters in the convents where they stayed had seen in years.[6]

Just as interesting to Madeleva, however, were the people she met. As she traveled, she went out of her way to strike up conversations with everyone from customs officials to fellow travelers. For Madeleva, travel was a type of ministry in which she listened to strangers and, when wanted, offered comfort. In her journal, she recorded snatches of such exchanges, conducted in taxis and trains, sometimes in foreign languages, as in the case of a singer who confided to Madeleva in French the details of her conversion.

Madeleva also recorded her observations on the appearance and customs of ordinary people. No one in Europe chewed gum, she noticed, and she observed that Belgian taxi drivers ate their suppers in their taxis. Wherever she went, she paid special attention to the children. In Belgium, they were "lovely, sturdy, well-dressed." The little girls with thick braids over their shoulders especially caught her eye. The German children impressed her with their reverence for nuns; they would, she recorded, run up to her and Verda Clare and take their hands or kiss their crucifixes.

Throughout Germany, Madeleva and Verda Clare witnessed massive parades in support of the new chancellor, Hitler, whose Nazi party had seized power and established the Third Reich only months before; they wondered at the enthusiasm and order of the crowds. In Cologne, Madeleva had a long talk about Hitler with the steward of their inn, trying to understand his appeal to the rank and file. The next day, not knowing what to think or exactly how to feel, she watched row after row of schoolboys march by in yet another great Hitler parade.

The Hitler phenomenon cast its shadow over what was in most ways for Madeleva a happy return to her roots. Although she traveled only to Aachen and Cologne, she "loved everything there."[7] Not only did the German children welcome her and her companion, but the first nuns they met on the street in Cologne invited them to stay at their convent, fed them, and put them to bed under feather comforters. "I have never met with cordiality to compare with all that we received in Germany," she wrote another German-American, Ben Lehman.[8]

On the journey, which supplied some new cause of wonderment at every turn, Madeleva celebrated small pleasures: strong coffee served with real cream in England; delicious regional beers in Belgium and Germany; a fine bed and good plumbing in Aix-la-Chapelle; and a deep sleep on spotless linen and under a soft down quilt in Aachen. She kept a list of unusual food she liked: quartered oranges filled with gelatin, tiny radishes whole in salad, fried bread for breakfast, hard boiled eggs stuffed with minced ham. She also began making a list of things not to forget: brush brooms, the unaccustomed shapes of bread. Not even a tiring trip from Cologne to Paris, made worse by a bad headache, depleted her zestful appreciation of the moment.

In Paris for only a few days, Madeleva tackled the Louvre, where she sought out the *Mona Lisa* and *Venus de Milo*, and the Pantheon ("so satisfying," she wrote in her journal), and still had amazement to spare for Sainte Chapelle, which she called the city's "jewel, perfect."[9]

Not far from Sainte Chapelle, she and Verda Clare took tea one afternoon with the Du Bos family in their apartment on the Île de France. In an elegant drawing room that overlooked the Cathedral of Notre-Dame and the river Seine, the American visitors basked in the company of Charles Du Bos (whom Madeleva described as "the prince of French intellectuals),"[10] his wife, Zezette, his daughter, Primerose, and his young secretary, Madge, who lived with them as part of the family.

Then in his early fifties, Du Bos impressed Madeleva as a dignified yet deferential man, soft-spoken, with drooping moustaches and a pipe never far from his mouth. During this first visit, Du Bos and Madeleva talked about Oxford, where he had studied as a young man—he had also attended universities in Florence and Berlin, she discovered—and before she left, he furnished her with letters of introduction to some of his British friends. Through his drawing room and library, where he customarily withdrew with his personal visitors, passed some of the best-known thinkers and writers from Europe and America: the Maritains, François Mauriac, André Gide, Paul Valéry, Rainer Maria Rilke, Edith Wharton, T. S. Eliot, Frank Sheed. Madeleva blessed the happy accident that had admitted her to an inner sanctum of European culture, if only for the afternoon. In fact, she would return to the apartment on the Rue des Deux Ponts and sit beside him in his library many times during the coming year.

It would seem that the Du Boses were as taken with Madeleva as Madge had been in their chance meeting on the *Aurania*. Madeleva would have been her best self in such company, especially in the presence of Du Bos , a recent convert who shared her religious devotion as well as her knowledge and love of literature and philosophy. Erudition such as his (he read widely in not only French but also in English, Italian, and German), coupled with spiritual depth (he began every day with mass at the cathedral), rarely failed to galvanize her own formidable mental and spiritual powers. Energized by the meeting, she felt primed and ready to enter Oxford.

"At long last, I am here," Madeleva wrote in her journal on the night of October 4, the Feast of Saint Francis of Assisi. In one of life's golden moments, reality wed desire. She had arrived in Oxford that evening and taken up residence at Saint Frideswide's, a hostel for Catholic women kept by the Sisters of the Holy Child at Cherwell Edge, a mansion that had once been the residence of historian Sir James Anthony Froude. More recently, and of greater significance to Madeleva, the daughter of Coventry Patmore had lived there as a nun.

Too tired to unpack, Madeleva took a hot bath and wrapped herself in a down quilt. After she read the pile of mail she found waiting for her, she wrote briefly in the little black notebook that served as a journal, and sank into a welcome night's sleep.

Madeleva awoke to breakfast in bed, which she ate from cerulean china with heavy silver flatware while the birds sang outside her window. She took time to arrange her things in what she described as her "lovely" room, then spent what was left of the day resting and praying. Her second morning in Oxford established a more typical routine: up early for a long walk followed by mass at seven, after which a good breakfast (usually, cereal in what looked to be a soup bowl, eaten with a similarly outsized spoon, an egg, marmalade, and good bread and butter), then on to the business of the day.

As its name suggested, Cherwell Edge (as the convent continued to be called) was situated to the east of the city, on the edge of the Cherwell River. Madeleva found the location conducive to repose and meditation. As she followed the meandering walks along the paths by the river or into the fields beyond, she found her prayer life restored and renewed. "I am saying all my prayers, office, spiritual reading with the enthusiasm of a novice and the seclusion of a Carmelite," she wrote Mother Vincentia shortly after her arrival.[11] She also began composing poetry again. Her idyllic first morning at Cherwell Edge inspired "I Enter Oxford," which she completed within two days of her arrival. "There were," she wrote, "that daybreak, in my new world only/ I and a bird."

Oxford, the "City of Bells," is also the city of towers and spires "in every architectural style from the twelfth century to the twentieth."[12] Gerard Manley Hopkins celebrated in verse the "towery city": "branchy between towers;/cuckoo-echoing, bell-swarmed, lark-charmed, rook-racked, river-rounded." In such particulars, the university and the town had changed little since he wrote those words toward the close of the nineteenth century. The bell at Magdalen, which sounded one stroke at nine for each of its graduates, might ring longer; since the recent war, the town might have added a factory and a suburb or two; motor-cars might now hum down "the High" and "the Broad"; but the verdant gardens within the silvery-gray walls of the ancient towers perpetually renewed the fragrance of past seasons. When Madeleva identified the "secret" of Oxford as its "stability, its persistence, its inheritance,"[13] she referred as much to its venerable demeanor as to its educational tradition.

In fact, the university had undergone profound internal changes in the first three decades of the twentieth century. The ease with which Madeleva, a foreigner, a Catholic, a nun, and a woman, could register for lectures at Balliol and Magdalen made those changes manifest. Long excluded from full participation in the university, women were now admitted to lectures outside their own colleges; moreover, from 1920 on, they could receive the Oxford degree. In the wake of the Oxford movement, Catholics, who had been officially excluded from the university from the Reformation until the middle of the previous century, once again attended the university freely. Priests and now nuns, the short Oxford gown thrown over their habits, were becoming a familiar sight in the lecture halls. Foreigners, still prohibited from enrollment in any except the summer term at Cambridge, could now study at Oxford during the entire year. Women continued to be subject to discriminatory practices, however; as Madeleva discovered, some of the dons refused to tutor females. Nevertheless, she could sign up for whatever lectures she chose.

Knowing she would be accountable to no one but herself (as a special student, she would take no exams and write no essays), Madeleva registered for lectures on a variety of subjects, attracted by the reputations of the teachers more than the content of the courses. She intended to sample as much as she could in the hope that further study would keep her from "petrifying" and open up "new points of view or fortify old ones."[14] Eight years past the completion of her doctoral studies, she felt remote from the scholar's life. Anticipating a return to college teaching after her sabbatical year, she hoped to recapture her enthusiasm for the life of the mind. This was her chance to stoke old fires.

Madeleva selected Theory and Extent of Knowledge, to be taught at Balliol by Father Martin D'Arcy, an English Jesuit legendary for his brilliance. She also put her name down for Milton and the Miltonic Tradition, English Literature and the Classics, and courses on Jane Austen, literary theory, Old English prose pieces, the later Genesis, and the Rune poem. Her course on Old English literature would be taught by J. R. R. Tolkien, later famous as the author of *The Hobbit* and *Lord of the Rings*. As she explained to Mother Vincentia, two of these courses were limited to four lectures, and most of the others met only once a week, so she was confident that she could manage the required reading.

At Oxford, Madeleva discovered an extended community of young American nuns from a variety of orders. "The place is a sort of novitiate," she wrote.[15] Most were at work on advanced degrees and intended to spend up to four years in the process. The modest tuition, favorable exchange rate, and of course the reputation of an Oxford education enticed a number of congregations to send sisters abroad as soon as the university admitted women to degree status. One of the justifications for Madeleva's year in Europe was to explore just such opportunities for Holy Cross sisters. Most of the sisters from other orders were "very young, just professed,"[16] which surprised her; her own order usually selected older nuns for advanced study. Madeleva liked the idea of choosing younger sisters and of allowing them ample time to earn the degree.[17]

A few days after her arrival, Madeleva called on four religious of the Sacred Heart who had been sent from Manhattanville College in New York to study at the university. One of them, Mother Margaret Williams, remembered the visit. Not only did Madeleva arrive at the convent at Norham Gardens without a companion, but she confessed quietly that she went most places alone, something that, according to Mother Williams, no other nun ventured to do at the time. She also astonished the others by asking in an off-hand way where she might buy a pair of tennis shoes to use on the Oxford courts—she intended to play for exercise and enjoyment. According to Mother Williams, "Sister Madeleva was a 'post-vatican II nun' without knowing it! She did many things which the rest of us, even the privileged Oxford students, had not yet begun to do!"[18]

The term began on October 10, and for a month, Madeleva lived the scholar's life. After she found the Bodleian library, she needed almost nothing else to make her happy. She dutifully attended her courses, surprised to find so few women in them (she noted that she was one of only two females in Father D'Arcy's philosophy class[19]). She took full advantage of the frequent public lectures sponsored by the university, which were often given by visiting scholars and writers. Among others, she heard Italian critic Benedetto Croce speak, and also John O'Connor, the original of G. K. Chesterton's detective-priest, Father Brown. Before the year was finished, she had attended lectures by some of the most distinguished men of her day, including prelate and author Dean William Inge and poet Walter de la Mare.

Although Madeleva savored each experience, she soon confessed that she was less impressed with the education at Oxford than she had expected to be. "Everything is much more specific, detailed here than in the States," she wrote to Mother Vincentia. In her opinion, "Not any of the lecturers in school or out, are better than our own." Even Father D'Arcy could not compare with Father Hagerty as a teacher, she added; Father Hagerty remained the best teacher of philosophy she had ever had. What she most admired about Oxford was its refreshing lack of emphasis on degrees and its imperviousness to "the wild orgies of experimentation,"[20] attitudes American schools would do well to emulate, she thought.

Bit by bit, Madeleva made her way into the circle of English Catholics connected with the university. The other sisters introduced her to their acquaintances, and her developing friendships with Father D'Arcy and Professor Tolkien allowed her to meet others. The one introduction she longed for, however, never came. She knew that Monsignor Ronald Knox, the noted theologian, was then in residence at Oxford, and she planned to seek him out to deliver greetings from mutual American friends. The English sisters discouraged such audacity, however, and uncharacteristically deferential, she never managed to meet him.

Soon after her arrival, the members of the Margaret Roper Club, a Catholic literary society, invited Madeleva to speak to them. Mother Williams, who was in the audience, described her talk as "low-key, amusing and thoughtful," adding that she was "at home in academic waters, without ever flaunting her own literary achievements."[21] Madeleva's reputation as a scholar and poet had preceded her, and she was gratified to realize that many of the medievalists at Oxford knew of her work and looked on her as a colleague instead of a student.

Requests for articles and books arrived regularly in the mail, and Madeleva mulled over which to pursue. Should she accept an invitation to contribute a volume to a series on science and culture? She wanted to explore the implicit Catholicity of Chaucer; she also longed to do a study of Coventry Patmore and his group, and even met with an editor at the Oxford University Press about such a project. But perhaps she ought to pursue her interest in mystics such as Dame Gertrude More or some of the "lovely Middle English ladies," like

Dame Julian. "Which," she asked herself, "when all fascinate me so?"[22]
She wrote to Father Hagerty about whether she should try to publish
a book during her sabbatical year. He advised against committing
herself to any project. "If you write at all, let it be for yourself," he told
her. "This is a year for you—not for others."[23]

A telegram halted all such deliberations. On the morning of
November 9, the day after her lecture to the Margaret Roper Club,
Madeleva received word from Paris that Sister Verda Clare had just
undergone an emergency appendectomy. Madeleva left immediately
for Paris.

Hyères

While Verda Clare spent the following three weeks in a Paris
hospital, Madeleva dealt with doctors and finances. Although the
patient was recovering well from surgery, her physicians feared that
she might develop tuberculosis of the intestines if she spent the winter
in Paris, rainy and cold; they recommended that she convalesce for at
least a month in the south of France. As the unanticipated costs
mounted—the hospital bill alone was more than one hundred dollars—Madeleva worried about how she could stretch the money they
had left (considerably less than the combined two thousand dollars
they started with) to pay for everything.

The superior of the convent on the Rue de Vaugirard, where
Verda Clare boarded while she attended the Sorbonne, stepped in to
help Madeleva handle their affairs. The kind nun, herself from Poland,
lent Madeleva French francs to pay the bills until the exchange rate for
the American dollar improved. She also helped Madeleva obtain re-
duced train fares to southern France and book lodgings in a pension
run by nuns in Hyères, France, on the Riviera. When Madeleva brought
Verda Clare home from the hospital, an event to which they jokingly
referred as "the triumphal return," the thoughtful superior had roses
in her room.

Two days later, Madeleva and Verda Clare left Paris for the south.
Madge Vaison came to the train to see them off, bearing a lunch basket
that contained a feast: chicken, sandwiches, cakes, wine, fruit, tea,
mint chocolates, and marron glacès. They shared their compartment
with a bridal couple, who found it impossible to keep their hands off
one another, and with an elegant young man, as reserved as the others
were demonstrative. Madeleva surreptitiously surveyed his books and
magazines, all on big game hunting in East Africa, and admired his
beautiful hands. She and Verda Clare, who chatted unself-consciously

during the trip, were taken aback when he bid them farewell in flawless English.

Their first stop, Avignon, reconciled the two nuns to their exile. They spent what in America was Thanksgiving Day at an inn whose twelfth-century dining room had once been a chapel built for the Knights Templar. They lingered over a unique holiday meal that began with a course of sardines followed by another of rabbit, and ended with fruit and cheese. At the table next to theirs, six Frenchmen from the Midi region, all wearing caps and with their elbows on the table, argued about Hitler as they ate.

While Verda Clare rested, Madeleva set out alone in the rain to explore the legendary town, home of popes and poets. "I go through gardens in the rain," she wrote in her journal. "Glorious walks, views over an ancient world and the dreaming splendour of a potent past. The roofs! the narrow winding streets. . . ." She passed through a gate in the thirty-foot-thick city walls to walk along the turbulent Rhône to the Pont d'Avignon, then circled back through another gate and up twisting, cobblestoned streets to the palace of the popes, the church of Notre Dame, and gardens from which she surveyed the city and valley beyond.

The next morning, the travelers arrived in Hyères, on the Côte d'Azur between Toulon and Nice, where they intended to remain until January. Madeleva described the town as "clinging precariously to the craggiest of the Maures Mountains, with its feet in the Mediterranean."[24] At their pension on the avenue Îles d'Or, kept by the Soeurs de Bon Esperance, they were led down labyrinthine corridors to "quaint pretty rooms," spotless, each with its own fireplace and double-shuttered window that opened on a panoramic view of the sea and the mountains.[25] They could take their meals in the dining room with the other pensionnaires, most of them elderly, aristocratic Frenchwomen who spent their winters there, or eat in their rooms, as they pleased. They were welcome to pray and to attend mass with the sisters each morning at 6:30. They were also at liberty to wander about the town and the countryside. For two entire months, they had nothing to do but take life easy.

Living well was surprisingly cheap. The American nuns found the south of France a far less expensive place to live than Paris or Oxford had been. On an average, they each paid twenty francs a day for their room, three meals, and all services: about one dollar American each when the exchange rate was good. That was almost half of what daily expenses were in Paris. Nevertheless, Madeleva continued to complain about the exorbitant cost of French postage: it took between nine and ten cents American to send one letter to the United States. She often spent entire days writing letters, then felt guilty about the expense of mailing them.

What Madeleva experienced of French convent life intrigued her, and she was grateful for a chance to witness it firsthand. Among other things, it gave her insight into the French origins of her own order and allowed her to view her own community life from a new perspective. The nuns who ran the pension preserved many old customs that made her feel as if she were living with those first sisters of the Holy Cross. One such occasion occurred when the mother superior "renewed her vows aloud and alone at the communion rail with a lighted candle in her hand," after which the rest of the community renewed their vows as a group, "as we do," she noted.[26]

Moreover, the architecture and atmosphere of the convent reminded Madeleva of earlier times, as did the lack of any modern conveniences. Without running water, flushing toilets, or central heating, she discovered the austerities of convent life in an earlier era. To bathe, she used a combination of pitchers and pails. A discretely decorated wooden box in her room disguised the commode. On rainy, cold evenings, she learned that her fireplace offered more than decoration. She gave special thanks for the curious, metal hot water bottle that made her bed bearable.

With time to wander and a gracious winter sun to invite her outdoors, Madeleva spent part of most days following the "involved little streets" that led "God knows where."[27] She window shopped, enjoyed antique store hopping, discovered candy shops that sold chocolate Santas on donkeys and small chocolate shoes with a tiny Infant Jesus in each one. On one of her perambulations, she ran into a priest who asked her where the nearest church was, inquiring about a few she knew to be Anglican. In her hesitant French, she gave him directions to a Catholic church and was about to lead him there by the hand when he laughed and said in English that mirrored her French, "That's splendid, sister. I live here. You know all your churches."[28]

On the brightest days, Madeleva sat on the rocks along the sea or climbed into the hills, whose vegetation reminded her of California. Sometimes she went alone, sometimes with a recuperating Verda Clare, sometimes with friends she met through the pension, foreigners like herself wintering at the convent or in nearby villas. She walked often to the house where Robert Louis Stevenson once spent winters, and to Fenauillet, the site of an old hermitage. Once, for the breathtaking view, she climbed eleven kilometers to the top of Mount Caudon, an ascent that took three hours; on her way down she visited the home of Napoleon's mother. That day alone, she noted with pride, she walked a total of sixteen miles!

One of Madeleva's most memorable excursions was a personal pilgrimage to an area not far from Marseilles to visit the shrine of her patron, Mary Magdalen. La Sainte Baume was a vast grotto where, according to legend, the saint had lived a life of prayer until her death. Madeleva walked over an hour each way to reach the shrine, following paths that she imagined the Magdalen herself walking. In her journal, she described the experience as "one of the privileges of my life."

Madeleva often recorded in her journal unique details of village life. On one of her first days in Hyères, she observed a funeral cortege wending its way through the streets. Everyone walked except the priest and the dead, she noted, with the women coming first and the men after. The advent season, during which she arrived, ended in a colorful display of regional Christmas and New Years customs. At Saint Paul's, a nearby church, she discovered an elaborate crèche, "absolutely local," which recreated a miniature Provence: its mountains, the Rhône and Pont d'Avignon, its artisans, peasants and gypsies—no Bethlehem, no shepherds. She joined the crowds at a Provencal shepherds' play enacted in the church, with young girls singing old Provencal shepherd songs. "I loved the music," she wrote. "It has a peculiar incisive rhythm, a way of starting in mid-air and ending there and leaving one buoyantly there after it is ended."[29]

The most distinguished inhabitant of Hyères was unquestionably the famous American novelist Edith Wharton, who spent part of each winter at Sainte Claire le Château, her venerable house with its lovely gardens. Madeleva learned with excitement that the novelist was at home for the holidays. With a letter of introduction from Charles Du Bos and a local priest acting as intermediary, the two nuns met Miss Wharton. Soon after, she invited them to tea. To their utter delight, a few days before Christmas Madeleva and Verda Clare sat sipping tea and discussing writers with the grande dame of American literature on her terrace overlooking the Mediterranean.

Miss Wharton, then in her early seventies, struck Madeleva as "quick, alert, direct," with warm hazel eyes. She wore her chestnut-colored hair, showing only threads of gray, wrapped around her fine head. The best American novelists, she told her guests, were all male. She singled out Sinclair Lewis and William Dean Howells as prime examples, although she added that she did not care much for Lewis's latest novels. In her opinion, the best American poets were women.

The author reminisced about literary friends, including Madeleva's long-time favorites, Alice Meynell, whom Mrs. Wharton had known well, and the wayward Francis Thompson, whom the author had almost met through Mrs. Meynell. Unfortunately, the day they were to have tea together, he was "too much under the influence of a drug" to join them.[30] At the end of the visit, Mrs. Wharton offered the nuns the use of her extensive library. They saw her often before they left Hyères, and she and Madeleva made plans to meet again in London in the spring, although the proposed meeting never occurred.

After the visit, Madeleva composed a sonnet to commemorate the occasion: "Hyères (From Sainte Claire le Château)." She described the view of the city from Mrs. Wharton's terrace as a "bravely blazoned shield" whose "proud device of avenue and street/ A hundred palms and plantane trees repeat." "There are so many things that one forgets," she wrote. "But never this sun-smitten shield of France."

To brighten what she called her "strangest Christmas," spent so far from friends, community, and family, Madeleva made a crib for her mantel, buying the figures at a local shop for five cents apiece. For gifts, she bought a few nuts, a little candy, and fruits. But the midnight procession and mass at Saint Paul's, thrilling with its tambourines, fifes, and "song, laughing and leaping," transformed the lonely holiday into a memorable one.

In the depth of the dark night, the meaning of Christmas occurred to Madeleva as if for the first time: the king for whom she waited was a sleeping child! "A holy experience, unforgettable," she wrote afterwards in her journal. She puzzled over the sense of peace this realization brought her and to commemorate it composed the poem "Midnight Mass," one of a pair of sonnets called "Christmas in Provence." "I had not known that night could be so holy;/ I had not thought that peace could be so deep," she wrote. In the poem, she struggled to convey the paradox of a love at once passionate and innocent, a further manifestation of the "virgin love" to which she had committed herself:

> O passion of night and peace, possess me solely!
> O passion of love, be mine this night to keep!
> O little climbing streets, lead me up slowly
> To where the King I wait for lies asleep!

In the second sonnet, "The Serenade," the speaker of the poem depicts herself as "bemused, song-shaken, weeping,/ A happy-hearted troubadour in tears" who contemplates "a Child cradled on the fresh-strewn hay" and hears the "music of a thousand lyric years,/ A serenade of love where love lies sleeping."

That night, the king, lover, and bridegroom of Madeleva's early poems began a gradual transformation into the sacred child of the later ones. She would spend years exploring in verse that transformation and its implications. All she knew at the moment was that Christ had been born again in her. Revivified, love for God refreshed her existence, and the certainty of God's love for her flooded her parched spirit with joy.

For Christmas dinner, a buoyant Madeleva, assisted by Verda Clare, decorated the dining room at the pension for the old women who lived there, making lamp shades and place cards out of red paper and arranging pryrocanthus leaves with their red berries on each table. It had been a "lovely, happy day" she wrote that night in her journal.

Late in January, Madeleva and Verda Clare, her recovery assured, left Hyères. Madeleva wrote that the little town had proved perfect for their needs. There, each had found a different kind of healing.

Pilgrimage

Madeleva and Verda Clare decided to spend a month traveling before they returned to their studies in early March. More than tourists, they particularly wanted to visit and pray at the holy places of Rome and Assisi. They became conscious pilgrims.

Again, a newly married couple shared the nuns' compartment to Cannes, and a party from Oakland, California, the only other American travelers they had seen so far in Europe, sat with them on the way to Genoa, filling the air with cigarette smoke. Madeleva did not seem to mind; cigarettes were to her a harmless and pleasant way to relax.

On their layover in Genoa, arranged by American Express, the pair ate their first American-style meal in months, with ice cream for dessert. Two distinguished-looking Italian businessmen traveled with the nuns to Pisa, one of whom gallantly offered them orange slices on a blue fringed napkin then returned the napkin to them so that they might wipe their fingers on it. The nuns decided that they liked Italy and Italians, even the woman who had planted herself before them on the pavement in Genoa and demanded in loud Italian to know the name of their order before she let them pass. "Italian in ten minutes— phrase book," Madeleva later scribbled in her journal.[31]

In Rome, the nuns met friends from Hyères who had traveled ahead, and with them began the formidable task of touring the city. It was the beginning of a Holy Year, proclaimed by Pope Pius XI, and visitors thronged the city. A few days after their arrival, Madeleva and

Verda Clare decided to attend mass at the Church of Saint Mary Major, where the Holy Year Novena would begin. When a priest finishing his private mass at one of the side altars turned for the blessing, Madeleva stopped, thunderstruck. She recognized him as Bishop Edwin O'Hara of Great Falls, Montana, a friend for many years.

Because of the chance meeting, Madeleva and Verda Clare spent most of February in Egypt and the Holy Land. Father O'Hara, they learned, was traveling on to Jerusalem with four others: Miriam Marks, who worked for Bishop O'Hara at the Confraternity of Christian Doctrine; her thirteen-year-old niece, Miriam Marshall; Archbishop Edward Howard of Portland, Oregon; and Father John Forrest, of Saint Anthony Guild Press. Father John, it turned out, had been cared for by the Sisters of the Holy Cross after the death of his mother; in gratitude, he invited Madeleva and Verda Clare to join them on the trip as his guests. Miriam Marshall Hemphill recalled: "Verda Clare demurred, saying that they must have permission from a superior to do such a thing and the superiors were in Indiana. . . . But Madeleva didn't hesitate. She said, 'I am the Superior of this congregation of two, and I grant us permission to go.' So our party of seven went by ship from Naples to Alexandria, saw the pyramids and sphinx, and walked in the holy places where Jesus had walked."

While crossing the Mediterranean, the girl asked everyone in the party to write something in her autograph album. Sister Madeleva kept it for a couple of days, then returned it with a poem written in it, addressed to "Drennan," Mrs. Hemphill's middle name, by which she was known at the time:

A Conversation—Mid-Ocean

Drennen speaks:
    No purse, no staff, no scrip have I,
    Only the ocean and the sky,
    And one clear star to travel by,
and asks:
    Shall I, with star and sky and wave,
    Find a small house, a midnight cave,
    A lonely hill, an empty grave?
To which I answer:
    Yes, girl; sky, star and sea are true,
    The ways that kings and prophets knew.
    I follow the child-soul of you.

If, wonder-hearted, we shall meet
A woman fair and brave and sweet,
A man with wounded hands and feet,

What purse or staff or scrip need we
When His one word shall spoken be,
"Let little children come to me"?
Yours in the Childhood of that Word,
Sister M. Madeleva[32]

Madeleva reacted to north Africa succinctly: she was glad to have seen it, but convinced after a few days that she had seen enough of it. "Mussolini's discipline has penetrated less evidently here," she commented.[33] Like other tourists, she rode a camel and had her photograph taken before the pyramids of Gezeh. She even mustered considerable intellectual interest in the ancient art and architecture everywhere evident; but the spirit of the place eluded her. The sand storms and broken train engine that interrupted her journey from Cairo to Jerusalem evoked a more colorful response from her than monumental sights and alien tongues. Her emotional barometer vacillated between discomfort and apprehension.

In Jerusalem, Madeleva's mood changed; the landscape impressed her as "more like Utah than any place I have ever been."[34] Spring flowers were in bloom when she arrived, wild tulips, cyclamen, flame-colored anemones as big as poppies. Elated, Father O'Hara bought a bunch for the ladies from a child at the train station; and so they "entered the holy city carrying flowers."[35] Madeleva appreciated the neatness and newness of the city, "all clean buff native rock," as she described it in her journal. Their accommodations at a Franciscan house were "clean and cold," but the hostel itself "cheery" with activity.

The group of pilgrims made its way to Bethlehem, Cana, Caphernaum, Nazareth, and Carmel, but Jerusalem, the scene of Christ's last days, impressed Madeleva most. The prayerful spirit of the Holy Sepulcher enclosed her; in it, a person could lose herself, she wrote in her journal. More often on the trip, she recorded her deepest impressions in poetry, as in "Suez Canal at Sunset," where she suggests the emptiness of a world without Christ:

Two long, low, level banks of sand and a long, low sky;
On a strong, straight leash of water a thoroughbred boat goes by.
Far to the south a single cluster of palm trees lifts itself like a cry.

Across the long, low, shifting levels and hills of sand comes no
    reply.
The light in the west that was gold and rose is dead now. I
    watched it die.

Even the simplest, most humble activities seemed to her charged
with meaning in this sublime context. Breakfasting on big, juicy oranges at Jaffa and shopping for mementoes in Nazareth, Cana, and
Jerusalem—she celebrated each with poetry.

On her return, Madeleva saw Alexandria in a different light.
Whereas on the voyage out, it had seemed total confusion in the bustle
of arrival, she now noticed the countryside, which was green and
alive; people at work filled the fields. But she reentered the West with
relief, literally staggering ashore after a stormy sea voyage that brought
Aeneas' and Saint Paul's turbulent crossings to mind.

Back in Rome, Madeleva was once again in her element. Here,
instead of numbing her, strangeness piqued her interest and sparked
her imagination. In her journal she could note with delight "the distance filled with the gray blues of Giotto." The literature, art, and
religion she loved served as cicerones. Subiaco, Benedict's first monastery, with his legendary cave close by; Assisi, home of Saint Francis,
where she at last knelt at his shrine; Florence: Dante! Michelangelo!
Siena and Saint Catherine—she had anticipated them since childhood
and now rushed to meet them.

Needing to return to Paris to resume her studies, Verda Clare left
Madeleva, who explored Italy for almost three weeks in the company
of various friends. Thanks to the economic windfalls of an inexpen-
sive winter in Hyères followed by three weeks without expenses of
any sort in Africa and Palestine, Madeleva could relax about money.
She decided to spend a final three weeks in Paris, with trips to Chartres,
to LeMans and nearby Solesmes, and to Mont Saint Michel, before she
returned to England in time for Trinity term in mid-April. She described European travel as three-fourths mystery and one-fourth miracle
as she made her way alone from Italy to Paris.

Madeleva's third stay in Paris allowed her to see again friends
she had made on earlier visits: Madge and the Du Boses; Bruce
Marshall, a young Catholic writer, and his family (Madeleva was cap-
tivated by his tiny, bi-lingual daughter, Josephine); and Maurice Denis,
a religious artist who had studied with Cézanne, and his cultivated
wife, who had translated the poetry of Francis Thompson into French.
Through these friends, she was introduced to many of the thinkers
and artists at the forefront of the burgeoning Catholic intellectual,
cultural, and spiritual revival in Europe.

One such luminary whom Madeleva had met the previous autumn when he happened to be in Paris was G. K. Chesterton, the genial British author and journalist. They shared many acquaintances: three years before, he and his wife had spent six weeks at the University of Notre Dame, where he delivered a series of lectures. After sitting next to him at mass one morning, Madeleva recorded in her journal that his presence had unfortunately made a poor sermon worse. As soon as the celebrant recognized the great man, intimidation set in and he entirely lost his train of thought.

After a Holy Week spent in Le Mans, the home of the founders of the Holy Cross congregation, Madeleva spent "my most beautiful Easter" at Solesmes, the Benedictine monastery famous for its Gregorian chant. With the monks, she attended the singing of all the offices, including matins and lauds at four in the morning. She assisted, she wrote, "with an expectant intensity and an attentive inner listening to every chanted text, every sung note."[36] Between services, as she walked from church, she followed a delicate fragrance to discover a little lane blanketed in blue violets. For hours, she sat among them, unable to leave, praying as well there as within stone walls.

A few days later, Madeleva followed spring to England. At Winchester, she visited Jane Austen's house, where she "saw spring: six virgin apple trees with their feet among unblossomed primroses and daffodils."[37] She recorded her itinerary in the poems she wrote: "Thus Found I Spring at Winchester," then "Stonehenge," inspired by her first experience of a skylark's song.

Madeleva traveled to London for a long-awaited visit with the elderly Wilfrid Meynell, widower of Alice Meynell, whose poetry she had first read as an undergraduate. The old man could have found no more appreciative audience than she for his reminiscences. Seated before the fire, he talked of Francis Thompson, Coventry Patmore, the Brownings, George Meredith: the friends of his youth and the inspiration of hers. As if in a dream, she imagined Alice Meynell at work in the very room where they sat and realized that Francis Thompson had once lain on the hearth rug before this same fireplace. As a keepsake, Wilfred Meynell presented her with a letter Alice had handwritten and an autographed picture of her. Madeleva visited him again a few months later at Greatham in Sussex, his country home, where she spent the weekend with members of the Meynell family and mutual friends.

Back at Oxford at last, this year of people and places offered Madeleva a plum. She signed up for C. S. Lewis's course on medieval poetry and hoped to tutor with him in this, her area of special interest. "Mr. Lewis refuses to tutor a woman," other women students warned her.[38] Then in his midthirties, Lewis had not yet published the books that made him famous both with old and with young readers. Madeleva knew him chiefly by reputation as a poet and a medieval scholar.

Determined, Madeleva looked for a way to approach him. According to Oxford etiquette, a student did not ask questions in lectures, nor did she stop a don after class for conversation. Always resourceful, Madeleva used the excellent intercollegiate mail service to write her suggestions for the course, to ask questions, and to request bibliographies. Lewis responded with copious notes and long lists of books—indeed, he sent her a history of the development of his ideas on medieval literature in several fat notebooks—all of which he addressed to "Dear Madam." These, Madeleva triumphantly regarded as her tutorial.

Referring in later years to his course and to the "beautiful academic magnanimity" that had prompted him to reply to her so fully, Madeleva wrote Lewis: "No experience in education has been richer for me than that."[39] "I believe that when they told you long ago of my refusal to take women pupils," he responded after reading her autobiography, "the true statement would have been, 'he has a full time-table and refuses *any* more pupils.'"[40]

Whatever the reason for his initial intransigence, the reluctant professor and the nun first became friends at a distance. Eventually, he invited her to come to him for any further help she might need, and she occasionally visited him in his rooms. "[He is] one of the most honest minded teachers I have ever had. You know my theory about working with teachers rather than subjects," she wrote Mother Vincentia.[41] She praised his course as "most concise and definite" and "about the best . . . I have ever had anywhere."[42]

Before Madeleva left Oxford, Lewis wrote her a farewell note in which, still the tutor, he cautioned her against being overly influenced by the ideas of Jacques Maritain and T. S. Eliot, who, he warned, were faddishly promoting neoscholasticism. She should, he cautioned, be guided by the much sounder ideas of Gilson.[43] He enclosed a poem he had written for her, which to her distress she later lost.

Until his death the year before hers, Madeleva and Lewis continued their correspondence. Without success, she tried every few years to lure him to the United States to teach or to lecture. They sometimes exchanged books and customarily wrote each other at important times in their lives.

In May 1957, Lewis wrote her that he had recently married and that his wife was dying, adding that he was constantly at her bedside. Two years later, he described his wife as "walking about our woods pigeon shooting," a recovery he regarded as miraculous. After the death of his wife in 1962, Madeleva wrote, "I think that the difference between our prenatal selves and our present selves is immeasurably less than the difference between our present selves and ourselves the moment after death. This difference your wife now knows."[44]

Madeleva received her last letter from C. S. Lewis just a few weeks before his own death on November 22, 1963. He told her that he had been very ill since his wife's death and had, in fact, almost died the previous July. He wrote: "I was, while unconscious, given extreme unction. It would have been such an easy death that one almost regrets having had the door shut in one's face." He then quoted Dante in Italian: "In His will is our peace," and concluded: "I am now retired from all work and live as an invalid, but am quite contented and cheerful. I am afraid laziness has more to do with this than Sanctity!"[45]

On one of her last Sundays in Oxford, June 3, 1934, Madeleva witnessed a historic procession between the Jesuit church and the chapel at Blackfriars, the Dominican residence and the center of Catholicism in the city. For the first time since the Reformation, priests openly carried the Blessed Sacrament through the city streets. "Like both the pelican and the phoenix the beautiful living body rose, one might think, from the blood and ashes of the past," Madeleva commented.[46]

By comparison, the commencement ceremonies of the university struck Madeleva as devoid of all significance "save that of antiquity." Still, she found the colorful procession through the Oxford streets impressive in its own way: "Silk braided broadcloth with full-crowned hats marched beside taffeta rose and cream brocades. Black velvet beside blue, gray with white."[47]

Her year abroad almost over, Madeleva gathered together the information about foreign study for which she had ostensibly been sent by her congregation. At a reasonable cost to the congregation, she reported, young sisters could be sent to study at Oxford. Madeleva estimated that about a thousand dollars a year would comfortably cover all expenses for others, as it had for her. She also explored the possibility of hiring one or more Oxford graduates to teach at Saint Mary's. For approximately sixty dollars a month, she thought, she could arrange for a young single woman to come to the United States for a year to teach philology. Such a person could help prepare the sisters chosen for foreign study by acquainting them with Oxonian methods and would infuse an air of culture into the Midwest atmosphere. Just the thought of the Oxford cap and gown gracing the commencement procession at Saint Mary's amused and delighted Madeleva. Transportation expenses seemed to be the only obstacle, and in a letter

to Sister Vincentia, Madeleva offered to use a gift of money that she
had recently received to finance the passage of a Miss Cunningham,
who was interested in such a position if she could be guaranteed
travel expenses.[48]

Madeleva was happy to learn that money had been found to
allow Verda Clare to stay on at the Sorbonne for another year to complete the work interrupted by her illness. Madeleva would return alone,
first traveling to London and Sussex, and then touring northern England in the company of her friends, the Peplers.

Madeleva had met Hilary Pepler, an English convert, in Utah the
previous spring when he visited the Wasatch. From his home and
workshop in Ditchling, Sussex, he traveled often to America to lecture
on liturgical drama and demonstrate the art of mime. Like Madeleva,
he wrote religious poetry and shared her love of medieval arts and
crafts. Through her friendship with him and his family, especially his
son Father Conrad Pepler, OP, and his daughter Susan, she had made
the acquaintance of Wilfred Meynell. Through them she also met the
family of author Hilare Belloc.

Young Father Pepler, who was a scholastic studying at Blackfriars,
visited Madeleva often during her stay in Oxford. One of his most
enduring memories was of visiting her at the convent at Cherwell
Edge, where the restrictions of the house forced him to drink tea alone
while she watched him. "That memory is always fresh in my mind,"
he wrote her almost thirty years later, "and you were rightly indignant
at the nunnishness of the place in not allowing you to take tea with
your guest!"[49]

On July 1, 1934, Madeleva wrote a single sentence in her journal:
"I leave Oxford—pulled up by the roots." Again she used the image
she had chosen to describe her departure from the Wasatch the year
before. This "blessed plot": Oxford, England, Europe, had given her
the time and space she needed to nurture both body and spirit. Could
her renewed strength sustain yet another transplantation? Could other
soil nourish her as this had?

In a little more than a month, Madeleva must sail from Cobh in
Ireland for Boston. Her passage was already booked on the *Scythia*.
Ruefully, she remarked on priests she had met, "especially Jesuits,
loose all over Europe and for unlimited periods of time. . . . They just
have years and years off."[50] Her mood darkened as she saw her money
and her year running out, and she had nightmares about returning
home. In one, she dreamed that she was back in America. "I felt as
though I was coming out of gas and someone was trying to help me
realize that it was all over!" she wrote.[51]

Letters from home convinced her that not only the finances but also the morale of the congregation were at an all-time low. The pettiness and back-biting of which she had been a victim seemed endemic. "When will we Sisters of the Holy Cross learn the heavenly lesson of mutual charity!" she exclaimed in a letter to Mother Vincentia. "That would be a greater contribution to our divine efficiency than a mint of financial endowments!"[52]

Affairs at the Wasatch had gone from bad to worse, Madeleva learned, and even Saint Mary's was hurting financially. Sister Irma, appointed president after Mother Pauline's retirement, was being hastened out of office after only three years. A successor had not yet been appointed. "Would that I could conjure up a College President for you!" she wrote her superior general.[53] Madeleva had asked for and received assurance from Mother Vincentia that she would not be considered for the position.[54] She had little desire to try college administration again.

Intensifying Madeleva's dejection was news of Father O'Donnell's death on June 4. His had been a long and debilitating last illness, which he described as a losing battle against "at least seven devils of infection running riot."[55] In his final days, paralyzed from the waist down, he had drifted in and out of consciousness. "How like a holocaust the burnt offering of his life has gone up to God," Madeleva wrote to her superior general.[56]

Madeleva recalled her last visit with him in his hospital room the previous August, only a few hours before she left South Bend for Europe. As he sat with his rosary in his hand, looking listlessly out the window, so weak that he was unable to stand, or even to read or write, he said ironically, "I live now in the beads." But by late fall, word had come to her in Hyères that he was better, well enough to spend the winter in Florida. Like everyone else, she dared to hope for his eventual recovery. He had returned to Notre Dame at the end of April, but the good that the Florida climate did him had no lasting effect. He died the day after commencement, just as his term as president of the university ended. He was not yet fifty years old.

Madeleva mourned for the man and for the poet whose career had ended too soon. The last six years of his life had been consumed by his responsibilities as president, a position that allowed him none of the sustained leisure his nature demanded. He had been a talented and successful administrator who sought to balance the extensive physical expansion of campus facilities with commensurate intellectual and cultural offerings. Because of his efforts, G. K. Chesterton and W. B. Yeats each spent part of a semester at the university. It was clear to Madeleva that the demands of his office had killed him as surely as the infection that at last overwhelmed him. In his death she saw a warning for herself: his presidency had been a "brilliant fatality."[57]

In Hyères, on the rainy days of the mild southern winter, Madeleva had read the mystics. Now she traveled to the anchor hold of her favorite, Dame Julian of Norwich. As she stood before the marker for her rose garden on the south side of the Church of Saint Julian, Madeleva felt a "loneliness for her" so poignant that she made note of it in her journal. The "common sense, intuitive knowledge, literary competence, and psychological analysis" that she admired in the fifteenth-century English woman were qualities she no doubt wished for herself.[58] But perhaps that day she yearned far more for the consoling wisdom that, according to legend, had been Julian's gift to others.

On this trip into the north of England, Madeleva also came to Whitby, site of the monastery of Saint Hilda, whose spirit she had consciously sought to resurrect at the Wasatch. The countryside at once welcomed her; it reminded her of her Wisconsin birthplace. She caught her impressions in her journal: "Brown, green, bracken, mauve of moors, cup-like valleys, fertile, vivid green heather, sheep with neatly set horns, long, high winding hills, the ruin of the abbey and the North Sea on the right—lovely winding approach, quaint fishing village. Harbor, nets drying." The inhabitants even looked American to her. The walls and the public buildings of the town had been built from the stones of the ruined abbey. It was still there, just rearranged.

During a visit to the moors and Haworth, with its obligatory stop at the parsonage of the Brontës, Madeleva and the English friends with whom she traveled shared a picnic supper. As they sat on the hillside enjoying the summer evening, the question of the efficacy of the religious habit came up. "My young English trio were strong for defrocking us all," she wrote.[59] Religious garb, they argued, was a barrier between the priest or the nun and the rest of the world. Madeleva, who loved her habit and had celebrated it in poems such as "Concerning Certain Matters of Dress," defended it staunchly, as a general might defend the military uniform. As she had traveled through Europe, often alone, she felt its effect on others, who hurried to greet her because of it or bowed reverently before its symbolic power. Yet she knew that even as it attracted some, it repulsed others: those who, as she put it in "Questions of a Nun's Habit," deplored her "world."

Madeleva made her way alone by train through northern Wales to Holyhead, where she caught the ferry to Dublin. She came at the invitation of poet and storyteller Seumas MacManus, a frequent visitor to the United States over the years on lecture tours that had brought him most recently to the Wasatch. She would go to Mount Charles, his village in Donegal, to stay with his cousin in her house across the road from Seumas. He promised to show Madeleva an Ireland few tourists see.

First, Madeleva would meet William Butler Yeats, to whom Father O'Donnell had shown her poem "Penelope" on his visit to Notre Dame the year before. Seumas made arrangements for Yeats to call on her at the convent at which she was staying in Dublin. He came directly from the Abbey Theatre, where he was directing a new production and took her to his home in Rathfarnum so that she could glimpse Irish rural life.

There, with his wife and teenaged daughter and son, Yeats sat her down to tea, then walked her through his garden and eventually escorted her to his library. He talked of Lady Gregory, gave his opinion of A. E., whose verse he was then reading, and spoke of Gandhi. Madeleva judged him to be a handsome man, with brown eyes, white hair, and a lovely voice. He read to her: his own poems and those of another Gaelic poet, Ella Young. But in the privacy of her journal, Madeleva called him "an Irishman manque: a man without a spiritual home."

As she had liked Italy and Italians, Madeleva liked Ireland and the Irish: a "dirty, disorderly, happy" people whose reverence for her habit and the faith they shared touched her. Many of those she encountered on the streets were ragged, obviously in want, but not one failed to tip a hat to her or salute her courteously—further vindication of her habit. At masses, which were packed, she saw rosary beads used for almost the first time since her arrival in Europe.

On the last day of July, Madeleva left Dublin for Bally Shannon in Donegal, town of the O'Donnells. The trip paid homage to her deceased friend, Charles O'Donnell, whose parents were born "seven Irish miles" from each other, his mother in the little fishing village of Killybegs and his father in Ardara. In one of his poems, "A Shrine of Donegal," he had written of Lough Derg, an island off the coast dedicated to Saint Patrick: "Here came my fathers in their life's high day/ In barefoot sorrow." Now Madeleva traveled against the raw wind to the holy place, to visit the basilica and do penance.

Madeleva's year of pilgrimage ended with the sight of wild swans in flight. She later reminisced: "My own dearest days were spent in Donegal with the North Atlantic beating upon the rugged coast and the fishermen ringing in their great nets of silver fish. The tinkers too were in the village of Mt. Charles while I was there. The setting could not have been more perfect. It came to a nostalgic conclusion as I sailed from Galway after seventy-two hours of waiting for a boat among sunshine, rain, and hundreds of swans flying from the river to the bay and back again."[60]

11

Harnessing Her Will

Madeleva's "wonder-year," as she called it, came to a close as she approached Boston Harbor. There, she disembarked and boarded a train to Indiana. In transit, she wrote a postcard to Ben Lehman: "Did I write you that I am to be at St. Mary's College, Notre Dame, Indiana this year? How I shall miss the west!"[1]

In a letter to Lehman written after her return to Indiana, Madeleva confessed: "To be lost in immensity is one of the great adventures of life, and to have that adventure has been my physical world too long to make this tame and ordered landscape surpassingly attractive." She explained that she longed not only for the friendships she had left out west but also for those "great sacraments of majesty and power and peace, the mountains, and the ocean."[2] Indiana, once the only horizon she craved, now seemed confining and predictable.

As far as Madeleva knew when she arrived at the mother house, she would teach at her alma mater, which was still without a president. "Have you found a President?" she questioned her superior general a few weeks before she left Europe. "It should be a *real* person, don't you think? One can't fool all the people *all the time*—and there has been a long period of second best expedients."[3] For thirty-six years, from 1895 until 1931, Mother Pauline had occupied the office that now, after three years, was again vacant. Enrollment in the college had fallen by more than a third in the previous two years, and while the depressed economy might explain the swift decline, strong leadership was the first necessity if the college was to survive.

Specific assignments, or "obediences" as they were called in the convent, were handed out on August 15, two days after Madeleva arrived at Saint Mary's. Only then did she learn that, in spite of what she had interpreted as assurances to the contrary, her superiors had chosen her to become the third president of the college. She was incredulous. Indeed, she felt betrayed. "The one position which our Superior General, Mother Vincentia, had repeatedly assured me would not be assigned to me she had appointed me to fill," she wrote later.[4]

"You will consider it quite as much of a disaster as I do," Madeleva wrote Lehman of her new assignment.[5] Although she realized that the position was, as she put it, "not without opportunity," she also recognized that it meant the end of her dream of a more reflective, prayerful life. The memory—still painful—of her failures at the Wasatch, coupled with her sense of the devastating physical and psychological effect on Father O'Donnell of a similar position warned her of the personal and professional pitfalls that lay ahead.

At the Wasatch, perhaps in part as an escape from the problems that beset her, Madeleva had yearned for a different, more contemplative way of life. In letters, she had often expressed her desire for greater solitude in which to pray and write, as when she wrote Lehman: "I think I told you once that if, knowing religious life and all life as I do now, I could choose again, my decision would be as it is, with the only possible alternative of the Carmelite convent. More and more one feels the imperative need of the interior life."[6] In those days, Madeleva had assented to Father Hagerty's intention to "make a mystic and a poet" of her as consonant with her own deepest desire.[7] If anything, her sabbatical year had strengthened that desire.

Unavoidably adding to Madeleva's sense of betrayal was the announcement that her new superior would be Sister Lucretia, the same woman about whose rigidity and narrow-mindedness Madeleva had complained bitterly during her last few years at the Wasatch. Further complicating their relationship was Lucretia's simultaneous appointment to the faculty of the college. Again Madeleva found herself in the awkward position of answering to a religious superior who was at the same time a professional subordinate.

The problems that the two women experienced at the Wasatch and which no doubt recurred at Saint Mary's were as much structural as personal. The authority of the president of the college lacked clear definition in relation to that of the local superior, who bore ultimate responsibility for an educational establishment that at Saint Mary's included an academy and an elementary school as well as the college. Should the superior concern herself primarily with the spiritual well-being of the sisters in her charge, or should she play an active part in the day-to-day operation of the institutions under her authority? Should the president merely inform her superior of decisions made within the college, or must she submit them for final approval? Such ambiguity inevitably caused conflict, especially when those holding the positions were strong-minded women with different temperaments and approaches.

Because of her experience at the Wasatch, Madeleva knew what to expect even before her first day in office, and she surely dreaded the confusion and tensions that arise when power must be shared without established limits or precedents. She also no doubt recognized that even though Lucretia's term might be brief (as in fact it was, ending within two years), the tensions between the superior and the president of the college were in a manner of speaking part of the job for each of them.

As every Holy Cross sister knew, the *Constitutions* of the congregation cautioned that the nun who holds back part of her will lives a life "full of unrest, of bitterness, and continual desires." She is "always troubled and a constant prey to sadness; she torments herself, disedifies her sisters, and crucifies her superiors."[8] Madeleva regarded obedience as a sacred obligation—the heart of her vocation, in fact, because it was the means by which she joined her will to God's. As she practiced it, true obedience required a willing acceptance of the decisions of her superiors, not just mindless acquiescence. Consequently, before she submitted to a decision, Madeleva saw no contradiction in wrestling with herself and sometimes with her superiors like Jacob with the angel or in arguing her case before God like Job.

In "Jail Bird," a poem written during this period, Madeleva voiced her frustration at finding herself in circumstances that, by denying her the full use of her powers, thwarted her nature. Longing to fly free, she fantasized about escape.

> For who am I
> To be in this wise made
> Thrall to a sweet-faced glade,
> I who am kin to mountain-top and cloud?
> Why not deal cunningly, devise some tool
> To freedom and escape from this adventureless school?
> Why not break prison bonds and fly
> Up, up to where
> The high hills and the high heavens lie bare
> With no tree nigh?

Trained to put the good of the community ahead of her own needs or wants, Madeleva assumed the presidency of the "adventureless school" with the appearance of good grace. Her ideals of "holy indifference" and the "relaxed grasp," espoused early in her vocation and practiced assiduously over the years, enabled her to master the inner struggle that the poetry and her letters revealed. Once again the harness-maker's daughter labored into harness. If she felt like a race horse condemned to the traces, who could blame her?

The college whose leadership Madeleva assumed had a recently expanded facility, with a large new building, Le Mans Hall, that housed under one roof most classrooms and administrative offices as well as a dining hall and a dormitory. As president of the college, she moved into a spacious office on the main corridor; it had wood paneling, casement windows, and a large fireplace. Her bedroom with a private bath was just down the hall. The new building, completed as the Great Depression began, was Mother Pauline's parting gift to the college— a bequest that carried with it a monumental mortgage.

If the institution were to thrive, Madeleva had to balance a budget that included a debt of more than $1 million, and at the same time preserve the integrity of the congregation's proudest educational establishment. Without undermining the traditions of the college, she must find a way to update an outmoded curriculum and modernize rules more appropriate to a convent than to a college. At the same time, she must bolster the sagging morale of a faculty, staff, and student body that had seen enrollment, personnel, and resources dwindle over the previous five years. The situation at Saint Mary's not only mirrored but magnified that of the Wasatch.

At the opening of the 1934 through 1935 academic year, student enrollment in the college numbered 252 students, an improvement over the 193 of the previous year, but still lower than the 300 students registered in the college at the start of the depression. The full-time faculty numbered approximately fifty, of whom almost two-thirds were Holy Cross sisters, many of them ill-trained for the positions they held. Among the others were seven Holy Cross priests "on loan" from the University of Notre Dame who served at the pleasure of their religious superiors. A few lay members, mostly single women, supplemented the religious faculty and staff. They often boarded at the college, living like poor relations on the fringes of the religious community.

The faculty and the student body welcomed their new president, who looked younger than her forty-seven years. They met a dignified yet unassuming woman who carried her reputation as a poet, scholar, and educator lightly, with grace and simplicity. Her distinguished record promised the resourceful and imaginative leadership that the institution needed in unpredictable economic times. She had the added advantage of knowing the college intimately, first as an undergraduate and then as a professor for more than a decade.

In her own estimation, Madeleva brought two qualifications to her position: her "ability to work" and her "capacity to dream."[9] She

FIGURE 11.1

Sr. Madeleva, c. 1935

Courtesy Saint Mary's College Archives.

also brought the varied experience and broadened perspective that she had gained on her recent travels. At Oxford, she had entered the "sanctum sanctorum" of higher education, and during her sabbatical year had come to know some of the most influential intellectuals and artists of her day.

Especially significant for her new position, Madeleva had made her way into the charmed circle of the so-called Catholic Revival, which flourished in Europe in the early thirties. Among her friends and acquaintances, she counted Charles Du Bos, Martin D'Arcy, Frank and Maisie Ward Sheed (whom she had met on one of her trips through London), Wilfred Meynell, G. K. Chesterton, Jacques Maritain, and Étienne Gilson. The minds and works of such individuals had expanded her vision of Catholic culture and, with her experience at the Wasatch, equipped her to assume a position of leadership in American Catholic higher education—even if initially it was one she neither sought nor desired.

Madeleva proceeded cautiously, taking time to reacquaint herself with the college. She began by getting to know its students and faculty and offering them the opportunity to know her. Unwilling to relinquish her desire to return to the classroom, she insisted upon teaching several courses that first year, even if it meant taking on extra work, and soon knew every student in the college by name. She set aside regular office hours when both students and faculty might drop in to talk with her informally. She also presided over weekly meetings of the faculty, which were more like seminars than business meetings.[10]

In frequent convocations, Madeleva shared with faculty and students some of her ideas on education. In particular, she emphasized the contemplative aspects of learning, stressing that education is "an end in itself" which must be realized through the cultivation of "habits of thinking" and "habits of quiet."[11] She added that students would never learn the joy of contemplation if not during the leisure of their college years. But, she said, the educational enterprise was not only interior; it was also communal. "This is our school," she told the assembled group, and she challenged students and faculty to collaborate on the creation of an environment conducive to the search for truth and the love of beauty.

Wary and consequently unwilling to assume control too obviously—perhaps to avoid the formation of factions like those that undermined her authority at the Wasatch—and in fact still lacking any comprehensive vision of what she wanted for the college, Madeleva was at first satisfied to imitate what she had already established at the Wasatch, where she had built a college from scratch. As she had at the Wasatch, she first turned her attention to the spiritual and intellectual well-being of the community.

To build a stronger sense of community, Madeleva set about integrating some of the spiritual exercises of the convent and the college. She convinced the college sisters to chant the office of the Blessed Virgin together three times a day in the college chapel instead of in the convent church; students and lay faculty could then join them in prayer. To minister to the spiritual needs of the campus, she created the position of resident chaplain, to which she appointed Reverend Matthew Schumacher, CSC, a colleague and friend from the days before she left Saint Mary's for the West.

As she had at the Wasatch, Madeleva focused on the importance of a fine library in which both faculty and students could "study and read and think" and assured the community that even though she was not quite sure how she would finance it, "[a new library] is only what you all deserve and it is something of which you are all worthy."[12]

Working with her dean of students, Madeleva instituted student government, even though like their counterparts at the Wasatch, the students seemed reluctant to assume responsibility for themselves. She sponsored elections of student officers, turning over to them the detailed working out of their system of self-government.[13]

In Sister Maria Pieta Scott, who became dean of women at the end of 1934, Madeleva found an ally for change as well as a close personal friend. Gradually, they relaxed the strict, convent-like rules that governed most aspects of student life. Madeleva's administration welcomed Notre Dame men to campus, encouraging not only a more active social exchange between the two campuses but also intercollegiate dramatics, music, and debate.[14] Perhaps the most controversial decision of her first months in office was to permit students to smoke openly on campus for the first time. Although some in the community decried the move as the end of "sacrosanct tradition and respectability,"[15] it established Madeleva's image among students as a tolerant, up-to-date administrator.

In her relations with the faculty, the new president devised a simple but effective strategy to initiate change: she used catalysts, which enabled colleagues to work together. Soon after taking office, she invited Reverend William Cunningham, CSC, a part-time member of the education department, to organize and lead a weekly seminar on the curriculum, which she herself attended. The group set as its goal the revision of the college catalogue, and in the process studied and revised the curriculum. Not only were course offerings reorganized so that introductory courses were clearly distinguished from advanced offerings, but new requirements, including a general comprehensive examination, were instituted. Moreover, for the first time, administrative policies and procedures were established and spelled out.

Granted, Madeleva reserved a large measure of power to the president, who for example decided whether and when to call meetings of her advisory council, but for the first time in the existence of the college such a council was mandated and its membership specified in the catalogue. When she referred to the college president as "someone to take the blame for things," she downplayed the very real authority of her office and emphasized instead her sense of responsibility and accountability.[16]

To a college used to Mother Pauline's benign autocracy, Madeleva's cautious innovations, mild as they may seem in hindsight, must have seemed bold. A hierarchical model of governance was taken for granted by a faculty and staff composed predominantly of sisters and priests accustomed to obeying superiors whose decisions were regarded as providential. Catholic colleges like Saint Mary's were often administered like the convents, seminaries, or monasteries that sponsored them. The monastic rule on which such government was founded theoretically gave power to the best, who parented the rest with counsel from the wisest and most experienced. Important decisions in such colleges and universities were usually made within the cloister and passed down when and as it suited those who made them. Although the president had to defer to the judgment of the religious superior, the authority of the president within the institution itself was usually absolute and unquestioned. Indeed, at that time it was a matter of serious discussion in Catholic higher education whether the faculty should take a formal vow of obedience to the president.[17] Consequently, Madeleva's involvement of faculty and students in decision making at the college, however limited, was a striking departure from accepted practice at the time.

By the end of her first semester as president, Madeleva had settled into her position and even expressed some enthusiasm for it. She wrote Lehman, "I have a faculty that will go all the way with me. Our student body, too, I think, can be met on other terms than the Notre Dame football schedule." She was determined to lift the sights of the academic community beyond the ordinary and mediocre, even though, as she put it, "limitations of time and energy, the finite in existence, keep us within standardized regulations, and the uninteresting pale of the North Central Association."

Proclaiming herself "wildly ambitious to recall peripatetic, trivium, and quadrivium curricula," Madeleva held up a venerable model of Christian education that drew upon her extensive knowledge of the medieval university.[18] She found herself able to apply her knowledge and interests to the situation at hand, and as time went by, to develop a vision of what the college might become. In the meantime, she invited intellectuals whose ideas excited her to organize seminars on teaching and learning both for faculty and for students. Two of her chief resources were Robert Hutchins, the young president of the University of Chicago and an advocate of liberal learning, and Mortimer Adler, a young associate professor of law at the same university.

In the spring of 1935, Madeleva arranged for Adler to address the faculty on "Metaphysics and the Liberal Arts." She specified the topic,[19] which, as she had mentioned to Lehman, intensely interested her. In his consideration of the nature and purpose of the liberal arts in a historical context, Adler outlined the medieval organization of the seven liberal arts into the quadrivium (consisting of arithmetic, music, geometry, and astronomy) and the trivium (which comprised grammar, rhetoric, and logic). In the question period that followed, Madeleva asked whether the trivium or quadrivium had any relevance in the modern university. From the ensuing discussion emerged the idea of a program of general education based on the medieval division of the liberal arts into grammar, logic, and rhetoric. Faculty response to the idea was as enthusiastic as her own.

Wasting no time, Madeleva invited Sister Miriam Joseph Rauh, who taught in the department of English, to take charge of adapting the trivium to the modern curriculum. Over a five-week period in April and early May 1935, Sister Miriam Joseph and several other sisters, one of whom was Madeleva herself, arranged to meet with Professor Adler in his Chicago apartment to study the matter further.[20]

Out of these efforts grew one of the distinctive curricular innovations of Madeleva's tenure as president of Saint Mary's: the Trivium in College Composition and Reading, required of all entering students. The course, which met daily, integrated the study of literature, composition, and logic and formed the interdisciplinary core of the Saint Mary's liberal education for the next twenty-five years. During that time, other colleges adopted aspects of the program, and the textbook written by Sister Miriam Joseph went through five editions. Once established, Madeleva turned the administration of her brain child, and the credit for it, over to her colleague.

Ironically, the desperate financial condition of the college when Madeleva took office probably made accomplishing such changes easier. Even if her superiors or other sisters opposed them—as some did in the case of a more permissive social code and a radically revised general education requirement—Madeleva had only to argue that the status quo no longer guaranteed survival in tough times. Moreover, the outmoded college to which she returned had failed to anticipate the needs of modern women in a changing world. Looking to the future, she approved plans for a five-year baccalaureate program in nursing, a degree completion program for registered nurses, and a continuing education program both for men and for women from the South Bend area.[21]

Although her first priority was to strengthen the college from within, Madeleva recognized that she must bring Saint Mary's before the public eye if it were to acquire a national reputation. As often as her superiors approved and her other duties allowed, she willingly traveled on college business. During her first year in office, in spite of the expense of time, money, and energy, she attended national education meetings in Atlanta and Chicago, the first of many such trips that took her all over the United States. She valued the fresh ideas and numerous contacts gained from such meetings, convinced that they would benefit the college, even when their effect was not immediately evident.

Like most other religious orders at the time, however, Madeleva's congregation questioned the propriety of such exposure.[22] When as president of the Wasatch she had requested permission to speak to various groups in order to promote the college, she was refused on the grounds that sisters were as a rule not permitted to lecture in public.[23] She argued tirelessly with her superiors then and later about the value of such contacts. Even though Madeleva gave occasional talks both before and after she left the Wasatch, she usually received permission to address only small groups affiliated with the Catholic church, as in the case of the Margaret Roper Society at Oxford. As president of Saint Mary's, Madeleva renewed her petitions to speak in public and persisted until her superiors granted her requests, however reluctantly.

In early February 1935, Madeleva addressed the Catholic Women's League and Business Women's Club in Madison, Wisconsin, where she had spent her first year of college. As was often the case when she traveled, she mixed business with pleasure. The visit introduced her to a number of educators, including Helen C. White, a well-known Catholic novelist and literary critic who taught at the university, from whom Madeleva promptly secured the promise of a lecture. The trip was also a joyful homecoming for Madeleva. Several of her former teachers attended her talk, among them the historian who had introduced her to Saint Benedict and his *Rule*. Several friends from town were also there, including her landlady of thirty years before, now an old woman. Revisiting Madison, Madeleva saw how far she had traveled in the intervening thirty years.

Madeleva requested and received approval to spend most of the summer of 1935 at the Catholic University in Washington, D.C., teaching graduate courses on the English mystics and Chaucer's poetry. Professionally, such work was imperative if she were to remain vital as a scholar, but the intense summer schedule and the pressure of preparing and teaching advanced classes further taxed her already depleted energy. "Washington was hot in temperature and exhausting as an experience," she wrote Lehman, "but I am glad for the illumination that it brought."[24]

Concerned for her health, Lehman routinely cautioned Madeleva to take care of herself. Soon after she assumed the presidency, he wrote to ask if her present life were not "more strenuous for the body and the spirit than ever? Did the European year, from Whitby to Rome, store you against the taxing routine? Having all that within, are you the more sought to give—too much perhaps?"[25] He received her assurance that in spite of occasional illness and fatigue (which necessitated at least one hospital stay during her first year in office, although she withheld that information from him), she was equal to the demands of her position. Knowing her, he continued to question her closely. "Will there be leisure for the genial spirit below the flow of the mind even in office? I hope."[26] In particular he wondered "if the presidency left room for the poetry?"[27]

In reply, Madeleva sent Lehman two poems she had recently written, "Survivors on the French Riviera" and "Things to Be Loved," both of which drew on her European trip for inspiration. "They will bring you slight evidence that I have not gone hopelessly executive," she wrote.[28]

Although her duties as president of Saint Mary's in fact left little "room for the poetry," Madeleva managed to assemble a third collection of verse, *A Question of Lovers*, during her first year in office. It appeared in mid-1935, published by Saint Anthony Guild Press, with whose editor she had traveled to the Holy Land, and contained some of her best work, "better in craftsmanship, imagination and restraint," as one reviewer put it, than many of the poems in her first two volumes.[29]

Only a fraction of the fifty poems in *Lovers* could be called new. Madeleva had written perhaps a fifth of them during her sabbatical year; most of the others were composed during her last five years in the West, usually while she recovered from various illnesses. "Details for My Burial," which she wrote in 1931 during a stay in a Salt Lake

City hospital, appeared in the collection, as did a sequence of poems on biblical women written around the same time. None of the poems composed in the Holy Land appeared, probably because they did not suit the theme of *Lovers*, but several written in England and Hyères were there, as were a few written after her return to Saint Mary's.

In contrast to the passionate verse in *Knight's Errant* and *Penelope*, the poems in *Lovers* are often wistful in tone and characterized by enigmatic brevity. In their evocation of the "poignance of love unspoken," the title poem and others such as "Song Silence" suggest the resignation, sometimes bitter, of one long accustomed to unsatisfied yearning. The speaker of "Riddles One, Two, and Three," which Madeleva considered one of her finest poems,[30] puzzles over the paradoxical qualities of Christ as lover and struggles to comprehend the meaning of a love that is "endless pain/ Or endless peace."

Stripped of the illusions of love but loving nonetheless, the female speaker of poems such as "And So I Am Betrayed" is undone by any reminder of prior fulfillment, which mocks her present deprivation:

> Hunger and thirst and loneliness have come;
> This wild, this poignant singing has unmade me;
> It is not pride but longing holds me dumb.
> The mocking bird, beloved, has betrayed me.

The speaker of "Protest Imperative" is both wary of her lover's power over her and weary of his elusiveness:

> Just what would it profit us, were I the oak, you, being the wind,
> Would buffet me, torture and shatter me, helpless to bend me to
>   mood of your mind.
> Or were I the pine tree, subduing to music your vagrant unrest,
> You, windwise, would slip the wide noose of my arms, the
>   intricate snare of my breast.
> And let us not speak of the grass, prostrate to be trampled by you,
> Scarce lifting its head as you pass to look after the feet it can
>   never pursue.
> Leave off being the wind! I, your lover, have no taste for these:
> The prostrate abjection of grass; the futile, the impotent power
>   of trees.

This is no longer the expectant love of a novice nor the ecstatic love of a bride, but love whose deep roots withstand the blasts of winter.

Set in deserts and prisons, speaking of silence, isolation, and suffering, many of the poems evoke images of desolation and destitution. Both the memory of past delight and the promise of future happiness are almost too painful to endure, as in "California Spring":

> Suppose such life, such beauty, hour by hour
> Came creeping on me, stealthily, like a thief!
> What weapon have I for a gradual flower
> Or what defense against a folded leaf;
> To parry long, sure thoughts of you what power?
> Yes, spring has shown me mercy, being brief.

In the grip of death, which she imaginatively embraces and desires, the speaker of "In the Face of Failure," "Concerning Death," and "Details for My Burial" resigns herself to an unhappy present only because it is temporary. She speaks of life as "a sword by which I cleave existence, birth to death, in twain."

As symbols of Madeleva's interior state, the earliest poems in *Lovers* enlarge upon the spiritual and physical malaise often referred to in her letters of the same period, from the late 1920s through the early 1930s. Still desiring the intimacy of love, she experienced instead the emptiness of its absence, hollowed out by the pain of longing and remembrance.

Shortly after the publication of *Lovers*, during the summer of 1935, Father Hagerty returned to the University of Notre Dame, transferred back from Saint Edward's University in Texas, where he had headed the philosophy department for the previous nine years.[31] That fall, he joined the part-time faculty at Saint Mary's, where he replaced a Holy Cross priest on leave for the year. Apparently their superiors, who previously had done their best to keep the friends apart, decided to allow them to work together, which meant that if they wished they could see each other daily.

Because all written correspondence between them ended with Father Hagerty's return to Notre Dame, where he remained until his death more than forty years later, when he was almost ninety-two, it is impossible to say with certainty what direction their subsequent relationship took. College records indicate that he taught various courses at Saint Mary's in the years following his return, teaching in the summer program beginning in 1937. He also conducted so-called "retreat Sundays" in the convent throughout the 1960s. But apart from a few general references to Madeleva and her family in his memoirs, no further record of their personal relationship remains,[32] even though they spent the rest of their lives on adjoining campuses.

By the time of Father Hagerty's transfer to Notre Dame, it seems clear that the intensity of his relationship with Madeleva had diminished. Although they remained in contact during her last years at the Wasatch and her sabbatical in Europe, they wrote less often to each other, and far less passionately, given the letters that remain.

The tone and content of a letter that Father Hagerty sent to Madeleva in Europe, apparently his last to her, suggests that they mutually agreed to distance themselves from each other. Addressing Madeleva simply as "Dear," Father Hagerty briefly alluded to their last meeting before she left for Europe, during which they talked about both human and divine love. As a conclusion to their discussion, he advised her to reflect on a passage from the Old Testament (Wisdom 8:21): "And knowing that I could not otherwise possess her except God gave it—and this, too, was prudence, to know whose is the gift—I went to the Lord and besought him, and [prayed] with all my heart."

In the Latin, the passage, which refers to wisdom, also connotes continence. "This concept is most important," he wrote her. "Otherwise there is nothing but disorder and weakness, an attempt to do the impossible."[33]

Apparently, love carried the friends full circle, to a reaffirmation of the faith that inspired and sustained their religious vocations and the chastity their vocations entailed. Age probably played its part in their ability to direct their passions to spiritual and intellectual ends: Father Hagerty turned fifty in 1935, and Madeleva was just two years younger. As her superiors no doubt hoped, the year in Europe had restored Madeleva's emotional equilibrium as well as her physical, intellectual, and spiritual energy. Moreover, her return to Saint Mary's had brought her back to an earlier self—one immersed in the love of God—and called forth a new identity, recommitted to community life. Father Hagerty, too, gave every sign of having re-examined his motives and found them suspect. Whatever their reasons, each publicly adopted a position of discrete silence concerning the other. Their silence most likely pays tribute to the depth of the feelings each mastered.

In her poetry, Madeleva continued to work out her own answers to the question of love. *Lovers* hints at a new direction for life and love to take: service. In *Knights Errant* and *Penelope*, celebration in the present moment characterizes a love that manifests itself sensually, in an exchange of glances, a shared embrace, words whispered or sung, fragrances breathed in, and feasts prepared and eaten. The speaker of the poems in *Lovers* longs and hopes for such love to return. But as she waits, as in "Song Silence," she serves by keeping house for God:

Yes, I shall take this quiet house and keep it
With kindled hearth and candle-lighted board,
In singing silence garnish it and sweep it
For Christ, my Lord.

In "A Nun Speaks to Mary," the speaker imagines herself serving Christ's mother by performing menial tasks: dusting, sweeping, running errands, and caring for the new baby. "Mother, all fair," she pleads, "Lay Him within my hungry arms to sleep;/ Lay Him within my hungry heart to keep,/ Adorable, holy,/ Little and lowly." Like all children, the divine Child must be nurtured, and she offers to perform the necessary task. Is such work a substitute for other satisfactions, or is it in fact the nourishment she desires? The speaker of these poems leaves this implicit question unanswered. It was a question Madeleva had not answered for herself when she wrote the poems in the early 1930s.

Only toward the end of *Lovers*, in the "Christmas in Provence" sonnets, does the speaker realize that the Child she serves is also the Lover, Lord, and God whom she seeks. By nurturing Him, not only she but others will experience the fullness of divine love.

A similar revelation seems to have gradually brightened Madeleva's perception of her new position at Saint Mary's, which she initially accepted not from desire but out of obedience. Years before, she had named service as her reason for joining the convent, a goal subtly reaffirmed by the poems in *Lovers*. Like the speaker of "Song Silence," who decides to make her "quiet house" into a home, Madeleva began to transform Saint Mary's into a place where Christ might rest "in every season."

In one of her presidential talks, later collected in *Conversations with Cassandra* (1961), Madeleva quoted from "Design for a House," by Father O'Donnell:

In my love I would give you liberty, confining you only in the
    Infinite,
I would wall you up in the beauty of God,
In the reach and range of God.
I can think of nothing better I could do for you
Than build you a house, out of my love.

"This can well be the design for your college as we build it with and for you," she told students and faculty.[34] Similarly, she often referred to the college as the "home" of Truth and Beauty, divine attributes that signify the presence of God.

As she had at the Wasatch, Madeleva looked to the model of Whitby and its abbess Hilda for inspiration. In an essay on Hilda, she wrote:

> [She] is under my roof, at the very heart of my living and being, this wise, versatile woman, this very Benedictine nun. If there is a problem of building under adverse circumstances, I look at the floor plan of her double monastery at Whitby. If there is a question of educating teachers, she is before me with her best students studying in Rome. If the matter is one of recruiting faculty, I find her drawing on episcopal scholarship from Tarsus to Carthage. As for going to conventions, she was hostess for a synod. Mothering Caedmon, she pioneered workshops of creative writing. She became the mother of English literature. Her universality encompasses me.[35]

At the Wasatch, Madeleva had aspired to create a world like Hilda's, where wisdom and creativity engendered the highest truth and most profound beauty. There, her efforts to build a center of Christian culture had failed. At Saint Mary's, she decided to try again.

12

ᴺARROW ᴳATES

Enter through the narrow gate; for the gate is wide and the road broad
that leads to destruction, and those who enter through it are many. How
narrow the gate and constricted the road that leads to life. And those
who find it are few.

—*Matthew* 7:13–14

The title poem of *Gates and Other Poems*, Madeleva's fourth volume of poetry (published in 1938), concludes:

> The world has narrow gates and wide;
> Men seek their loves through all of them
> And I have come here, seeking mine,
> Jerusalem, Jerusalem!

Written in the holy city in 1934, the poem provides an apt metaphor for many passages in Madeleva's life: her entry into religious life, her discovery of the West and of the scholarly life at Berkeley; her experience of Oxford and European culture; her passage to Jerusalem itself. As president of Saint Mary's, Madeleva found herself—not for the first time—before a narrow gate to be entered alone and with difficulty. She squeezed through only by leaving much behind: dreams as well as reality.

In the poems in *Gates* written close to the time of her return to Saint Mary's, Madeleva contemplated the sacrifices demanded of her. "Meditation on Atlas" parallels its female speaker both to the mythological figure who supports the world and to the Christian divinity who through suffering and death resurrects it. Like them but also like the burden they bear, she describes herself as "stretched out and uplifted." Speaking to herself in the guise of Atlas, she concludes with the paradoxical mix of anguish and triumph characteristic of the martyr:

Be strong and glad as God is;
Open your great arms wide
And set your feet against God's feet,
Atlas. Be crucified.

The speaker of "Love and the Law" gives as much as she of "Meditation," but demands something in return from the God she serves:

Your word is law. You lift these high horizons
Of mountains; stretch this long line of the sea;
Set me enamored and elate between them;
Then, with a breath, you take them all from me.

Your word is still my law. I vow to follow
What path you point, whatever trail you show.
Take when you will these blue stars of December,
This strange and silent loveliness of snow.

No, I retract. I will not sell the ocean;
My mountains and the blossoming stars above;
Peace and the snow and all my wild, white freedom
Except you swear by God your word is love.

Like her personae, obedience might have brought Madeleva through many of the gates through which she passed, but love alone kept her on the narrow way: both the love of God for her, in which she trusted implicitly, and her love for God, which she hoped would reveal itself in new ways in changed circumstances.

In another sense besides self-sacrifice, Madeleva stood before a narrow gate when she took on a position that conferred a measure of worldly power and of public recognition. Her dream of a great college, which made the onerous demands of office bearable because they served a larger purpose, depended for its fulfillment on a knot of personal traits that she had spent her life as a religious trying to unsnarl: her competitiveness, perfectionism, and at times caustic critical acumen. In many ways, her longing for a more contemplative life bespoke a longing for a better self—one more like her father, perhaps, or like her image of the "dream lady" of her youth, Sister Rita.

"Limitations" and a group of poems called "Epitomes" respectively suggest Madeleva's predicament and hint at its solution. In-

stead of feeling trapped and thwarted by the narrowness of her circumstances, she must learn to simplify, and in place of multiplicity,
aspire to unity. Although life in a convent guaranteed a certain external simplicity, ensured by her vows of poverty, chastity, and obedience, her emotional needs—which in another poem from *Gates*, "October Birthday," she referred to as her "tangled moods"—seemed to be
more complex than ever. Her professional life too pulled her in a
dozen directions. Nevertheless, in her poetry as in her inner life,
Madeleva set out on the painful journey toward simplicity, seeing in
that movement "one way of moving toward God," as she put it in a
letter to a sister poet.[1]

     Madeleva's love of nature gave her a starting place as she began
her search for new ways to connect with God. The beauty that she
rediscovered in the "tame and ordered landscape" of northern Indiana
moved her to silent tears. In "Beech Trees," she wrote:

> I passed a wood of beech trees yesterday
> And I am shaken with its beauty yet.
> Why should my breath catch and my eyes be wet
> Because a hundred trees some yards away
> Know simply how to dress in simple gray,
> Are poised beyond the need of epithet,
> And beautiful past power to forget?

     On daily walks that prompted free-flowing meditation, Madeleva
followed the paths that wound for miles along the river and into the
woods beyond the convent and college. Occasionally, in the quiet
moments between appointments, she scribbled down images and
thoughts that stayed with her, and from such jottings came the few
poems that she found time to write.

     Ironically, even though Madeleva wrote no more than several
dozen poems during her first decade as president of Saint Mary's, her
reputation as a poet swelled during those years, thanks in large measure to a single poem, "Snow Storm." She wrote the poem during her
first winter back at Saint Mary's, when a sudden winter storm revived
memories of the hundreds of white swans she had watched as they
flew, crying, from the river to the bay and back again as she waited to
sail from Galway:[2]

> The air is white and winds are crying.
> I think of swans in Galway flying.

Winds are wings; snow is a rover;
Swans of Galway are flying over.

Winds are birds; snow is a feather;
Wild white swans are wind and weather.

Wings drift downward; snow is falling;
Swans are wild winds crying, calling.

Winds are white with snow but alway
Mine are white with swans from Galway.

The poem won a National Poetry Center gold medal for the best poem submitted by an Indiana poet and was placed on display at the New York World's Fair. On January 30, 1939, the *New York Times* printed it.

The publicity that ensued astonished Madeleva. "You speak of the poetry award," she wrote Lehman more than a year later. "That was quite inadvertent and a matter of complete surprise. The simple snowstorm resulted in quite a blizzard of publicity."[3]

Individual poems appeared frequently enough in anthologies and journals, both secular and religious, to keep Madeleva's poetry before the reading public, even though she seldom wrote more than two or three new poems a year. To fill a new volume she sometimes obtained permission from her publishers to include poems that had already appeared in earlier collections, as in the case of *The Happy Christmas Wind and Other Poems*, published in 1936. In a few instances she even included previously unpublished poems that she had written as early as the novitiate.[4] Collected editions of her poems, the first of which was issued in 1939, kept her verse in print.

The poems that Madeleva wrote during those years recorded, however briefly and obliquely, her inner progress as she sought her "loves." In a chastened state as her image of God and of her relationship to God changed, Madeleva seems to have questioned her prior experiences of the divine, including the validity of the ecstatic visions that fired her early poetry. The speaker of "Mirrors," collected in *Christmas Eve and Other Poems* (also published in 1938), tells the creator of nature: "I seek you always," and asks, "Have I never seen you?" By implication, she goes so far as to suggest that her visions of God may simply have been the product of her own imagination, reflections of overwhelming inner needs. In response to this terrifying possibility,

she dares God to become more—not less—obscure, even to the point
of absurdity:

> Choose any veil you will. Set it between you
> And my beholding. Know it shall not screen you
> From me. What occult vesture you may wear,
> Too dread or dull or difficult to bear,
> Are mirrors meaning naught unless they mean you.

The sestet of the sonnet offers a minimalist's credo, cast in the
interrogative:

> Is beauty something I cannot discover?
> Is truth a thing that only children know?
> Are you not mine who are the whole world's lover?
> Can I not find you in all winds that blow,
> In the wild loneliness of lark and plover,
> In slender shadow trees upon the snow?

Coming into her office after a trek along the river, Madeleva
might explain to a waiting sister or student, "God and I have been out
walking together,"[5] a remark whose pious sentimentality masked the
intensity of her inner quest for peace. She downplayed the jarring
contrast between her meditative excursions and the flurry of activity
in her office or classroom with comments such as: "One sees God
everywhere," but realistically cautioned both herself and others that
too many distractions, too much noise, and in particular what she
sardonically referred to as "this preoccupation in the name of the advancement of education," drove God out of one's mind and heart.[6]
True education, she often reminded students and faculty, leads to God
by way of contemplation, which best occurs in serene, uncluttered
surroundings.

For this reason alone, that it would reserve a space for contemplative learning, Madeleva wanted a new library. There were also
pragmatic reasons for the haste with which she undertook a project
that meant increasing the indebtedness of the already financially over-
burdened college. When she took office, two crowded reading rooms
along with a couple of adjacent offices in Le Mans Hall served as the
college library; because of its inadequacy, the application of the college
for membership in the American Association of Colleges had been
refused in 1932.

"If the teacher is the soul of the school, the library is its mind and heart and stomach," Madeleva told students and faculty early in her administration. "Through the library a school breathes and is fed. A school is as great as its teachers and its library."[7] Obviously, if she were to build a great school at Saint Mary's, one recognized as such by peer institutions, she must begin with a new library.

Books and their repository, the library, tangibly represented all that Madeleva cared about most: culture, the life of the mind, the world of the spirit. As a child, she had treasured books, and one of her favorite places was the corner of her grade school classroom that served as its library. As a student at Wisconsin, Notre Dame, and Berkeley, she had visited their large libraries almost before she had unpacked her suitcase; at Oxford, more than "anything or everything," she anticipated the "wonder of the Bodeleian Library."[8] By begging books from friends such as Lehman and Noel Sullivan, she had built up the library at the Wasatch, so dear to her that she referred to it as her child.[9] But could she finance the library she envisioned for Saint Mary's with Le Mans Hall still unpaid for?

A gift of $25,000 received early in her presidency[10] allowed Madeleva to proceed with fundraising. "[This project] has made a mendicant of me," she wrote Lehman.[11] Braving criticism from sisters and alumnae who objected that publicly asking for money was beneath the dignity of women, and especially nuns, she turned to alumnae for support, incidentally launching the first development campaign in the history of the college. Her goal was to begin construction by 1941, the centennial of the founding of the Congregation of the Sisters of the Holy Cross in France. In this way, she justified her effort to the congregation in spite of what must have been serious reservations on the part of her superiors about the timing of such a project.

Funds were raised and ground was broken for the new building on schedule. As Madeleva wrote, "Five minutes later would have been too late. Suddenly, we were in war. The library was the last major building done in this area for the duration."[12] It rose as a tribute to the scholarly life that she personally relinquished so that others might find it.

Another costly essential of Madeleva's plan for a great school was the creation of a great faculty. Like Mother Pauline, she believed that "great teachers are the first requisite for a good school" and set about "finding them, making them, and keeping them."[13] Although the financial situation of the congregation as well as the college was still far from secure, Madeleva fought to convince her superiors that promising young nuns should be released from other duties and allowed ample time and money to pursue advanced degrees in the best universities.

Madeleva's year in Europe, filled with stimulating people, ideas, places and events, had broadened her nature and taught her to think on a large scale. The gifts of time, beauty, and knowledge that Mother Vincentia had generously secured for her had restored her body and her spirit. She knew the worth of such life-giving bounty, and wanted it for others. She made her case so successfully that several young sisters were approved for graduate study, and in the fall of 1935, she had the pleasure of escorting one of them, Sister Maria Renata Daily, to Yale to begin work on her doctorate in history. Others went off to the Art Institute of Chicago, the Catholic University, and Columbia.

Even before she became president of Saint Mary's, while she was still in England, Madeleva devised a plan to augment the faculty. It occurred to her that recent Oxford graduates might welcome an opportunity to spend a few years teaching in America. Young Bridget Cunningham, who completed her degree in the spring of 1934, offered herself as a candidate. Madeleva worked for months, first to convince her superiors of the wisdom of the plan and then to find money to pay the young woman's passage—which she did by contributing a personal gift of money sent to her by a friend. Miss Cunningham taught in the English department at Saint Mary's until 1936, enhancing the credentials of the faculty with her prestigious degree and brightening academic processions with her distinctive regalia—in other words, adding a touch of class to the small, midwestern college.

Madeleva's enduring fondness for England and the English manifested itself in various ways, from her patronage of young Miss Cunningham to the maps of London and Oxford on her office wall. It showed itself in the design of Riedinger House, built in 1937 for the use of home economics majors on the plan of an English cottage, and in its lovely garden. The rock garden that replaced the old boat house on the bank of Lake Marian was also modeled on the English gardens Madeleva loved.

Instead of leaving Europe behind, Madeleva was determined to import something of its intellectual and cultural life by bringing as many Europeans to Saint Mary's as possible. Close collaboration with Reverend John O'Hara, CSC, Father O'Donnell's successor as president of the University of Notre Dame, and with subsequent presidents of the university, allowed her to expand the academic world of the college with distinguished speakers and visiting professors for whom, acting alone, she could not have found funds. British journalist Arnold Lunn, British historian Christopher Hollis, and Shane Leslie of the

Dublin Review always stopped at Saint Mary's when they visited Notre Dame. Waldemar Gurian, a distinguished journalist and an expert on Russian politics and language, taught at both schools as did French philosopher Yves Simon before he moved to the University of Chicago.

Madeleva's Irish friend Seamus MacManus became a frequent lecturer on both campuses as did Father Martin D'Arcy, the Jesuit scholar who had taught her philosophy at Oxford, and both Frank and Maisie Ward Sheed. In 1933, the Sheeds had opened a branch of their press, Sheed and Ward, in New York City, which in effect introduced the Catholic Revival to the United States. Frank, Australian by birth, was a brilliant speaker, energetic, ebullient, and passionate about religious questions. Maisie, born into a prominent English Catholic family, was an idealist whose cause was her militant Catholicism. Rarely a year went by when one or both of them did not visit Saint Mary's and Notre Dame, doing their part to keep faculty and students of both schools in touch with the Catholic intellectual world beyond their gates.

Oxford-educated actor and author Robert Speaight became one of Madeleva's favorite and most frequent visitors. "Bobby," as she affectionately called him, paid his first visit to the college in the late 1930s, when he spent a year as a visiting professor at Notre Dame. He had originated the role of Thomas Becket in T. S. Eliot's *Murder in the Cathedral* and also had written a biography of Becket. Madeleva admired his talent, but even more, she respected the strong faith and exemplary Christian life of the Catholic convert, in spite of the temptations of theatrical life. She also loved the play of his mind and variety of his interests.

Through Speaight, Madeleva laid the foundation for a program that would eventually bring the finest English drama to life on the Saint Mary's stage. In the course of several decades of working together, which culminated when Speaight twice spent several months at Saint Mary's as a visiting lecturer and artist in residence, the actor and the nun became genuinely fond of each other. On his visits, Madeleva invited the lively Englishman, brimming with urbane wit and good talk, to her office for tea. He later recalled the room as "a wise and hospitable 'refugium peccatorum,' " a place of rest and respite. Seated before the fire, surrounded by books, pictures, and memorabilia that ranged from a collection of walking sticks to bells of all sizes and shapes, the friends conversed for hours at a time. "Like so many people who have a genius for getting things done," he wrote, "she never seemed to have anything to do."[14]

One of the most illustrious of the European visitors during the early years of her presidency, and probably the one who meant the most to Madeleva personally, was Charles Du Bos. In the fall of 1937, he arrived from Paris along with his wife and daughter, and with them his secretary, Madge Vaison, Madeleva's good friend. Du Bos had accepted a visiting professorship at Notre Dame, and he also arranged to offer courses at Saint Mary's and deliver a series of lectures on literature to the Saint Mary's faculty. As he told Madeleva, he came expecting to make Notre Dame and Saint Mary's a center of his life.[15] In turn, Madeleva hoped that Du Bos would become the cornerstone of her great school.

Soon after she met them in Paris, Madeleva had raised the possibility of such a visit with the Du Bos family, and she and Madge had combined forces in the intervening years to smooth whatever obstacles arose on either side of the Atlantic.[16] Although Du Bos's health was poor and he had in fact been "several times at death's door"[17] during the spring of 1937, the family came as planned the following fall. Madeleva helped them rent a house near campus and arranged for their daughter, Primerose, to enroll as a first-year student at Saint Mary's.

Routinely, the family and Madge joined the sisters for daily Mass at 6:30 A.M., followed by breakfast. Madeleva described how every Sunday morning she and "Charlie," as she called him, would then sit down together for a long conversation, he with his row of pipes before him on one side of a table in her office and she on the other.[18]

Madeleva recalled: "One pipe after another was lighted, smoked and cooled as we talked of ominous world conditions, the epistle or gospel of the Mass of the day, a current book, a line from Julian of Norwich, the light that is life. You can easily guess that my contributions to these conversations were chiefly monosyllabic. Charlie needed oral expression and a listener before he fixed his clarities of thought into the clarities of prose."[19]

What Is Literature? a collection of essays written by Du Bos and delivered in English to the faculty at Saint Mary's, took shape in those long Sunday conversations. When it was published, Du Bos dedicated the little book to Madeleva in acknowledgment of her inspiration and in gratitude for her friendship. But it would be impossible to decide who benefitted more from their intellectual exchange. "I can only say that I am a different I because of it," Madeleva asserted.[20] Their talks lifted her above the necessary but mundane tasks of her office, as did the Sunday afternoon salons that Du Bos and his wife Zezette hosted for faculty and students from both campuses.

As her professional scholarship languished without the time and energy to sustain it, Madeleva found an outlet for her questing mind in her conversations with Du Bos and his circle of family and friends. She enjoyed exchanges with a dazzling array of visitors, the most frequent of whom was Jacques Maritain, who with his wife, Raïssa, and her sister Vera, came often to South Bend to see the Du Boses, usually staying as houseguests at Saint Mary's. Madeleva made sure that not only she herself but the entire campus community benefitted from such visitors, conscripting them to deliver lectures and conduct seminars for faculty, students, and convent sisters.

Madeleva's friendship with Madge Vaison flourished during Madge's year-long stay in South Bend. They saw each other daily and continued the conversations that had begun on the *Aurania* four years earlier, taking up where their frequent letters left off. After Madge returned to France in the spring of 1938 to be married, the two women resumed their correspondence, which continued throughout the rest of Madeleva's life, with occasional visits marking the years apart.

Madeleva embraced the younger woman as a spiritual daughter, writing consoling letters to her as war threatened to break out in Europe soon after her marriage. "One has to practice constantly the sacrament of the present moment to preserve peace," Madeleva wrote the distraught young wife. "It enriches even our distractions."[21] To Madge's fears for a baby daughter born shortly after war began, she responded, "What a blessed refuge infancy is against the bewilderments of our time!"[22]

During the winter and spring that followed Madge's departure, Madeleva saw her hopes for a long collaboration with Du Bos dashed. He was so desperately ill that he could neither lecture nor teach and was finally hospitalized. Although he improved enough to make the voyage home in June 1939, he barely survived the difficult journey. By August, he was dead. Primerose wrote Madeleva from Paris: "Father died last Saturday, the fifth, on the feast of Saint Mary of the Snow. He had the death he deserved, the death of a saint. He was quite conscious and asked himself for the sacraments. He had time to speak to each of us in particular, to tell us about his unfinished work. It was so great, so beautiful, that it gives courage to Mother and to me."[23]

"It is reassuring to have M. Du Bos . . . with God in this crisis," Madeleva wrote of the war that disrupted the lives of her friends.[24] Their firsthand reports kept her abreast of conditions in Europe, about which she often spoke to students in her weekly convocations. In one such address, she diagnosed the cause of the war as "a state of spiritual world-bankruptcy" that could be cured only by "a return to supernatural values" and not by a victory through arms.[25]

Far from quiescent, however, Madeleva offered practical help to refugees, especially to those of Jewish blood, with whom she felt an affinity. Several of the teachers she most respected at Berkeley were Jewish, including Ben Lehman. She traced her membership in the National Conference of Christians and Jews back to 1930, and later served on the board of trustees of this ecumenical organization. Several times during the war years, she cooperated with Mme Du Bos to help Jewish women escape from Europe, offering them a place to stay when they reached the United States.[26]

However much Madeleva deplored its effects and prayed for its end, World War II proved to be an ally in her desire to strengthen Saint Mary's by grafting something of European culture onto American stock. Religious and political exiles who were often scholars of the first rank thankfully accepted teaching positions at colleges such as Saint Mary's and Notre Dame, and many more passed through. Archduke Otto of Austria came, as did Contesse de Chambrun. The von Trapp family performed, and Baroness Catherine de Hueck addressed the students. Madeleva spent time with each visitor, gently questioning and avidly listening and learning; some, such as economist Barbara Ward, returned often and became friends.

Among the Europeans who joined the faculty at Saint Mary's during the war years was Otto von Simson, a young art historian who held a doctorate from the University of Munich. The Catholic convert, of Jewish descent, arrived at Saint Mary's in 1943 with his wife, a daughter of Prince Schonburg-Hartenstein, the former Austro-Hungarian ambassador to the Holy See, and their small son. During his tenure at Saint Mary's, von Simson wrote *Sacred Fortress*, a study of church architecture that established his reputation as a scholar and distinguished art historian. Madeleva's hope that in von Simson she had found a star to light her college flared brightly but briefly. Within two years of his arrival at Saint Mary's, the University of Chicago offered him a position on its faculty. Madeleva dug deep in her pockets. "We will meet any offer,"[27] she told him, but to no avail.

In her autobiography, Mrs. von Simson praised the excellence of the college her husband had nonetheless chosen to leave and recorded her impressions of Madeleva as she was in her mid-fifties, when the von Simsons knew her: "The President of the College was an impressive woman of great culture and a distinguished poet herself. She knew and corresponded with a number of scholars and intellectually outstanding personalities and when she entertained some distinguished lecturer in her elegant little drawing room with its big fire place, she herself dressed in the becoming habit of her Order, one would have rather thought of a great lady conversing on intellectual and artistic topics than of a nun."[28]

No doubt, Madeleva would have been flattered to know that blue-blooded Mrs. von Simson perceived her to be "a great lady"; nevertheless, she described herself and her concerns quite differently in a letter to Lehman, written at about the same time, when she was fifty-five. She was, she said, "maintaining a certain inner peace" but felt harried and appalled by the "importunities of every day" that swept "weeks and months before them." She lamented, "We are precipitated into another year with no time for the luxury of experienced living."[29]

Once again, Madeleva felt discouraged by overwork and by poor health. Her susceptibility to fatigue, colds, and depressed moods had returned, accompanied by several new complaints, including problems with her liver and thyroid. No longer young, she took longer to recover from even minor illnesses, sometimes spending weeks at a time in one of the Holy Cross hospitals, laid low by a virus, a bronchial infection, or what she described as "a very unforgiving nervous system."[30] She blamed her declining health on her job. "Graduate work may have been devastating in its demands," she confided to Lehman, "but it cannot compare with the position in which I am now inundated."[31]

Personal considerations paled, however, before the "agony" of war, as she phrased it, that somber backdrop for everything else at the time. Lehman wrote to express his anxiety for his son Hal, who planned to enlist. Madeleva shared with her fellow educator her concern not only for Hal, whom she had known as a child, but for an entire generation of young people burdened with "premature maturity and what strange wisdoms!"[32] Their educations, she pointed out, had been "fearfully wrested from our hands" by the events of recent years.[33] Continued prayer promised some fortification, she hoped, commenting, "How badly we remember our Macbeth, adverting so little to the essential trap 'Security is mortal's cheapest enemy.'" She asked him, "Do you remember quoting in class years ago from Cornelia A. P. Comer's *The Preliminaries*, 'We are secure when we can stand everything that can happen to us'?"[34] She found this spartan philosophy consoling, and in her convocations passed it along to her students.

In December 1943, Madeleva sent Lehman a typescript of a recent poem, "November Afternoons," as "a small sign of life." The poem celebrates a peaceful moment in an otherwise bleak season:

Now they have come, these afternoons in November,
When all the air is still and branches are bare,
And the long, lovely light that I remember
Invades with luminous peace the untroubled air.

Off to the west a dozen trees together
Stand in gray loveliness, bemused with light;
Slender and silver they stand in the autumn weather,
Waiting the inevitable winter, the inevitable night.

Blossoming light they bear as a single flower,
And silence more singing sweet than a lone bird's call.
Off to the west I stand, sharing their hour,
At peace with beauty and needing no song at all.

For a brief moment, the speaker of the poem—whose time of life parallels that of the season and the hour—sees past darkness, even death, transfixed by momentary beauty that has the power to carry her out of herself and beyond her own limitations and needs.

Such epiphanies refreshed the poet and restored the inner vision that gave her life purpose and meaning. They occurred unexpectedly, perhaps infrequently, but just the memory of them revitalized her. She told the story of a train trip through the Rockies in a snowstorm that offered one such moment, which she called "one of the great moments of my life." She recalled, "As I looked out over the great immensities of mountain peak and snow, a bald eagle swept into view, descended slowly and settled on a great naked branch of fire-blackened pine. Perhaps no one in all the world saw this lone king on his stark throne except myself." She concluded: "We find our great teachers and our great lessons everywhere, even from a train window."[35]

The image of the solitary eagle on its ruined branch surely represented to Madeleva something of her own condition. The loneliness of leadership was especially present to her following her unilateral decision in 1941 to integrate the student body of the college. Convinced that integration was the right thing to do, she refused to debate the issue, even with her superiors, relying on several sympathetic clergymen for support in the firestorm that followed.[36] Implemented by Saint Mary's in 1943, years in advance of most other residential, private colleges and universities, the policy infuriated many parents, students, and members of the congregation, as Madeleva knew it would. She refused to back down. "If it emptied the school, we would enroll Negro girls in residence," she declared.[37]

As Madeleva wrote in her autobiography, "Southern parents wrote enraged letters telling me that as a Northerner I did not know what I was doing. I answered that, however conditioned by my own upbringing, I was acting under the direction of Cardinal, then Archbishop, Stritch who had been born and reared in Memphis. A round robin of protest went to him. He sent me a copy of his reply, with the reassurance, 'You are right, Sister. Stick to your guns!'"[38]

A single African American student arrived on campus in September 1943, a light-skinned Creole whose obvious mixed blood made the brouhaha caused by her admission even more ridiculous to Madeleva. The young woman was a brilliant student. "By the third semester she led the school academically," Madeleva wrote. "She stood first on the Honor Roll, with a major in science."[39]

By ones and twos other black students followed, their number soon augmented by international students of color from Africa, Southeast Asia, India, and Central and South America. Late in Madeleva's administration, foreign students at the college represented thirty-eight different nations. Madeleva justified the many scholarships granted to international students with the comment that to fulfill the Christian obligation to go forth and teach all nations, the college must improvise and "bring all nations to us."[40]

A few years after the integration of the college, Madeleva went so far as to question the unspoken segregation in her congregation, writing to her superiors: "Our students are asking if the Sisters of the Holy Cross accept properly qualified Negro postulants. In at least one case the inquiry comes from a girl who will make application only to a community that does. What answer shall we give?"[41]

"The red man, the black man and the white man should come together bringing their gifts to the dear Lord God," Madeleva wrote,[42] seeing in the three wise men a prototype of interracial unity. In her comments on the subject of race, she reserved pointed irony for the sometimes blatant discrimination practiced by Catholic schools and churches. "Some day, please God," she wrote an African-American friend, "we will be truly Christian."[43]

Madeleva extended her desire for unity to those of other religious sects, priding herself on her ecumenism. In part because of her Lutheran father, she was, in her own words, always "keenly conscious of the text from the New Testament, 'Other sheep I have that are not of this fold.'"[44] She wrote C. S. Lewis, an Anglican, "No matter what our faith or creed we all share the great basic realities of life and love and death."[45] Shortly before her death, she told a newspaper reporter,

"I'm eliminating the word 'Protestant' from my vocabulary because I believe we are all children of God."[46]

Like that of most people, Madeleva's tolerance had its limits. Apparently, she had little exposure to or understanding of Islam, as her diary entries during her trip to Egypt and the Holy Land reveal. She had no sympathy whatsoever for Communism, which she regarded as the antithesis of Christian faith. Indeed, she was so adamantly opposed to it that late in life she threatened to withdraw from a panel on poetry if Langston Hughes, whom she heard was a Communist, took part. Until she was informed of Hughes's political sympathies, she had been pleased to appear on the program with him. In the end, Hughes stayed home.[47]

For the most part, however, Madeleva kept an open mind and practiced forbearance in her dealings with those of other cultures, creeds, or races, however different from her own. "Her universality encompasses me," Madeleva wrote of Abbess Hilda of Whitby, imitating her ideal in this quality as in most others. Constantly challenging her own cultural biases, Madeleva began to think and write about the need for westerners to learn Asian languages and master at least the rudiments of Asian history and philosophy.[48] Recognizing a future world power in China, she eventually overcame even her hatred of Communism to favor publicly the admission of The People's Republic of China to full membership in the United Nations. She also kept abreast of tumultuous political developments in Africa in the 1950s, and before she retired, appointed a specialist in African history to the faculty.

But, undeniably, Madeleva was most at home in Western culture and centered her educational efforts on it. In the early days of the Great Books Program, she invited Robert Hutchins and Mortimer Adler to conduct frequent seminars on the classics at Saint Mary's. Along with faculty, students, and staff of the college, adults of the local community participated in these experiments in liberal education. Perhaps influenced by her experience at the University of Wisconsin, with its commitment to continuing education, Madeleva opened the resources of the college to the local community from the earliest days of her administration.

In 1941, the college had observed the centennial of the Sisters of the Holy Cross with the construction of the new library. Marking the end of her first decade in office, Madeleva celebrated another centennial, the anniversary of the founding of Saint Mary's in 1844. To commemorate the event, she invited many of the distinguished scholars and educators who had served the college as unofficial consultants to deliver a series of lectures on liberal education, later published as *A College Goes to School.* Jacques Maritain spoke on moral education; Robert Hutchins discussed education for freedom; and Mortimer Adler chose character and intelligence as his subjects. Madeleva herself sounded a Christian theme, education for immortality. In his lecture, Father Hugh O'Donnell, president of the University of Notre Dame, praised Saint Mary's as a citadel of Western culture, which as he put it "has its roots in Christ"—that is, in the values and institutions inspired by Christian faith and tradition.[49]

Father O'Donnell articulated the aspect of Madeleva's emerging vision for Saint Mary's that, in the course of the next two decades, revealed itself as central: the college as a center of Christian culture. That ideal, which first took shape in the design of a core curriculum based on the Trivium, an essential component of medieval Christian education, acquired further definition with the advent of Otto von Simson's replacement, a young Austrian immigrant named Bruno Schlesinger, who was completing his doctoral studies in history and political science at the University of Notre Dame when Madeleva hired him in 1945. She wrote in her autobiography of her plans for the college: "Gradually I began to see light." Her new member of the faculty brought his own vision to strengthen hers.

A Jewish convert, Schlesinger had fled from his home near Vienna six months after the occupation of Austria by the Nazis in 1938. Traveling first to Yugoslavia, he eventually made his way to France, where he obtained entry to the United States with the help of an American clergyman. Attracted to Notre Dame by Waldemar Gurian's work on the *Review of Politics*, Schlesinger was finishing a dissertation on the ideas of English historian Christopher Dawson when Madeleva appointed him to teach both in the history and in the art departments. He stayed to found the Program in Christian Culture, which Madeleva dubbed "the department deluxe."

Based on Dawson's educational ideas, the program (renamed Humanistic Studies in the late 1960s), exemplified all that Madeleva thought best and loved most about Western culture. Designed to counter the fragmentation of the contemporary college curriculum, which Dawson interpreted to be the result of increasing specialization and secularization, the program was centered on a study of the dynamic and formative role of Christianity in the development of the intellectual and cultural traditions of the West.

Ironically, the program almost died before it was born. For months that stretched into years, Professor Schlesinger's proposal, which would have instituted the study of Christian culture as an alternative to the traditional history major, lay in limbo, first on the desk of Sister Maria Renata, who headed the history department, and after Schlesinger appealed directly to the president, on Madeleva's desk. Although Maria Renata did not publicly voice her objections to the proposal, she most likely feared the loss of many of her best students to the new program. In any case, she opposed it with silence. Apparently unwilling to move against the opposition of a department head and a member of her community, Madeleva delayed.

Schlesinger credits Frank Sheed with convincing Madeleva to decide in his favor. As he put it, "Frank Sheed was her messenger from the outside world."[50] Sheed knew Dawson well, reinforced the value of his educational ideas, and encouraged Madeleva to support the innovative program. Her own knowledge and love of medieval culture did its part to convince her of the value of the experiment. In 1956, she finally authorized the program as an interdisciplinary major, entirely separate from the department of history. At Professor Schlesinger's suggestion, she approved Dawson as a consultant to the program, bringing him to campus from Harvard, where he was the Charles Chauncey Stillman Guest Professor of Roman Catholic Studies from 1958 through 1962.

With Madeleva's encouragement, the Program in Christian Culture—which she described as second only to theology in importance in the curriculum[51]—became one of the distinctive offerings of the college and remains the only successful incorporation of Dawson's educational theories in American higher education. Christian Culture exemplified Madeleva's conviction that contemporary education need not be dissociated from Christianity but that, on the contrary, the Christian tradition offers a coherent focus for the interpretation and integration of knowledge. In collaboration with Bruno Schlesinger, she brought what she considered to be the best of European culture home: a crucial piece in her plan for a second Whitby.

13

ʻEducating ʻWomen

Growing up, Eva Wolff resented being referred to as Fred or Vern's sister;[1] she insisted on an identity of her own. Both in grade school and in high school, she relished her frequent academic successes over male classmates who were expected to out-perform their female peers. At Wisconsin, Berkeley, and Oxford, she prided herself on holding her own as one of few females in a predominantly male environment. As a woman, Madeleva seems to have thought of herself as something of a David among Goliaths, invariably emphasizing her young age, small size, or lack of experience when comparing herself with men. Her weapons were an intelligence and a determination that few could match.

Not that Madeleva thought of herself as an enemy of men—she enjoyed male companionship and, even in the convent, satisfied her need for it. She related to Father O'Donnell, Father Hagerty, and Ben Lehman as most women of her time related to men, with a sense not of equality but complementarity and an expectation of courteous respect rather than camaraderie. Nevertheless, particularly in her autobiography, Madeleva often portrayed herself as the triumphant underdog, revealing traces of the irony that those who are underestimated and know it bring to relationships with those who assume superiority.

In contrast, a sense of solidarity marks Madeleva's comments about women. She identified with them, liked them, and looked to them for inspiration. "All that I or any of us can do," Madeleva often said, "is what one good woman can do." Far from deprecating the power of women, she knew what a high standard she set when she made such a statement. She looked to a pantheon of good women who demonstrated a seemingly limitless capacity to make a positive difference. Abbess Hilda was only one among scores of committed women whom Madeleva regarded as exemplars of the highest values. They included holy women of the church, past and present, among them members of her own Holy Cross congregation.

Madeleva often called to mind the "pageant" of fine leaders who had preceded her at Saint Mary's, "too many to cite but too brave and dear ever to forget."[2] Regal Mother Pauline, who died within a few months of Madeleva's inauguration, set the benchmark for her as president. Above all, Sister Rita remained for her a model of all that women should and at their best could be, and she honored her memory. In all the years after Sister Rita's death, Madeleva had never failed to celebrate her feast day. As the president of Saint Mary's, she hung an oil painting of her beloved teacher above the fireplace in her office and memorialized her in an essay published in *The Ave Maria*.[3]

Inevitably, Madeleva's style of leadership betrayed the influence of the female models she emulated, as shaped by her experience of authority in the convent. Moreover, a childhood spent in a home where a decisive mother with high expectations ruled had its effect on her. "I still have difficulty in this day and age of expecting others to stand a little longer than they find comfortable, of kneeling without padded benches, etc.," she admitted, describing herself as a strict disciplinarian.[4]

Two traditional types of female power, those of the queen and the mother, merged in the model of governance with which Madeleva was most familiar, that of the mother superior or abbess, a model reinforced by the image in church tradition of Mary, Mother of God and Queen of Heaven. As practiced in the convent, this style of leadership was based on the practice of discernment, a subtle blend of intuition and inspiration involving prayer, empathy, and openness to individual need, rather than on logic or precedent.

In defense of her decision to send Madeleva to Europe, Mother Vincentia had struggled to articulate the concept of 'discernment.' "For the community," she had written, "not for favoritism." For the community, yes, but through the good of the individual. The qualities that Madeleva attributed to Abbess Hilda, which she characterized as "wisdom," "versatility," and "mothering," also exemplified discernment in action.

Madeleva spoke of her role as president and her vocation as a sister and an educator as a type of "motherhood"[5] and often referred to the college as the "mother" of the minds of its students,[6] redefining these concepts and expanding upon their usual connotations. Through the influence of their teachers and their alma mater, she said, young women learned "the dignity of obedience, the nobility of sacrifice, the sanctity of selflessness, the wonder of beauty, the joy of goodness, the freedoms of truth, the securities of faith, the sanities of hope, the divinity of love" that enabled them to become mothers themselves, and, as she put it, "do the things that a mother must be able to do."[7]

FIGURE 13.1

Sr. Madeleva under a portrait of Sr. Rita in Madeleva's Office

Courtesy Saint Mary's College Archives.

Correspondingly, Madeleva usually conveyed her vision of education through traditional images of feminine work such as homemaking and child-rearing, connotative of nurturing, and through concepts such as 'beauty,' 'wisdom,' and 'goodness,' which are often identified as feminine as well as noble or divine.

The introduction of such imagery into Madeleva's language suggests a gradual shift in her personal perspective. Instead of looking for God in potent, masculine manifestations of the divine as King, Lover, or Lord, as she once had, she began to seek the divine in more unexpected manifestations. In the weak and humble, exemplified in Christian iconography by the images of the Child and the Woman, she learned to identify the divine presence.

Translated into practice, such a realization explains in part Madeleva's determination to give herself fully to her work, seeking meaning in an active life of service rather than a solitary, contemplative existence. Surely she experienced moments of regret at being cast as a Martha instead of a Mary, but instead of conceiving of her work as a detour on her path to God, she began to speak of it as the way itself—her "progress to Eternity"—emphasizing in numerous talks the spiritual benefits of work and the active life it implies.[8]

Studying successive generations of the young women whom she had taught over the course of many years, watching them, listening to them, speaking with them, challenging them, and being challenged in return was at the heart of Madeleva's mission as an educator. "My essential work has been the education of girls," she wrote in an autobiographical statement in 1940. "This I begin by believing in them and loving them. Whatever else may have been the results, they have succeeded fairly in educating me."[9]

When asked what she had missed most during her year in Europe, Madeleva promptly replied, "The American girl!"[10] She preferred modern American women to those of Europe or of an earlier generation because they seemed to her "more simple"; they entered freely into "the give and take of conversation" and refused to be "intimidated by position or overpowered by glory."[11] She especially appreciated the "fugitive loveliness of the final teens," but in all female beauty she saw a special reflection of the beauty of God.[12]

Female beauty was a frequent theme in the president's addresses to the student body of Saint Mary's. She attacked the image of beauty promulgated by the media of her day. In her opinion, this image pressured women to look "not like themselves, but like pitiful parodies of the motion picture deities of the moment."[13] She redefined the notion of "true beauty" as "beauty of being—apart from hairdos and cosmetics,"[14] and stressed that only Christian education conferred it.

Specifically, Christian education alone provided the knowledge of a woman's "supernatural stature," according to Madeleva, and conferred a sense both of her true worth and of her true identity. Alert to the images of women conveyed in popular culture, she was quick to speak out, as when she discovered that her publisher, Macmillan, had also published *Forever Amber*, a best-selling novel that in her estimation demeaned women. She wrote a scathing letter to the editor of the company, in which she protested: "Because my life has been spent teaching girls and young women I speak almost instinctively in protest against this prostitution of their integrity of mind and thought."[15]

Like her favorite mystic, Julian of Norwich, Madeleva believed that women manifest unique aspects of the divine, which she consistently identified as "mothering." In the *Revelations of Divine Love*, Dame Julian associates specific acts of nurturing and teaching with Jesus as mother. Madeleva regarded the development of the intellectual and emotional qualities necessary to such mothering as the essential aim of and justification for the education of women. She offered as an example to be imitated the image of Mary, the perfect expression of the feminine.[16] "The quintessence of womanliness [is] the very flower and fruit of the education of women,"[17] she professed; moreover, the development of her womanliness is a woman's way to God.

In amplifying this theme over the course of many years, Madeleva stressed intellectual development as the key to spiritual maturity for women. In a talk titled "The Intellectual Virtues," for example, she praised the "right reason about doing and making" of women such as saints Helena, Paula, Eustochium, and Hilda. These women used their mental strengths: wisdom, understanding, knowledge, imagination, and prudence, to do God's work. "Are they too remote in time and place to move us to imitation?" she asked.[18]

One of Madeleva's favorite mottos became, Just think! She used it as a call for intellectual virtue and as an antidote for the stress on physical appearance that in her opinion corrupted many young women. She cautioned women, especially those who found themselves caught up in the demands of home and family, to save time for what might seem like "luxury" activities: reading, music, art, including the fine art of conversation. "I do not absolve . . . women on any intellectual level from putting their minds in order," she told a reporter, "planning for them as they do for their meals, their clothes, their recreations. Their minds deserve even better treatment than their bodies. This they rarely receive."[19]

Madeleva also used her platform to emphasize the responsibility of women to teach "our daughters to think ethically, honestly, morally about civil rights, about segregation, about the sacredness of human life, about power, wealth, truth."[20] She warned against the tyranny of conformity and the obsession with security that rob women of their ability to think independently and that compromise their sense of themselves as individuals. She identified as goals of women's education to rectify the "feminine vices: vanity, self-indulgence, fear of humiliation,"[21] and to strengthen young women in their "battle for personal identity and freedom against the gregarious disease of togetherness."[22]

Long before psychologists defined women's distinctive ways of knowing, Madeleva described as one of the chief advantages of a woman's college its recognition that "girls study, learn and respond to teaching differently from the way boys do, and differently in classes with boys from in groups of girls only. Whatever the reasons for the delicate psychology governing these facts, they are facts."[23] The substance of an education for women should match that of their brothers, she maintained, but should differ significantly in approach. The recognition of this difference, which Madeleva equated primarily with emotional differences between the sexes, allowed women to explore their "womanliness" fully and freely, both in terms of interests and in terms of abilities. It also prepared them to enter any profession with confidence in themselves as women, thanks both to the quality of the education they had received and to the affirmation with which it had been imparted.[24]

Madeleva thought that women who chose co-education short-changed themselves. She spoke of them as Sabine women who willingly transported themselves into an alien land. As she put it, "We women have reversed the story of the Sabine women; we have put ourselves in a somewhat unintellectual position in our very endeavor to prove our intellectual position with men."[25] Men, she pointed out, apparently felt no need to colonize institutions designed for and by women. Why should women submit themselves to an education defined exclusively by and for males?

Anticipating the threats to single-sex colleges as well as to religious education several decades before they became imminent, Madeleva made a coherent, positive case for women's education and for Catholic education tailored to the specific needs of women. In the process, she offered Catholics by example and precept an image of women as the intellectual and spiritual counterparts of men, distinguished by supernatural qualities that identify them in a distinctive way with God and Christ—and which have the power to redefine patriarchal images of the divine. Although couched in the rhetoric of her era, her ideas on women exceeded those of most of her contemporaries (so much so that few at the time appreciated their implications), and in many respects anticipated those of later feminist theorists. They continue to offer insight into ways of constructing the feminine.

As an educator of women, Madeleva paid close attention to the condition of women in her society and, in particular, in the church. She saw much to be optimistic about. As she told a reporter in 1962: "All areas of living have opened up to women—politics, social service, law, medicine, diplomacy. That scope has been realized in the religious life as well."[26] Neither a revolutionary nor a radical, she tolerated the status quo. As she told the same reporter, "We shouldn't brood over the past, or get desperate over the future. We should accept the present and give it everything we have that is good."[27] However, when she identified a need she could fill or an injustice she could rectify, she acted swiftly and decisively. Even though her primary goal was usually something other than to improve the situation of women, in fact women as a group often benefitted from her actions.

For many years, Madeleva had been acutely aware of the deplorable state of theological education in most Catholic schools. This was a subject that touched her personally and concerned her profoundly as a nun and as a Christian educator. She wholeheartedly endorsed John Cardinal Newman's assertion in *The Idea of a University* that theology is the queen of the sciences and should be a linchpin in the curriculum of the Christian university. Yet too often, as she had found at the Wasatch, priests—the only formally trained theologians at the time— were not always available to teach such courses. Consequently, they were entrusted to well-intentioned sisters whose only preparation was their training as novices and their life in a convent. Madeleva spoke scathingly of the expectation that a religious vocation of itself qualified one to teach theology—as though eating three meals a day qualified a person to teach nutrition!

Madeleva assessed the inevitable consequences: "The courses of religion that were offered in our colleges were the dullest and most poorly taught in the curriculum. We had no graduate schools in which to prepare young teachers of Theology on levels equal to their preparation in profane subjects. Priests qualified to teach Theology were occupied otherwise. Religion was the last and least interesting of all subjects taught by the least prepared and frequently poorest teachers."[28]

To Madeleva, this neglect of the religious education and by implication the spiritual lives of students of all ages was an abomination. She wrote, "If, through lack of instruction on the part of the teacher,

the child fails to know and love and serve God, fails to enter into
[God's] great Christian heritage, the error reaches far beyond the range
of pedagogy. Jesus may have had our teachers of Christian Doctrine in
mind when He said, 'Suffer the little children to come unto me.' They
come largely through their teachers."[29]

When her friend Frank Sheed pointed out that there was no
place in the United States where a lay person, male or female, could
enroll to study theology, Madeleva saw the reason for the situation she
deplored. "[His] statement gave me no peace," she wrote. "Were we
to let these flagrancies continue?"[30] Working through the Problems
Committee of the National Catholic Education Committee, of which
she was a member, Madeleva brought the issue to national attention.
In 1943, she was appointed chair of a committee to investigate the
possible remedies for this situation.

As Madeleva understood, the exclusion of women and laymen
from graduate study of theology was not so much a matter of official
church policy, as in the case of the exclusion of women from the priesthood, as of certain previously unchallenged attitudes and circumstances. The church assumed that the "science of theology devolves
primarily on the clergy, those men who have been chosen as 'the
ministers of Christ and the dispensers of the mysteries of God.'"[31]
Consequently, most schools of theology were connected with seminaries. In the late nineteenth century, the Vatican founded the Catholic
University as a "Chief Seminary" where priests or young men studying for the priesthood who evidenced "outstanding talent and virtue"
might spend several years of concentrated study in theology, canon
law, or philosophy;[32] its curriculum eventually set the standard for the
formal study of theology both in universities and in seminaries. Such
study was regulated and overseen by the Holy See.

The years preceding the formation of Madeleva's committee by
the NCEA had been marked by debate in academic circles over
whether religion (defined as a study oriented to the application of
Catholic faith to life) or theology (defined as a science devoted to a
study of the truths of Catholicism) should be taught to lay people. In
1939, the National Catholic Alumnae Federation adopted a resolution calling for the inclusion of the formal teaching of the science of
theology in the curricula of Catholic colleges and universities. It also
recommended that some of the Catholic universities establish graduate departments of religion to prepare lay leaders.[33] Madeleva applied such thinking specifically to women, both religious and lay,
and to their institutions—a leap the framers of the resolutions had
not themselves made.

In conducting her investigation, Madeleva worked through the hierarchy of the church instead of against it. She shrewdly obtained support for the work of her committee from her long-time friend Bishop Edwin O'Hara, with whom she had toured the Holy Land in 1934; his position as chairman of the Episcopal Commission on the Confraternity of Christian Doctrine virtually guaranteed the cooperation of her own bishop, John Francis Noll, of the Diocese of Fort Wayne.[34]

Madeleva first contacted the Catholic University and graduate schools of the large midwestern Catholic universities: Notre Dame, Saint Louis, Marquette, Loyola, and De Paul, to see if they would agree to set up a graduate program in theology for lay people. All refused, citing various difficulties connected with wartime enrollments in these all-male institutions. She then contacted the Catholic University with the request that religious and other women be admitted to their divinity school. The request was denied.

When Madeleva discussed her disappointment with Bishop O'Hara, visiting Saint Mary's for the day, he looked around the spacious campus with its new library and suggested that she consider beginning such a program there and assured her of his backing. At the time she demurred, fearful of what she described as "presumption." At the next meeting of the NCEA, with all other possibilities exhausted, she responded to "a strange impulse outside [her] will." Rising, she announced: "I do not know how we will do it, but this summer we will offer at Saint Mary's a six weeks' graduate program in Theology. . . . We will send you details in a fortnight."[35]

How did she do it? At the Wasatch, Madeleva had instituted a summer program for sisters that she hoped to develop along the lines of a sabbatical program, with every seventh summer devoted exclusively to a consideration of the spiritual life. Her schedule for the sabbatical program included not only sessions on prayer and liturgy but also on dogma and Scripture studies, with an emphasis on teaching. The program met with great success, but she left the Wasatch before her plan took root. However, she had done a great deal of thinking about not only the need to educate sisters to teach theology but also the shape such an education might take. That preparation enabled her to move quickly to organize an experimental program in Scripture and theology in the summer of 1943.

Madeleva found two Jesuits and a monsignor willing to teach in the program, which at first offered no academic credit and charged no tuition. Monsignor William Newton and Father Gerald Ellard, SJ, each taught for one week, and the gruff, portly Father Michael Gruenthaner, SJ, who reminded Madeleva of Chesterton, took over for the final month. Eighteen sisters from diverse congregations registered. After initial reluctance, Father Gruenthaner agreed to help Madeleva design a curriculum and establish requirements that would meet with hierarchical approval (schools specializing in Catholic theology were authorized not by state or national accrediting bodies but by the Vatican); he also agreed to serve as the first director of the School of Sacred Theology, which was formally established with the approval of Pope Pius XII during the centennial of the college in 1944.

For the next twenty-two years, the school offered two regular sessions and a six-week summer session. The doctoral program, which required a minimum of two years in residence and three sessions of summer school, entailed eighty-five semester hours of postgraduate study chosen from among courses on the Old and New Testaments, fundamental, dogmatic, moral, ascetical, and mystical theology, church history, papal encyclicals, biblical archaeology, hagiography, and canon law for religious. A public comprehensive examination and research project were also required for the Ph.D. A master's degree in Sacred Doctrine called for attendance at four summer sessions and a total of thirty-two semester hours of course work.

For the first few years of its existence, priests alone taught in the school, among them several Dominican priests: Reverends James Mark Egan, William O'Beirne, and Leo A. Arnoult. Several sisters of the Holy Cross and a few lay teachers joined the faculty after they completed their degrees. Dynamic Sister Charles Borromeo, who had been an undergraduate at the college before she entered the convent, became one of the mainstays of the graduate program and a superb teacher of undergraduate theology.

Enrollment in the School of Sacred Theology rose steadily throughout the 1940s and early 1950s, with an average of between twenty and thirty students registering in regular sessions, and more than a hundred participating in most summer sessions.

Madeleva regarded theology as the "science of God" and thus the most perfect of all the branches of knowledge. Like Cardinal Newman, she believed that "a Christian college should, if consistent, give [theology] the place of pre-eminence in the curriculum, make it the integrating subject, giving sequence, importance and validity to all other subjects."[36] Two years after she founded the graduate program in theology, which supplied the trained theologians she needed, Madeleva instituted an undergraduate degree program in theology at Saint Mary's, the first women's college in the country to offer theology as a regular college major.[37] "We are here, Cardinal Newman, at Saint Mary's," Madeleva wrote. "Theology is the queen of the sciences and the integrating core of the entire academic life of the college. Once Saint Thomas might have had to prove that women have souls. Now he can regard happily their Thomistic minds and the home in which they honor his *Summa*."[38]

In her comment, Madeleva glanced at the chief limitation of the school as well as its greatest strength. Even though it formally admitted women to an area of study that had previously been denied them, thus theoretically expanding their access to positions of power within the church, the content and approach of the courses (mandated by Rome) guaranteed that traditional views on women and their place in the church would be upheld. Yet Madeleva also understood, as she implied in her comment, that opening the intellectual tradition of the church to women must necessarily change it, as would the circumstances in which women acquired it: on their own ground, so to speak, and in their own way. As at least one alumnae of the program, philosopher Mary Daly, demonstrated, a conservative curriculum did not necessarily guarantee religious orthodoxy.

Madeleva repeated often that she regarded the School of Sacred Theology as "the most important work that we are doing."[39] For a decade and a half it served as the center of graduate studies in theology for women, not only in America but in the entire world, drawing women to campus from across America and around the globe.[40] Sisters and priests representing a wide spectrum of religious communities congregated at Saint Mary's, some as teachers, and others as students, recreating a Whitby-like atmosphere of collaboration and universality in the modern world.

That Madeleva's decisive action enjoyed the acceptance and commendation of most Catholic educators, priests, and bishops, and quickly gained papal approval, suggests that she filled a pressing need in a nonthreatening if unconventional way. Madeleva called such approbation "pentecostal" in its spontaneity and enthusiasm.[41] Her genius lay in finding a solution that offered an acceptable alternative to traditional avenues of theological study, thereby initiating change in a way that a conservative hierarchy could accept. Like women's education in general, the school carved out a niche that allowed women a place in an exclusive system. Once religious women, who held a special if ambiguous position in the church, had been admitted to such study, lay men and lay women found it easy to follow.

Within a decade, after close consultation with the faculty of the School of Sacred Theology, the Vatican set up its own graduate school of theology for women at Regina Mundi in Rome, patterning it on the Saint Mary's program. At the request of the Holy Father, Madeleva turned over all of the documents pertaining to the School, including its curricular plan, to his representatives. Furthermore, Saint Mary's agreed to validate the credits of graduates from the United States who completed their studies at Regina Mundi.[42] Only after more and more Catholic universities began to admit women to their theology programs was the decision made, in 1966, to phase out the school.

Between 1946, when the first degrees were conferred, through 1970, when the last degrees were awarded, the school granted 76 doctoral and 354 master's degrees both to religious and to lay graduates, including several men. When Notre Dame and the Catholic University finally designed graduate programs of theology for lay people, Bishop O'Hara commented wryly that they were only following a suit that Madeleva had already played.[43]

Madeleva's primary concern in establishing the School of Sacred Theology had been a practical one: to ensure adequate preparation for those actually teaching theology in the Catholic school system, most of whom were nuns. At the ceremony celebrating the tenth anniversary of the School of Sacred Theology in 1953, Bishop O'Hara pointed out: "There are at present in the Catholic School system in our country 9,000 elementary schools with nearly three million children; 1500 high schools with 500,000 teenagers; 150 women's colleges with 100,000 women students; in the teaching staff for all of these schools there are approximately 100,000 women teachers. How overwhelming the demand for the advance of religious education on the part of teachers in our Catholic schools! How many times the facilities of the Saint Mary's School of Theology must be multiplied throughout the United States if this need on the highest level is to be met."[44]

Madeleva never forgot her own experience as a young sister of having been thrust into a classroom on a day's notice, before completing either her novitiate or her college degree. She had no time even to glance through the books she was expected to teach. As a fledgling teacher, she was assigned classes in French and Latin even though she had mastered neither language and could speak French only haltingly. As the need arose, she also took over classes in theology and philosophy, painfully aware of her lack of preparation to teach either. Unfortunately, her experience was the rule, not the exception, among young nuns.

The broad issue of "sister formation"—the preparation of religious for their vocations—was a passionate concern for Madeleva and one closely associated in her mind with the School of Sacred Theology; both were responses to the larger issue of adequate professional training for sisters. "The Sister Formation movement grew out of a

proposal on the part of the committee of the NCEA to provide a graduate school in Sacred Theology for women, lay and religious," Madeleva
wrote. "The first solution to this problem came in the formation of the
School of Sacred Theology at Saint Mary's College in 1943."[45]

The second solution officially began with Madeleva's appointment to the leadership of another NCEA committee, this one formed
to investigate the preparation of nuns for teaching careers. For years,
Madeleva's had been the loudest voice among those asking for a special section devoted to this concern. She called for the intellectual
formation of sisters, which she described as parallel to and just as
important as their spiritual preparation.[46] To her way of thinking, a
sister's work was a crucial component of her religious vocation, and
she should be prepared for it no less carefully than for her life of
prayer. Madeleva stressed that superiors and other leaders within the
religious community bore the responsibility for ensuring such professional preparation.

Madeleva was asked to chair a special session devoted to the
preparation of sister-teachers at the NCEA in April 1949. She solicited
papers from six different teaching orders; the papers offered practical
suggestions for such preparation, including a specific plan of study for
a hypothetical "Sister Lucy" drawn up by Madeleva herself. Her plan
integrated the intellectual, spiritual, and cultural formation of a young
sister-teacher, with state certification an essential part of the plan. In
both quality and quantity, the professional preparation of Sister Lucy
would not only match but surpass that of her secular counterpart.

To Madeleva's dismay, the section devoted to Teachers' Education at the NCEA convention was scheduled at the worst possible
time, which she described as "the last hour of the last day of the
convention." She recalled: "The room assigned proved absolutely too
small. We moved in and out of the cafeteria for the same reason. We
settled in the gymnasium with people sitting on the steps and in the
aisles. 'The Education of Sister Lucy' proved the big event of the week.
The tremendous, spontaneous response to the cause established its
importance and its need."[47] The demand for copies of the six papers
delivered that afternoon was so great that Madeleva arranged for their
publication; *The Education of Sister Lucy* offered in embryo the agenda
for the Sister Formation movement.

The First National Congress of the Religious of the United States,
held August 9 through 13, 1952, at the University of Notre Dame,
formed the link between the ideas published in *The Education of Sister
Lucy* and the actual Sister Formation program, established in 1954.
Over two thousand religious, including priests, brothers, and sisters

representing more than four hundred religious establishments, gathered—a first in the history of the American church. Madeleva served
as one of the organizers of the conference and presented a paper on
the Saint Mary's School of Sacred Theology before the assembled group.
On the floor of the congress and behind the scenes, she stressed the
need for other organized programs to improve the professional status
of religious women.

Thanks in part to Madeleva's politicking, a national committee
was subsequently formed, from which grew the Sister Formation
program, established to promote cooperation among the many congregations involved in teacher preparation and to serve as a national
clearinghouse for information.

Over the next ten years, Madeleva served as a consultant to the
official organizers and saw to it that the Holy Cross congregation
played an active part in the leadership of the organization. Following
the general outlines of the program designed by Madeleva for Sister
Lucy, a formal five-year program for sister formation was started by
the Holy Cross congregation in 1958.[48] Developing a team approach,
Holy Cross sisters organized training sessions to help superiors from
other religious congregations set up similar programs for their own
communities. In 1959, the college established a graduate program in
religious education to prepare those who actually administered and
taught in sister formation programs across the United States.

Madeleva's efforts to educate religious women were intended to
improve the quality of their service and to enhance their personal lives
through education. She also expected her efforts eventually to improve
the lot of women in the church. She wrote that efforts like hers, especially her work in the Sister Formation movement, had finally exposed
"the facts of sister-shortage, sisters' education, sister's salaries."[49]

Although the School of Sacred Theology and the Sister Formation movement filled a pressing need in Madeleva's lifetime, the subsequent decline both of Catholic education and of religious orders in
the United States raises the question of the lasting significance of
Madeleva's efforts. Certainly, her leadership made it possible for religious women to join forces to change the circumstances, especially
limited access to higher education, that contributed in earlier times to
the image of the nun as an uneducated, subservient handmaid, fit
only to cook and clean for the clergy. Madeleva was among the first
to introduce the idea of the nun as a well-trained professional woman
and a public representative of the church.

Ironically, Madeleva's efforts to broaden the opportunities and
lift the expectations of women in the church may have played a part
in hastening the departure of women religious from their communi-

ties. She nevertheless helped to prepare a generation of women ready and qualified to push forward in church leadership, and permanently opened a way for all women, both religious and lay, into the graduate study of theology, which had previously been restricted to members of the clergy.

Deepening the irony of Madeleva's achievement is the fact that, while she became widely known as an advocate for the professional welfare of sisters, a number of the lay faculty at her own institution, most of whom were women, perceived her to be unsympathetic and unresponsive to their needs, especially on the matter of wages and benefits. Through the years, stories accumulated of the harsh treatment petitioners could expect when they approached Madeleva for a raise or asked for some other special consideration.[50]

A young woman who had recently completed a degree that she hoped would bring her more money was said to have been kept standing while Madeleva silently contemplated her nervous request for a raise. The answer came in the form of a question: "Have they turned you too into a materialist at Columbia?" To another request, this time from a member of the staff, Madeleva reputedly responded with the offer of an additional five cents an hour—the best she could do, she said.

Another lay faculty member found Madeleva chillingly unresponsive when he approached her for a raise after several years at the same salary in an inflationary economy. "Have you thought of moving?" she asked coolly. During the long silence that followed her question, she stared into the fireplace. "If you move," she said finally, "you will find that moving itself is very expensive."

Mrs. von Simson, the wife of art historian Otto von Simson—one of the few offered more money—recorded a different sort of unresponsiveness. Because of a wartime housing shortage in South Bend, Madeleva had offered the von Simsons a two-room basement apartment at the college. According to Mrs. von Simson, it was cramped, dark, cold, and without a kitchen—quite an ordeal for anyone, but especially for a member of the Austrian aristocracy. Just before the birth of their second child, she went to Madeleva to implore her to find better lodgings for them. Madeleva's response: "Oh, just like the virgin Mary—no place to put the child," struck the expectant mother as coldly detached. "It was too long since she had known any worry about the details of life, she could not understand my problem," Mrs. von Simson concluded.[51]

No doubt, the indebtedness of the college through much of Madeleva's tenure accounts in part for her tight-fisted policy. Moreover, her upbringing in a thrifty German family, with parents who denied themselves and demanded self-sacrifice from their children, certainly contributed to her fiscal conservatism. What the faculty did not know, however, was that behind the scenes, Madeleva constantly petitioned her own superiors for the means to improve the lot of the lay faculty and staff. In her estimation, they were invaluable adjuncts to the religious faculty, dedicated to the institution in spite of low salaries by their exceptional commitment to Catholic education.[52]

When vocations to the convent began to decline in the mid-1940s, Madeleva urged that raising faculty salaries and benefits become a top priority of the college. "Unless salary is adequate," she wrote her superiors in 1947, "[we] cannot command the service of distinguished teachers." She went on to recommend retirement insurance, which would help to attract "a good type of teacher and procure for her social justice."[53]

Although Madeleva's preferred solution to the problem of a growing shortage of sister-teachers was to increase the number of vocations to the congregation,[54] she was realistic enough to foresee a day in the near future when lay faculty would outnumber religious at the college. From 1947 through 1948, a full-professor's salary at Saint Mary's was approximately five-thousand dollars,[55] which was at the low end of the salary scale nationally.[56] Even though most lay faculty at Saint Mary's as at other women's colleges expected to receive lower salaries than their counterparts at all-male or coeducational schools (as did most women at the time, compared with men), Madeleva insisted that finding and keeping good faculty members would be increasingly difficult without competitive salaries.

By 1957, when lay faculty outnumbered religious by fifty-seven to forty-six, Madeleva again stressed to her superiors that "a fund to improve faculty salaries is vital if Saint Mary's is to attract and keep the outstanding professors needed to maintain a high academic level."[57] Even a matching grant of more than $300,000, obtained from the Ford Foundation in 1955 to improve faculty salaries, was insufficient to raise compensation to a level Madeleva regarded as adequate. Thwarted in her efforts to offer the sort of wages she would have liked, she complained late in her administration that "the uncertainty of economic conditions had made it difficult to establish fixed salary scales during recent years."[58] She had no choice but to determine salaries individually year-by-year based on amounts designated by her superiors, who until the mid-1950s set the budget and controlled the finances of the college.

Her hands tied by circumstances over which she had little control, Madeleva no doubt preferred to appear unsympathetic to the concerns of lay faculty than to make promises she could not keep. Nor did she wish to shift the blame for low wages within the college to her superiors, who struggled no less than she to make ends meet. With no endowment and no substantial external grants or contributions on which to rely for income, the college counted on student tuition supplemented by subsidies from the congregation to meet its needs. As Madeleva frequently reminded the parents of students, the faculty of the college subsidized the educations of their daughters. Each year, half the salary of each college sister was returned by the congregation to the operating budget of the college; and with their substandard wages, lay faculty members also subsidized the institution.

By the mid-1950s, Madeleva was convinced that a professionally organized fund-raising effort, along with the establishment of a permanent office of development for the college, was the most effective way to address the immediate needs and to ensure the future well-being of Saint Mary's. With an advisory board of lay trustees, which she appointed in 1952, lending authority to her voice, she committed the college to a comprehensive development and public relations campaign. Representatives of the John Price Jones Company, a national consulting firm, arrived on campus to design and implement a long-range program that would raise $10 million over ten years. The fund would enable the college to increase faculty salaries, support sabbatical leaves and study, underwrite student aid and scholarships, and set aside over $2 million for a general endowment.

"I was ever a fighter, so—one fight more," Madeleva wrote, quoting poet Robert Browning.[59] Scathing criticism from all constituencies of the college—alumnae, faculty, parents, students, sisters, and even her superiors, who had acquiesced to her desire for a development effort with great reluctance and serious misgivings—fell on her. The objections she had heard fifteen years earlier, when she had solicited funds for the library, repeated themselves with added force because of the magnitude of the campaign. That nuns should publicly solicit funds, and such large amounts, on behalf of their own institution was considered by many not only indecorous but scandalous.

Once again, as she had on racial integration, Madeleva "stuck to her guns." As the chief fund-raiser of the institution, she wrote dozens of letters each day to prospective donors, and traveled thousands of miles each month to visit groups of alumnae and friends of the college. She attended scores of luncheons, dinners, and teas, and visited countless foundations and corporations. In a letter to prospective donors, she joked: "Saint Mary's has come to you by mail, by rail, by day, by night, by TWA, or United Flight," signing herself, "Yours with wings."[60]

Although the term of the campaign extended beyond her tenure as president, Madeleva succeeded in establishing fund-raising as a legitimate activity of a Catholic women's college. It was a costly enterprise in terms of time and energy. She wrote: "The president, her vice presidents and our alumnae have studied and served a stiff apprenticeship in college development, public relations, fund raising. The lessons have been hard, long, unrelenting. The tuition has been high. No one regrets any part of the process. There are no easy ways. The development program at Saint Mary's is now as integral a part of the college as its science department and as indispensable."[61]

In fact, Madeleva saw both the financial woes of the college and her particular difficulties in dealing with them as part of a larger problem that originated in the status of women in her society. Assessing conditions at her own institution in the context of American higher education, she wrote:

> [The women's colleges in the United States] are the most expensive to maintain, the last to benefit by philanthropy. Present educational crises are being met by colossal gifts from corporations, foundations, individuals. At a recent meeting of the American Council on Education, the question was asked, 'Where in the order of these gifts do colleges for women stand?' This is the answer which was given, not without embarrassment: 'Gifts for education go, first, to schools with big names; second, to big schools; third, to co-educational schools; fourth, to women's colleges.' We might add, last of all to Catholic women's colleges.

Colleges such as Saint Mary's, Madeleva concluded, "are monuments to the enterprise, the sacrifice, the fortitude of women."[62]

But however positively the existence of such colleges reflected on the women whose extraordinary strength and sacrifice sustained them, Madeleva pointed out that their obvious need reflected just as poorly on a society that neglected them, especially on the men who controlled its wealth. "Considering that half the parents of the world, all the mothers, the wives, the daughters, and the sisters are women," she wrote, "this does not reflect gloriously to the generosity, the chivalry, the gratitude, or even the justice of the manhood of our country."[63]

As a woman and an educator, Madeleva labored to build the room of her own that writer Virginia Woolf claimed every woman needs to dream her own dreams. But like most of her generation, whether in the convent or not, she often struggled to acquire the £500 a year that Woolf deemed essential to realize them.

14

In the Country of the Soul

Madeleva referred to herself as an "extrovert," by which she seems to have meant that she took pleasure in contact with people, both face to face and through writing. Making friends easily, she formed during her long life countless relationships that were based, as she put it, on "mutual interests, enthusiasms, objectives."[1]

Having chosen a way of life that emphasized community and hospitality at the expense of personal relationships, which were officially discouraged as "exclusive," Madeleva nevertheless pursued friendship openly and actively, observing its obligations to a remarkable degree, given the obstacles she encountered. During most of her time in the convent, visitors and correspondence were limited and monitored, "idle" conversation was discouraged, and personal travel— even to visit family—was restricted. The many friends Madeleva made and kept indicate both how gregarious she was by nature and how convinced of the value of friendship.

Certainly, religious life had its effect on Madeleva, teaching her to value solitude as well as companionship. She wrote: "I had to do my own thinking, make my own decisions, with proper deference to others. This gives one a capacity to be alone. Sometimes it almost imposes aloneness on one."[2] Not only her religious vocation but also her scholarly interests and poetic gifts required time alone. Perhaps because she found it so easy to become involved with others, she expressed the need to distance herself from too much human contact. "I'm interested in ideas and then if I get bogged down with people, you see, the ideas get crowded out in the human setup," she explained.[3]

In spite of her responsiveness and charm, Madeleva was and always had been at heart a private person who kept her deepest feelings, both positive and negative, to herself. Some of that reticence may be attributable to the conventions of the age in which she lived, but the old woman who in her autobiography refused to speak about her religious experiences was the same Eva who had told none of her friends, either at Saint Mary's or in Cumberland, of her decision to enter the convent. She also had been the young nun who from time to time expressed her wish that she had chosen a cloistered community such as the Carmelites. Even though she knew and cared for many people, those to whom she revealed herself were few. As her poetry and letters suggest, those few she loved with the same passion she saved for God.

Calling people "the best mirrors" of God, Madeleva no less than the poet Keats held sacred the affections of the heart. Although she might speak casually of her relationships in terms of shared interests, her frequent depiction of friendship was one in which each individual reveals the image of God to the other. This was the concept of "chaste" love that she shared with Father Hagerty; it was personal and physical in the sense that it admitted the part the body plays in love, including its subtle role in relationships between members of the same sex.

Many of Madeleva's relationships were sustained at a distance through voluminous correspondence, supplemented with occasional visits, frequent tokens of affection—a poem for a birthday or a book at Christmas—and daily prayer. She often maintained such friendships for years without seeing her correspondents. In truth, such relationships are often conducted in solitude, sustained by ideas and emotions divorced from the physical person. They lack the often tense give and take of relationships carried on face to face. But the continuance of such relationships betokens commitment: an implicit assertion of continuing connection in the present moment in spite of physical separation.

Madeleva often assured her friends that she met them daily at mass, where she not only prayed for them by name and remembered their intentions, but actually joined them in spiritual communion. For Madeleva, this was the theological heart of friendship: a coming together in Christ, which in its most perfect form occurred in the Eucharist.

Thus, Madeleva's faith kept even far-distant friends such as Ben Lehman and Madge Vaison Mouton—or long-absent friends such as Sister Rita—close. What was exceptional (and to some of her superiors, objectionable) about Madeleva's practice of Christian love is the extent to which she singled out individuals both within and outside the convent and made her preference for their company known. Rather than detaching herself emotionally from the people she cared about, as her training in the novitiate had taught her to do, she frankly admitted her need for them and devoted hours to tangibly showing her affection through the letters and poems she wrote. She summed up her approach when she wrote a friend, "Presently we are going to find that we have missed some of the joy of friendship in not seeing one another and talking together often enough."[4]

Eliciting an exquisite sensitivity to others, Madeleva's friendships brought out the best in her. Other concerns slipped away as she gave herself entirely to the person beside her. As one friend put it, "She *chose* people, and made her way in. She treated people with great honor."[5] In a few instances, however, her friendships failed, exposing the darker, more remote regions of her personality.

Madeleva's friendships encompassed a broad range of individuals, of assorted ages, races, and backgrounds. Among the least likely of her attachments, perhaps, were Edward Hansford, a black porter she met on a train, whom she informally counseled on his marital difficulties, and Robert Heineman, a convict sentenced at age sixteen to life imprisonment in a Pennsylvania penitentiary, whose poetry had been sent to her by his publisher.

Madeleva visited Heineman several times in jail, and sent him long letters of consolation. "You know that there are many persons in the world who have chosen the cloister as an opportunity for a more perfect and more profound living than secular life would permit them," she wrote soon after they met. "You have an opportunity to make your life an anchorhold, to fill it with the presence of God, contemplation, and union with Him."[6] When Heineman was paroled to Los Angeles in 1958, Madeleva prevailed upon a nephew who lived there to watch out for him.

Some of Madeleva's happiest friendships went back to her college days. To her delight, the presidency of her alma mater gave her the opportunity to renew them, and they often proved not only personally gratifying but also beneficial to the college. The closest of these was probably with Evarista Brady Cotter, one of the group known as "the bunch" during their student days. Evarista was active in the alumnae association, and Madeleva began visiting her regularly on trips to New York City, usually staying with her and her husband, Bill (who as a Notre Dame student had once called the two Evas his "pin-up gals"). She regarded the Cotters' Beekman Place apartment as a second home and grew so close to the couple's three children that she referred to herself as their "grandmother."[7]

Throughout Madeleva's administration, she and the Cotters collaborated informally on college business, especially fund raising and development efforts. Evarista often traveled to campus for alumnae gatherings, and she opened her apartment for various college receptions. When Madeleva instituted a lay board of trustees for the college in the early 1950s, Bill Cotter was among her first appointments and served as chairman of the new board. Madeleva relied on Bill's business acumen (he was a counsel for Union Carbide) and trusted his probity, grounded in his deep religious faith. Evarista she loved for her "buoyant spirit, her high heartedness, and her generosity."[8]

Madeleva's presidency also reunited her with another close friend, Mother Rose Elizabeth. Madeleva's former pupil and protegee had herself become a college president, of Dunbarton College in Washington, D.C., which she founded in 1935. In 1943, her election to the position of superior general of the congregation, which she held until 1955, brought her back to Saint Mary's and into close contact with Madeleva.

In Rose Elizabeth, Madeleva found someone with an imagination and intelligence commensurate with her own. Too often, her superiors had lacked one or both qualities, responding to her unorthodox ideas and bold innovations with suspicion and inflexibility. A woman of cultivated tastes and diverse interests and abilities, Rose Elizabeth combined vision with practicality. According to a friend: "Whether it was a matter of securing a permission from the Holy See, negotiating with a bishop about a meeting, finding a parking place in the District, or doctoring an undiagnosed ailment—Mother Rose Elizabeth could do it when no one else could, and she thanked you for importuning her."[9]

Rose Elizabeth's experience as a college president allowed her to appreciate Madeleva's perspective and anticipate her needs. In return, Madeleva offered Rose Elizabeth the benefit of her frank opinions and often shrewd advice. Their respect for and trust in each other enabled them to talk frankly and freely about shared problems and lightened the weight of their respective offices. Reflecting on their long relationship, Madeleva wrote: "I think we were both helped by sharing common problems and somewhat parallel situations. It is interesting to watch things unravel and untangle in that great dimension of time."[10]

Even though the nuns were subject to frequent moves dictated by the needs of the congregation, the religious community offered its members the opportunity for deep and long-lasting relationships. The Rules might warn against the dangers of particular friendships to community life, but in practice they sprang up and were tolerated if not encouraged by superiors, especially among established members of the community.

Madeleva had many friends among the Holy Cross sisters, perhaps none closer in her years as president than Sister Maria Pieta, who served in various positions at the college. Loved by colleagues, staff, and students alike for her kindheartedness, Maria Pieta became indispensable to Madeleva for her humane and sensible counsel. According to one colleague, everyone could tell how close the two women were "just by watching them together."[11]

Sitting next to Madeleva at table or recreation, Maria Pieta laced her conversation with the droll anecdotes and witty repartee for which she was famous, delighting her friend and often making her laugh out loud. Tall, lanky, long-faced, with flashing dark eyes enlarged by wire-rimmed glasses, Maria Pieta offered a dramatic contrast to an increasingly fragile Madeleva, with her small-boned frame, pale skin, and cool, blue-gray eyes.

Maria Pieta had entered the order in her late twenties, after working for several years as a stenographer to pay her way through college. When Madeleva became president, Maria Pieta, who had completed a master's degree by then (she later earned one of the first doctorates conferred by the School of Sacred Theology), was teaching in the journalism department at the college. She was soon appointed dean of women, and she and Madeleva worked together for four years to reorganize student life. During that time, an innovative, five-year work-study program was instituted at the college, the brain child of the college dietician, to allow needy students to finance their own educations by working in the food service while they attended classes. For thirteen years (1942–1955), Maria Pieta lived with the students in the program and served as their counselor, bringing them together with popcorn and lemonade and opening her door to their loneliness.

Working behind the scenes, Maria Pieta often tempered decisions and influenced policy with her characteristic concern for others. Typical of her approach was the manner in which she inspired the student-supported Martin de Porres fund for minority women. In one of her theology classes, she pointed out that a penny a day from each student would, by the end of the year, underwrite an annual scholarship for a black student. When one student responded with particular enthusiasm to the idea, Maria Pieta encouraged her initiative and directed her energy so effectively that within a year, the first Martin de Porres scholar arrived at Saint Mary's.

Especially after 1955, when Maria Pieta became Madeleva's vice president, the two women collaborated closely in the daily business of running the college. According to colleagues, after Maria Pieta spent an hour or two alone with Madeleva, seemingly unalterable decisions were revised and sometimes reversed. Maria Pieta's compassion tempered Madeleva's harsher judgments, and her robust sense of humor dispelled even Madeleva's most ominous mood.

Although the distance between Madeleva and the students in the college lengthened in proportion to her years in office, she shared with

FIGURE 14.1

Sr. Madeleva before LeMans Tower, 1957.

Courtesy Saint Mary's College Archives.

Maria Pieta a fondness for and a faith in the younger generation. "I believe in youth," she said in an interview. "I believe in its sincerity and generousness. . . . Above all else, there is a fundamental reverence about young people. They do a great deal of wise-cracking, but this is merely a protective covering they assume."[12] Toward the end of her life, she wrote, "I believe in [the younger generation] with almost an exaggerated faith, I think, because I want so much the perfection in the future that we have not been able to realize in our generation."[13]

Over the years, Madeleva welcomed several of her young relatives to Saint Mary's and Notre Dame: two of Fred's children, Mary Lucia and Fred, Jr., and eventually Mary Lucia's daughter "Sissie" and other grandnieces. Through them and their friends, she kept in touch with the younger generation. She also made a point of dining with the students each night. A believer in the advantages of good conversation shared over a leisurely meal, she had begun the custom of formal, sit-down dinners on week nights soon after her return to the college as president. As did the other college sisters, she continued throughout her administration to head a table of students, in her case specially selected seniors, and conversed with them as they ate from china and silver.

Every now and then Madeleva struck up a close relationship with a male or a female student or one of the younger sisters with whom she felt a special bond. She had an eye for talent and concentrated her attention on those who in some way showed exceptional promise. Young Tom Dooley, who later returned to lecture on his experiences as a medical missionary in Southeast Asia, was one of these. As a Notre Dame undergraduate, he came to Saint Mary's to attend Sunday afternoon tea dances and play the piano in the lounge. At her invitation, he soon moved into her office for long and lively talks, as did a number of other Notre Dame men, among them Henry Rago, who became the editor of *Poetry* magazine.

One of the young women to whom Madeleva became attached was a brilliant student who later realized in her own life Madeleva's dream of entering a contemplative religious order. Mary Barbara Kain, who became Sister Mary of God, recalled that at the end of her senior year, in the spring of 1946, Madeleva summoned her to her office with the sole intention of encouraging her to continue her studies. Would she consider enrolling in the School of Sacred Theology? When Mary Barbara expressed reluctance, in part for financial reasons—both her parents had died when she was young, and she was dependent on a brother and his family—Madeleva listened in silence. At graduation a short time later, Mary Barbara was astounded to hear that she had won the "Sister Madeleva Scholarship"—an award for which she had not applied and of whose existence she had not been aware.

"A most extraordinary experience at Loretto College in Denver convinced me that your mind and preparation and aptitudes and aspirations quite as much as my own can find their best fulfillments as a teacher and in what we call an active community," Madeleva wrote Mary Barbara after she completed her graduate studies in theology. Madeleva added that she thought that the young woman would be happy as a Holy Cross sister.[14] As her own teachers had nudged her toward religious life, she sometimes did the same with young women who showed a bent for it. When Mary Barbara chose instead to join a contemplative convent, Madeleva accepted her decision graciously, even though she obviously had hoped to welcome the young woman into her own community. "I find such reassurance in knowing that the tides of time cannot wash up on your shores with quite the insistence that they do on ours," Madeleva wrote her. "Even so, your boundaries are greater. It is once upon eternity even now for you."[15]

Madeleva wrote and visited Mary Barbara as often as she could, filling in for an absent mother. She made a special trip to attend Mary Barbara's first profession of vows, when she became Sister Mary of God. Madeleva commented approvingly on the Dominican community the young woman had entered, especially the fact that, even though cloistered, the sisters could upon occasion eat with their guests. As much as she admired the Carmelite way of life, she told Mary of God, she intensely disliked the spiked grilles that separated the Carmelites from the outside world; the Dominican openness was more to her liking.

On the occasion of Mary of God's profession of solemn vows, Madeleva wrote: "I read the simple statements and wonder how pen and ink can tell, even by announcement, of dedications so high and so holy, of the marriage of humanity and Divinity realized in one young girl with God."[16] She commented that she experienced the contemplative life "by proxy" through her young friend. Receiving a photograph of the cloistered area of her convent, Madeleva wrote that it was "as much of your world as I shall ever see," but added, "It is not, however, a hidden world nor one to which I have no access. Indeed, I think we are impervious to walls and screens. This is one of the joys of the freedom of the children of God, the utter reality of the spiritual life."[17]

A number of Madeleva's younger friends came to her through her poetry. Because of her reputation as a writer, she frequently received manuscripts from aspiring poets, in particular from nuns and priests or from their superiors. She read and responded to each manuscript, looking upon such work as a type of ministry devoted to beauty. Occasionally, she singled out young writers who in her opinion showed promise, and often became their friend and adviser.

The work of a contemplative nun, a Poor Clare named Sister Mary Francis, was sent to Madeleva in the mid-1940s by the young woman's aunt. Madeleva read the poems with amazement; they were, she said, "among the finest religious poems in contemporary writing."[18] She wrote to Sister Mary Francis to encourage her to continue writing and offered to help her find a publisher.

Madeleva simultaneously corresponded with Sister Mary Francis's religious superior, who was in a quandary about the young nun's talent. The superior feared that writing poetry—and even worse, publishing it—was inappropriate for a contemplative nun. Madeleva urged the superior to accept and nurture the young nun's gift. As she once had to her own superiors, she argued that writing poetry should be thought of as the "apostolate of the Word," and added forcefully, "It is hard to understand the inconsistency by which we cherish even mediocre talents in others and are so prone to suspect and fear them among ourselves."[19] She wrote, "I often wonder at the lack of trust we show in these gifts [of God] when they are bestowed within the beautiful security of the cloister."[20]

Madeleva visited Mary Francis several times in her convent in Chicago and kept in touch with her after she was assigned to a new foundation in New Mexico, offering unstinting encouragement of her calling both as a sister and as a poet. "The cloistered monastery is of all places the most perfect home of the most perfect poetry," she wrote. "You can give back there the loveliness of God's gifts to you."[21] Mary Francis's poems, Madeleva wrote, reflected the depth of her love for God and reached "to the width and breadth and the depth of God and our life and world in Him."[22]

Although she freely offered advice on publishers and on the business side of publication, Madeleva was cautious about suggesting changes in the poems themselves. She carefully read through one of Mary Francis's manuscripts, which was subsequently accepted for publication, proposed a few revisions and corrections, then wrote her young friend: "Don't let [criticism] hamper you . . . when it does violence to an intuitive rightness that you yourself experience in a certain way of fitting words to thoughts and thoughts to words. The theorist is not necessarily the seer nor the singer. The poet must defend the integrity of her own experience."[23]

Madeleva feared that, as she put it, the "impact" of her own experience as a poet or a nun might interfere with the "freedom and joy and spontaneity" of the gifts of younger poets[24] and preferred to say too little than too much. When, however, she came across writing that she considered inferior, she could be harshly critical. "My comments you may find very severe," she responded to a superior who had solicited her opinion of the poetry of a priest in his order. She defended her candor as the best compliment she could pay the poet, because "[it is] the truth, however disappointing it may be."[25] She wrote directly to the priest himself to recommend that he destroy all his material so as not to "blaspheme by the mediocrity of [his] work."[26]

A young Thomas Merton wrote from the Abbey of Gethsemani to request copies of Madeleva's books, in particular *Collected Poems*, which had received favorable reviews in *The New York Times* and elsewhere. She in turn read *The Seven Storey Mountain*, his spiritual autobiography, soon after its publication in 1948 and wrote to tell him that his account of his childhood in France revived memories of her days in Hyères. Not long after they began corresponding, Madeleva arranged for the press at Saint Mary's to print one of the first things Merton wrote on the contemplative life, a small pamphlet titled *What Is Contemplation?* She took an interest in every detail of its publication, from the paper on which it was printed to the pentecostal red she chose for its cover (with apologies to his superiors in case they found the color too audacious).

Madeleva's epistolary friendship with Merton—they never met—spanned almost fifteen years, their letters at first politely deferential, with Merton bowing respectfully before the older, established poet and Madeleva addressing the talented young priest with kindly solicitude. She confessed to a "holy jealousy" for his contemplative vocation[27] and mused wistfully that saying mass must be an experience "more annihilating and sublimating than even your original correspondence to your Trappist vocation."[28] When he won a poetry award, which he protested gallantly should have gone to her, he offered his opinion that he had received it only because he was a "novelty"—a Trappist poet.[29]

As did other young poets who wrote as members of religious orders, Merton tacitly acknowledged that the publication of his verse relied on the precedent set by Madeleva's. Even so, Merton's Cistercian superiors ordered him to publish under his secular name in order to preserve his religious anonymity and possibly to protect themselves from guilt by association.[30]

Although she thought that Merton edited too little ("It takes a whole field of flowers to make a gram of perfume," she commented on his work[31]), Madeleva liked his poetry enough to make it the subject of one of her lectures on contemporary verse. In response, he advised her not to waste her time on his work.[32]

As years passed, Madeleva adopted a grandmotherly tone in her letters to Merton, alternately teasing, encouraging, and scolding him. When he sent her an inscribed copy of *Seeds of Contemplation*, she wrote playfully to thank him: "The inscription puts it among the rarest of all rare books. I shall have to exercise a special virtue of detachment sooner or later regarding it. I know, however, that it will be later." More seriously, she applauded the spiritual insight of the book, especially his ideas on the sanctity of nature.[33]

In connection with another of his publications, Madeleva hailed Merton's comments on the "crucial subject of peace" as no less than "prophetic," saying that she wholeheartedly agreed with his condemnation of the "awful silence" of the hierarchy and clergy on such matters. She thanked him for his visionary writings, which she said supplemented her own "slower mindedness."[34] She drew the line at certain types of unorthodoxy, however. When he began signing his letters to her "Tom Merton," she persisted in addressing him as "Father Louis," as if to remind him of his true identity. After a few such salutations, he quietly resumed his religious signature, at least in his letters to her.

Late in their correspondence, Madeleva received an unsigned treatise from Gethsemani on mystical theology and the "great" mystical writers, which she immediately recognized as Merton's from its style. She took him to task for excluding the English mystics, especially Julian of Norwich, from his study. "She is I think a unique woman in the world of spiritual experience," Madeleva wrote.[35] Caught in an oversight, Merton shot back a letter to assure her that he deeply appreciated Julian's writings, and in fact had come to prefer her to St. John of the Cross and all the other Spanish mystics.[36]

Most found Madeleva to be an exceptionally faithful, attentive, and loyal friend, but several—Lucy Hazard at the Wasatch, for example, and a few of those with whom she worked at Saint Mary's—did not, accusing her of suddenly withdrawing her affection without provocation or warning. According to their reports (Madeleva never referred to such incidents), her manner could suddenly become distant and her remarks cutting. Sometimes the coldness passed without noticeable consequence; she seemed to hold no grudge and never spoke behind anyone's back. Occasionally, however, the breach remained and silently widened with time. She may for some reason have felt disappointed, betrayed, or emotionally crowded; according to those rejected, she never explained her behavior.

One such instance seems to have involved a member of Madeleva's administration, a sister, and at one time a close friend. The sister perceived herself to have been suddenly dropped by Madeleva, unfairly and without explanation. According to a friend of the woman, Madeleva "turned a cold shoulder to her and engineered her college assignments to minimize their contact and prevent her from ever again sharing any of the college spotlight. Although her official title stayed the same, the sister's responsibilities were curtailed." According to her friend, she regarded Madeleva's treatment of her "as a total and unexplained personal betrayal."[37]

"Who can tell us how love is parted?" Madeleva asked in "At Winter's End," one of the poems in *Gates*. Her own puzzlement or disappointment over her occasional changes of heart may have exceeded her capacity to explain them. Or perhaps the reasons for them were so painfully clear to her that she thought others saw them, too. Usually frank and constructive in her criticisms of others about professional matters, she could be reticent about emotions, expressing them only obliquely, usually through her poetry.

In "October Birthday," written for Ben Lehman, Madeleva commented indirectly on the limits of friendship. Wishing that she could offer each of her friends tokens "casually infinite," she confessed that all she had to give were.

> A little, human-hearted song to sing you,
> My arms to comfort and my lips to trust,
> The tangled moods that, autumn-wise, I fling you,
> The frail and faulty tenderness of dust.

In "If You Would Hold Me," an earlier poem, published in *Penelope*, Madeleva probed her own psychology more deeply:

> It is so very strange that, loving me,
> You should ensnare the freedom I find sweet,
> Catch in your cunning will my flying feet.
> I will not barter love for liberty;
> You cannot break and tame me utterly.
>
> For when your careful conquest is complete
> Shall victory be swallowed in defeat.
> You hold me only when you set me free.

Always independent, Madeleva resisted those who demanded more of her time or attention than she wished to give. Beyond the limits set by her religious vocation and the demands of her professional life lay personal boundaries, across which others dare not intrude. She in turn respected the freedom of others by observing a scrupulous courtesy both in her correspondence and in her personal relationships, even with members of her immediate family.

The enigmatic and paradoxical in Madeleva, closely tied to her poetic and mystical gifts as well as to her wry wit, flashed out unexpectedly, catching others off guard, baffling some but just as often summoning others to her. A student made famous the story of how, taking a shortcut across the lawn, she unexpectedly came upon Madeleva. Flustered, the young woman apologized for walking on the grass. Madeleva excused her with a question: "Of what have we more?" One balmy March 25, according to an alumna, Madeleva invited a group of students to accompany her outdoors. "She looked happily at the budding beauty of the campus on that day, the feast of the Annunciation, and said, 'This is the beginning of the Christmas season.'" To the alumna, "this was a memorable example of her touching humanity blended with deep spiritual insights."[38]

When one of the young sisters died, her parents were brought to meet Madeleva. Taking their hands in hers, she told them: "You are indeed privileged to have given your daughter twice to God."[39]

According to a colleague, Madeleva spent hours each Christmas season over the many gifts, usually fruits, candy, and flowers, sent to her by friends and acquaintances. Meditating on each day's arrivals, she thoughtfully redistributed them according to her perception of the needs of others in the community. To one sister she might bring candy, to another the gift of a plant. Roses, she often distributed one by one to sisters confined to the infirmary. When asked why she spent so much time on the gifts, she replied, "We must baptize these things."[40]

Madeleva had little patience for those with a diminished capacity for wonder. "To look at everything as though you saw it for the first time takes courage," she said.[41] When others reacted to beauty in a way that Madeleva regarded as obtuse, she did little to conceal her irritation. The failure of even so close a friend as Maria Pieta to appreciate the "wilding flight" of birds or the "petalled peace" of flowers earned her sad contempt.

Because of their freshness of soul, Madeleva delighted in children, and they responded to her without apprehension or inhibition. As a young nun, she doted on various nieces and nephews, romping for hours with them on trips home, crawling into their tents, and, on one occasion, allowing little Mary Lucia, Fred's only daughter, to dress up in her nun's habit and have her picture taken. During her student days at Berkeley, she had made friends with Ben Lehman's small son, Hal, and in France was charmed by writer Bruce Marshall's tiny bilingual daughter, Josephine. Every Christmas at Saint Mary's Madeleva invited the families of the lay faculty to a party, where she personally dispensed candy to all the children. When children visited the campus, she hurried to greet them, knowing just what to say and how to treat them so that they behaved naturally in her presence. Late in her administration, when the drama department produced *The King and I*, she often stopped by rehearsals to watch the children perform.

Madeleva wrote to a friend about a conversation she had with one little boy. "We were talking about how far we can see. We both agreed that we can scarcely see objects of any size a mile or two miles away. Yet we can see the sun ninety million miles away. At that distance, the sun looks as big as a penny in an immense sky that can hold millions of such pennies."[42]

In *Conversations with Cassandra*, a collection of essays on education, Madeleva included an entire chapter on her conversations with children. She recalled an hour spent in the company of twins named Rebecca and Rachel, who were, she wrote, "as unalike in appearance as Esau and Jacob might have been at their age." Allowing them to explore her office, she noticed that Rebecca "needed no induction into the amenities of administration. She promptly settled herself in the biggest chair in the inner room and gave herself up to considering her new environment. The globe on the window sill was a big enough world for her."

On the other hand, according to Madeleva, Rachel "lost and thoughtfully tried to find herself in terms of each of the many things" in Madeleva's rooms. Silently looking at and carefully touching many of the vases, statues, and books in the office, she finally remarked, "Everything here has been made into something beautiful." Madeleva concluded, "With what vision does this child look out on the world!"[43]

Inseparably connected to Madeleva's love of children was her love of Christmas. Each year, even when she wrote no other poetry, she celebrated the embodiment of all children, the Christ child; it was the only subject that unfailingly inspired her. "It is strange that year after year something comes to me to be said of the greatest of all nativities," she wrote Lehman in 1955. Four of Madeleva's volumes of poetry: *The Happy Christmas Wind* (1936), *Christmas Eve* (1938), *American Twelfth Night* (1955), and *A Child Asks for a Star* (1964) were primarily devoted to meditations on the mystery of a God incarnate in the form of a weak and helpless baby. "You could not fear this God at all," she wrote in "Ways."

Meeting new people constantly, Madeleva welcomed Christ in the stranger, as her own inclination as well as the Benedictine *Rule* instructed her to do. She had a knack for anticipating and discretely satisfying the needs of her guests, whether they came alone or in groups. She might order a simple lunch of tea and raisin toast because she knew her guest would prefer it, or serve an array of courses in the dining hall, as she did when she invited the entire cast and crew of *Knute Rockne: All American* to lunch at Saint Mary's. She lavished as much time and attention on the most humble visitor as on the most famous, of whom there were many in the course of her long presidency. She might spend as much time with a shy young girl (one recalls sliding down a haystack with Madeleva on the convent farm) as with a visiting bishop or well-known politician.

Not that Madeleva ignored or dismissed celebrities; she received them gladly, aware that their glow lit up the college. She had a particular affinity for those connected with the performing arts, enjoying the company of actors such as Robert Speaight, Helen Hayes, and Irene Dunne, all of whom became good friends. Without doubt, Madeleva astutely gauged the importance of publicity in building a famous school and knew that someone of the stature of Hayes or Dunne would bring throngs of reporters and photographers to campus. She also perceived the power of the cinema and the stage to touch the emotions and engage the imagination of the audience and may have wished to influence those who wielded such power. But unquestionably, on some level she was still the star-struck girl who had stood in the streets of Madison to watch Sarah Bernhardt drive by. She had also been the young woman who starred in her senior class play, and the teacher who wrote, directed, and produced dozens of plays for her high school and college students. All her life, she had loved the dramatic arts, and she knew a great deal about them.

At their first meeting, Madeleva so impressed director Leo McCarey, winner of two academy awards, that he sent his assistant and her secretary to South Bend to gather material and ideas for a possible picture. McCarey asked Madeleva to serve as a consultant on the project, which he intended to be a sequel to his Oscar-winning film *Going My Way*; she refused, pleading lack of time, but she recommended a Holy Cross sister studying in California to collaborate on the project that became *The Bells of Saint Mary's*. According to a friend of McCarey's, Madeleva served as the model for the nun played in the film by actress Ingrid Bergman.[44]

Madeleva met Clare Boothe Luce when the playwright, who was at the time also a congresswoman from Connecticut, came to Saint Mary's in 1947 to deliver the commencement address. She later told Madeleva that she had asked her friend and guru Bishop Fulton J. Sheen which from a pile of invitations to accept, and he told her, "Go to Sister Madeleva."[45] For both women, it was a "magical visit" and the start of a friendship that brightened both lives for the next seventeen years. The elegantly dressed, fashionably coiffed blonde beauty, a former editor of *Vogue* and *Vanity Fair*, was an unlikely intimate for an aging nun in widow's weeds. Married to Henry Luce, founder of Time-Life Enterprises and one of America's richest and most powerful men, Clare had wealth and fame of her own, several absorbing careers, and even less time at her disposal than Madeleva. Nevertheless, in spite of the obvious differences between them and the circumstances of their respective lives, Clare and Madeleva recognized in each other a kindred spirit. "The country of the soul is a land so beautiful that one rejoices to greet one's companions in it," Madeleva wrote soon after they met.[46]

Madeleva visited Clare at her home in Connecticut within a month of her stay at Saint Mary's, and the following November, Clare was back at the college to see Madeleva and talk to students. The visits continued, with Henry sometimes accompanying Clare; he even consented to join the board of trustees in the mid-1950s. On one occasion, he turned over to Madeleva his winnings, all twenty seven dollars, from an after-hours bridge game at Notre Dame—conscience money, he joked. Soon after meeting him, Madeleva began addressing him as "Harry," unusual for a woman who studiously avoided presumption, and Clare became "My Dearest." Clare referred to herself in letters to Madeleva as "Sister Trés Sophisticata," and enlisted the aid of her spiritual sister in praying for Harry's conversion to Catholicism.

Clare explained that she had converted because of her devotion to Saint Joseph Cupertino, whom she described to Madeleva as her filthy, louse-infested medieval monk.[47] Instructed in the faith by Bishop Sheen, she formally joined the church in 1946. Two years earlier, the accidental death of her teen-aged daughter Ann, born of her first marriage and her only child, had sent her in search of spiritual sustenance.

Both figuratively and literally, Madeleva ministered to the lost child in Clare. Appalled to learn that as a little girl Clare had never had a Christmas crèche, she sent her one. Clare in turn lavished gifts on Madeleva: money for a trip to Rome, which Madeleva gave with Clare's permission to an Irish nun so that she could return home after forty-seven years; works of art and small gifts of stock in her husband's corporations, which Madeleva turned over to the college. Madeleva explained, "My beautiful Lady Poverty leaves me with no material gift for you," but she sent "the riches of prayer" along with poems for birthdays and copies of her books for Christmas.[48]

When she first met Madeleva, Clare told others how happy she and the other nuns seemed. To Clare and perhaps also to Harry, the child of missionaries to China, Madeleva represented an ideal existence whose possibility her way of life confirmed. Clare regarded Madeleva as she regarded all priests and nuns, as something of a talisman who held the answer to the riddle of suffering and the secret of peace. Moreover, Madeleva's cultivated tastes, lively intelligence, and personal magnetism mirrored Clare's and subtly united them and their disparate worlds.

Madeleva regarded Clare as "one of our brilliant women not in a convent!"[49] She often remarked on her radiance, both inner and outer, and saw this quality reflected in her name. "Her name is a brightness, a light so right for her," she wrote. "'Clare' and 'Luce' are both words for the luminous elation which to me is so much herself."[50] These in turn reminded her of her own mother's name, "Lucy," always dear to her. In many ways, Madeleva identified with Clare, not only because of her name, with its spiritual and personal associations, but also because she represented the woman Madeleva might have become had she not entered the convent. Rare in their time, both were self-made women who had risen to the top in different ways using similar talents. "I often wonder what I would be doing if I were twenty-one and just out of college now," Madeleva confessed to Clare.[51] Built on parallel abilities and tastes, Clare's life represented a plausible answer.

Although she might make new friends, Madeleva did not neglect those of many years. She and Ben Lehman, her former teacher, carried on by mail the conversations that had begun at Berkeley in 1922, managing a visit every year or two. In 1937 he remarried, to Australian-born actress Judith Anderson.[52] On their honeymoon, which took them through South Bend, they stopped so that he could introduce his bride to Madeleva. The marriage ended a brief two years later, after a year spent in London hobnobbing with a theatre crowd that included Lawrence Olivier, Vivien Leigh, and John Gielgud. Late in life, when he was almost seventy, he married for the third time, to a woman his age, a wealthy widow and long-time friend—a happy marriage that lasted until his wife's death in 1973.[53]

In the days before air travel was common, Lehman's trips to the East Coast permitted stopovers in South Bend, and Madeleva's more frequent trips west also brought them together. "How quickly and easily all accidents fell away, leaving us in the presence of a friendship that gives by receiving and receives by giving spontaneously, almost intuitively," she wrote him following a visit in 1948.[54] After an afternoon at his home the next summer, she wrote: "Few friendships have fulfilled themselves in my life more richly than this of ours during the past twenty-five years. The quiet certitudes, the inner and outer vision that have come to both of us through the years . . . are part, I think, of what we have been able to share so spontaneously, so directly."[55]

When Lehman retired from his teaching post at Berkeley in 1955, Madeleva contributed an essay on Julian of Norwich to a festschrift in his honor. Unable to attend the celebration, she wrote her own tribute:

> There are things in our friendship of three decades that I shall not forget: the first, my mistake in stumbling into your seminar at all, my first report, your visits to the Wasatch and to Saint Mary's, and now your letter that brings me back to the heart of things as they touch the lives that you have influenced most. You are right in saying that I have had over and over an almost palpable experience of having been with you and your goodly company on the evening of January twenty-first. The boundaries of the mind, the areas of the spirit are gracious in giving us this gift of agility, this experience in omnipresence. I think I am only one of the entire group humbly grateful that as a group and as individuals we have been able to do anything that can slightly compare with what you have done for us, that can begin to express the gratitude that shall always be incompletely expressed. To have changed the minds and the hearts of others for good and for better is to have been a great teacher. We have all experienced that growth under your tutelage.[56]

Those closest to Madeleva might have said the same about her. According to them, she unfailingly gave her best self to them. As Madge Vaison, her friend of three decades, put it: "You give—you give with love."[57] When she was with her friends, Madeleva lavished her attention on them, drew them into conversation that focused on their lives and interests, listened carefully, and remembered well. When she was apart from them, she spent her talent and energy composing long and thoughtful letters that elicited their best selves in response, and, of course, prayed for them.

Mary of God mentioned how Madeleva had once given her a book of poetry inscribed with the words: "In the mystery of love that

knows no beginning and no end." The only explanation for her friendship that she ever gave her young friend, Madeleva's inscription suggests that she regarded friendship as a reflection of and as a way of
participating in God's infinite love for humans.

15

The Relaxed Grasp

These small things upon which my heart is set
Are matters for a heart's relinquishings.

—Sr. Madeleva, "Ballade on Eschatology"

As a young nun, separated from her family, bereaved by the death of Sister Rita, and inspired by the ideals of religious life, Madeleva had adopted as her motto "the relaxed grasp." Aspiring to the ideals of holy simplicity and religious detachment, she set as her goal to strip life of all pretense and of unnecessary attachments (or, in the language of a later time, of all "dependencies" or "addictions") in order to encourage the spirit to grow toward God and the body to reverence itself and all material things as creations of God. To Madeleva, the paradoxical image of the relaxed grasp represented joy in creation even as it signified acceptance of the truth that nothing earthly lasts.

Throughout her life, what Madeleva referred to as "new worlds of the mind and of the soul" had successively opened to her as old ones closed: Indiana succeeding Wisconsin, Utah exchanging with Indiana and California, Oxford replacing the Wasatch. As she wrote in her autobiography, all of these worlds taught her the necessity of relaxing her grasp as she grew to love each in turn and eventually had to leave it behind.[1] Taking hold of each new experience, she foresaw and accepted the necessity of its end even as she cherished it. But, as she ruefully pointed out, she was always "en route" to the ideal, never arriving.[2]

Madeleva's life at Saint Mary's proved to be no exception. Rising to the challenges of her office, rediscovering the beauty of the Indiana rivers and woods, making new friends and returning to former ones, both hands filled to overflowing. She took pleasure in many aspects of her administrative job, such as encouraging and overseeing new projects and programs, not only academic programs such as the Trivium, the graduate program in theology, and the Christian Culture Program, but also architectural projects, such as the building of the library and later the fine arts building.[3] She learned to enjoy public relations and fundraising for the college, both because she believed in her cause and also because they brought her into touch with a wide variety of people. For the same reasons, she took pleasure in traveling on college business.

By the early 1950s, Madeleva had taken hold at Saint Mary's. Devoting herself, Martha-like, to her work, she received as the rewards of service numerous honors and awards, which she accepted with pleasure and gratitude as tokens of labor in the vineyard: the Siena Medal in 1948, awarded by the Theta Pi Alpha Society of Pittsburgh to a "Catholic woman who has made a distinctive contribution to Catholic life in the U.S.," and two years later the Women of Achievement Award from the Women's International Institute, presented to her and to Eleanor Roosevelt at the same time. She also carried home a total of seven honorary degrees from Catholic and secular universities.

In 1953 Madeleva was especially pleased and excited[4] when the new president of the University of Notre Dame, Father Theodore Hesburgh, CSC, invited her to receive an honorary Doctor of Letters degree at a special ceremony commemorating the dedication of the new fine arts building. She admired her young counterpart, then in his midthirties, whom she described as "a very remarkable person, simple, good, unspoiled in any way, honest and direct, and concerned with the good of others."[5] The award cited Madeleva's contributions as "a Catholic educational leader, a poet, the founder of the first graduate school of theology for lay persons and women of religious orders, and a patron of Christian culture."[6]

Many of Madeleva's honors recognized her achievement as a poet. She was the only woman invited to lecture in a series on poetry at Boston College in 1957 that also included Robert Frost, Ogden Nash, and T. S. Eliot. In 1959, she received the Campion award of the Catholic Book Club for her extended contribution to excellence in Catholic writing, an award that had been previously conferred on her friends Jacques Maritain and Helen C. White and which later went to Maisie Ward and Frank Sheed. The next year, the Catholic Poetry Society of America honored her with the Spirit Award of Merit. Syracuse University expressed the desire to establish a permanent collection of her manuscripts, and other colleges and universities wrote to request original materials for their libraries.

During these years, Madeleva was often called on to lecture on poets and poetry and to review the work of younger Catholic poets such as Thomas Merton and Daniel Berrigan. She also met with groups devoted to reading and discussing her poetry, which had been organized not only in South Bend but across the country. One woman who belonged to such a group in Chicago wrote to say that she and other poets in the area looked upon Madeleva with "something like awe."[7] A non-Catholic fan wrote to the Catholic Poetry Society of America to offer his services in making her work better known and to inquire how to nominate her for canonization![8]

Madeleva personally shrugged off public recognition, even though she valued its benefits for the college. Although she was proud of her accomplishments as a college president, she knew that she had paid for them by sacrificing other loves: her writing, research, and teaching. She described the poetry for which she was honored as one of the chief casualties of office. "Because of my overwhelming duties during the past years, I have had almost no time even to think of poetry, much less to write the simplest kind of verse," she told a friend.[9]

"The impact of prosaic demands is all but fatal to lyric thinking and expression,"[10] she wrote in 1950. The little time she had for poetry, she snatched as she "walk[ed] through corridors" and "recover[ed] from colds."[11] As she told an interviewer, ideas for poems came at random, on a trip, on a walk, between appointments.[12]

Writing C. S. Lewis in 1951, Madeleva attributed her lack of scholarly publication to the same cause: "The impact of administration for these past seventeen years has been desolating so far as adventures in thinking are concerned."[13] After teaching several advanced courses in the early years of her presidency, she later confined herself to occasional academic lectures on favorite medieval topics such as Julian of Norwich or Chaucer's nuns. Most published lectures and essays, such as those collected in *Addressed to Youth* (1944) and *Conversations with Cassandra* (1961), focused on education.

Striving to relax her grasp, Madeleva wrote to friends that the *Collected Poems* of 1947 contained the best of her work and predicted: "It will be the last thing of any consequence that I shall do in verse."[14] She stated flatly that the days of her best verse writing were over,[15] and she assessed her limits as a poet: "I am not a major poet. I have neither the talent nor the time to be one."[16] She further admitted, "It is a great surprise to me to be considered a poet. I can never bring myself to talk of myself as a poet."[17] In fact, she said, she considered her ability "more critical than creative"[18] and time and again deprecated her verse, describing it as just her way of saying what she thought.[19]

Yet Madeleva admitted that there "have been, still are, books that I should like at least to try to write, cuds of song upon which I still hope to chew."[20] Unable to let go completely of the writing and studying she loved, she regularly deprived herself of sleep to write one last poem and devised a form of speed reading to keep up with scholarly and professional publications. Pressed for time, she dictated first administrative correspondence and then personal letters to her secretary, squeezed visits to friends into layover times at airports and train stations, and prayed as she walked.

When her "three lives," as she called them—her "religious life, human life, professional life"—collided, as they inevitably did almost daily, she called to mind the relaxed grasp, which allowed her to control her feelings of frustration and inadequacy.[21] "Thinking of things to be done, hopes to be realized, persons to be helped, I say laughingly that I go to a multitude of funerals daily, burying so many deceased projects, so much of what I have had to let die and must bury without regret."[22]

But as soon as Madeleva admitted that she was no longer able to write the poetry she once had, she scheduled lectures on poets and poetry to spread her love of the word in a different way. Shelving her research in medieval studies, she eagerly undertook a new field of study connected with the School of Sacred Theology. One of her colleagues wrote,

> When Sister Madeleva established the School of Sacred Theology at Saint Mary's, she persuaded some of the best American theologians to come to teach at the only graduate school of theology in the United States to admit women. Her plan was to prepare teachers for the faculties of religion for Catholic colleges. In fact *she* may have informally become one of its best students through her long conversations and planning with distinguished scholars, and in particular some very influential liturgists. Jesuit Father Ellard, Holy Cross Father Mathis and bishops who were at that time active in the National Catholic Education Association spent long visits on campus. During this period of fruitful discussions she read deeply and extensively.[23]

Even though Madeleva called herself an "unconscientious reader" and characteristically downplayed the amount of study she was able to accomplish, she admitted that she managed to "take the tops off a good many things." With almost no leisure in which to read, she hit upon the solution of skimming the first hundred pages or so of a book, after which she read only every other page. Reading, as she put it, only "the things I can least afford not to know," she kept up with publications in a wide variety of fields.[24]

Never a lover of fiction—she had once written Lehman, "All novels I divide for myself into two classes; those that make me sure that I don't like fiction, and those that make me wonder why I don't like it"[25]—Madeleva stated that she neglected "almost all" contemporary literary works, but she made time to read *To Kill a Mockingbird* (which, defying her classification, she liked) and *Catcher in the Rye* (which she did not), along with dozens of others. She preferred plays, which she read for relaxation, delighting especially in the work of Christopher Fry and Bertolt Brecht. Out of a sense of compunction, she pushed herself through some of the classics she had not read in her youth. During one hospital stay she finished *Moby Dick*, but admitted that, using her technique, she had skimmed it. "I would forget much in *Moby Dick* anyway," she said. "Why should I travel all those miles across the pages when what I want is the essence of the book? . . . By the time you get to thirty-five, you know enough not to have to fill your mind with all of that."[26]

Drawn by people and activity, spurred on by her perfectionism and need to achieve, Madeleva often voluntarily turned away from the solitude and leisure she idealized but in fact usually avoided. Complaining that convent life did not allow "undistracted time in large quantities"[27] and that the work assigned to her left little time for anything else, she seldom considered that the standards and goals she set for herself guaranteed that she would invest every spare minute in work.

Even when Madeleva's schedule was most crowded, life in a convent assured times of quiet reflection, one of the reasons she valued religious life. It protected her from her tendency to overwork and, as she herself described it, "get bogged down" with people. She assisted at mass every morning, where as she put it she met Christ in the Holy Eucharist, and devoted periods of each day both to communal and to private prayer. She started each work week with an hour of meditation and at least once a year withdrew for a formal religious retreat. On most days, no matter what the weather, she found time to work in a little garden she planted or to walk around campus, to pray in the presence of nature. In spare moments, she learned to meditate on whatever life offered: an envelope or pen from her desk, a pattern of reflected light on the carpet, the sound of rain on the window, the smell of fresh air or good food. Being driven to an appointment (she never learned to drive, saying she took enough risks as it was), she would open a Bible that she carried with her and select at random a passage on which to meditate, apparently unconcerned that some of the other sisters considered the practice eccentric.[28]

For the most part, Madeleva expressed content with her life. Writing to a young woman uncertain about whether to enter a convent, she told her: "The decision may be hard for you to make now. Ten years from now [those who enter a convent] will be the happiest of all your friends and schoolmates. Of course happiness is not your major consideration," she added. "God's will is."[29]

Madeleva's confidence that nothing can be amiss in a life dedicated to serving God went deep; it shaped her philosophy and transformed any and every circumstance, however unpleasant in itself, into an opportunity for spiritual growth. Ironically, it also impelled her to work hard, certain that her every effort was supremely meaningful because it served a higher purpose than her own. Her faith in the providence of God reassured her that all would be well in the end, if not according to human valuation then according to a higher law. In "Fare Well," the final poem in *Gates*, she wrote:

> Fare infinitely well,
> You who have valorously dared
> This last, unshared
> Unending and all-perfect quest;
> You who at length can tell
> The things God has prepared
> Are best,
> Are best.

However optimistic and complacent such a philosophy might sound, Madeleva knew from experience how difficult and demanding it could be in practice. Her faith in God's providence rested on her sense that choosing alone, by and for herself, she could not have done better than God's choice for her, based on perfect knowledge and designed and directed by love. Believing as she did that love, especially Christian love, cannot be made at a distance;[30] that it is, in its very essence, personal, singular, and one-on-one, Madeleva had faith that God's love was tailor-made for her, and for each individual—with this proviso: it is made for one's greatest self. Unlike Procrustes' bed, it molds itself to the individual, who is not forced to fit it.

Madeleva did not consciously raise the question of whether her religious vocation in any way hindered her development as a poet, and by implication, as a person, but she answered the unspoken question by insisting that whatever she wrote was because of, not in spite of, her life in a convent, without which, she said, she would not have been a poet at all. In any case, she said, she did not create art for its own sake, or even for her sake, but as a way to praise God, valuable only insofar as it pleased God and furthered God's will for her.[31]

Therein lay the contradiction, which continued to split the Martha in Madeleva from the Mary and divide her active from her contemplative life. Poetry had from the first been Madeleva's way to God, intimately connected with her life of prayer ("[Poetry] is as much a means of sanctification for me as my prayers," she had written Mother Vincentia from the Wasatch. "Indeed, much of it is prayer to me."). When she expressed a desire for time to write poetry, she betrayed her desire for union with and wholeness in God and, by implication, her sense of distance from the God she knew and loved. Knowing and loving, she sought to serve, but service itself seemed to separate her from the One for whom she declared herself willing to sacrifice everything—except love itself.

Madeleva coped with her contradictions by collapsing. Forced to relax her grasp, she then consented to spend anywhere from a few days to several weeks in a hospital or rest home—an annual occurrence in midlife. Seldom allowing herself to do nothing even there, she used the time to read, meditate, and write an occasional poem or two.

Madeleva's health veered dramatically during these years of intense activity. Sometimes she went for months without serious illness. Then for no apparent reason fatigue and depression sabotaged her energy and her peace of mind. Her hospital stays became in a sense retreats for the body and the mind, which whether Madeleva consciously recognized it or not, were as necessary for her as the spiritual retreats scheduled regularly for all sisters.

In 1949, because of what she described as a "terrible inundation of fatigue,"[32] Madeleva traveled to Boston at the suggestion of Clare and Harry Luce to visit the Lahey Clinic, a Catholic hospital that treated religious free of charge. Doctors John Norcross and John Daley became her regular physicians and her good friends. They diagnosed some liver damage and disfunction, which though slight required rest. She ruefully commented, "With normal conditions in all vital parts I have a distressing capacity for developing accidental ailments that undo me."[33]

Through most of 1950, Madeleva complained of insomnia, and after a bout of "very bad depression" that left her mind like "a mud puddle,"[34] she returned for more tests. This time, the liver abnormality showed itself to be "considerable," and test results revealed low thyroid and a low basal metabolism. She also showed signs of mild diabetes and, although she was not overweight, began a modified diet to control it.

One or the other of her physicians wrote often to Madeleva, encouraging her above all to slow down. Just being Sister Madeleva, Norcross commented, was in itself a "pretty exhausting experience," for which she should compensate with extra rest.[35] Cautioning her doctors that there was much in their profession "to which medicine itself does not give the whole answer,"[36] she answered their prescriptions with doses of poetry and spiritual reading, sending them copies of her own books ("which you will certainly never read," she said[37]) as well as personal favorites such as Merton's *Seeds of Contemplation* and de Chardin's *Divine Milieu.*

However much her uncertain health exasperated her by undermining her capacity to work as long and hard as she would have liked, Madeleva tacitly acknowledged that it kept her aware of her own limits and effectively compelled her to relax her grasp. In "Holy Communion in a Hospital," written during one of her illnesses, she reflected on an unanticipated consequence of her fragility:

All of my life I have come to You, walking erect, hands clasped,
    head a little bowed;
Finding my way to you through the Sunday, the every day crowd;
Kneeling to wait till You came to me in your own inexplicable
    way,
Leaving me shaken with love and with less than nothing to say;
Always I came to You so; always until today.

Today you will come to me here in this room half-lighted,
    curtains a little drawn.
Never before have You sought me so, brought me Yourself at
    dawn.
Now You are helplessly here more than I, to feed me, to comfort,
    to bless;
Infinite, patient to bear with me pain's relentless caress;
Clothing me with Yourself, in the vesture of helplessness.

Illness taught the independent, supremely competent woman more than simple endurance; it did what her best intentions could not, carrying her beyond physical pain to spiritual comfort. The certainty of Christ's sustaining power in spite of inevitable personal loss encouraged her to let go willingly of what would otherwise be wrested from her: youth, physical possessions, emotional attachments, and life itself. Only then would other, more essential gifts come.

Visits to her parents, which Madeleva continued to make regularly, also provided periods of much needed rest. However old she herself grew—she was in her sixties when her parents died—she became "a little child again"[38] when she was with them. When "Sis," as they still called their daughter, came home, they put her to bed under handmade quilts, fed her cream and fresh eggs, and plied her with town and family gossip. As she had as a girl, she helped her mother in the garden and the house and sat with her father in the harness shop, where he worked until 1945, when he retired at eighty-eight.

Being with her parents comforted Madeleva, but it saddened her, too; she ached to do more for them. Neither Lucy, who lived past her ninety-fourth birthday, nor August, who died at ninety-six, wanted to leave Cumberland, where they continued to live in their apartment above the harness shop until 1946, negotiating a steep flight of stairs each time they went in or out.

When the Wolffs finally moved to Duluth to be close to Fred and his family, they suffered from acute homesickness. "I think of the old home all the time and wander around in old familiar places," her mother wrote Madeleva.[39] "There's lots of God's will be done."[40]

When Madeleva fretted over her parents' unhappiness and her inability to help them, Lucy wrote to comfort her daughter: "I think you are doing yourself a great injustice when you speak of the *meagerness* of what you are doing for what we as parents did with the greatest joy and pleasure not to mention the duty parents owe to worthy children. Are you not rewarding us every day in the good you are doing in your daily life? Could any calling in your life have done more than you are doing now to prove your gratitude? Just one short prayer means everything to us, so forget your helplessness. We thank God every day you are where and what you are."[41]

Lucy died in February 1948, alert enough at the end to ask her daughter's advice on what she should say when she saw God.[42] The burial took place three months later in Cumberland, when the ground thawed.

August lived for six more years, writing regularly to his daughter when Lucy could no longer write for both of them. In his humble prose and crabbed handwriting, he recorded the simple facts of his daily existence. He reported that he was the first one up and dressed in the retirement home and that he continued to enjoy his "eats." He paid close attention to the weather, reporting on each change, and kept track of how the crops were doing. He continued to follow politics from a distance and confessed that even though he was a Republican he would have voted for Harry Truman if he had not "lost all political ambition."[43] When Madeleva mentioned in a letter to him that, to her astonishment, someone had given her four pints of Kentucky whiskey as a gift, he promptly wrote to request that she send him some for a nightcap. Another time, when she sent him a box of chocolates to give to the nuns who attended him, he wrote to confess that he first gave some to the garden crew, but that only ten or so were missing.

August faded from this life gradually and peacefully, as though nodding off to sleep. His mind went before his body did; in his last letters, he boasted to his daughter that he was three hundred years old and the oldest man alive. "Whatever happens," he wrote, "I am going to keep on living and growing old."[44]

Madeleva spent her father's last birthday with him. On the September afternoon of his party, celebrated with cake, candles, and presents, the two of them walked in the orchard and garden for a pleasant hour. In her words, "The ripening fruit, the laden branches pleased him. Again and again he would point out lovely colorings or beautiful groupings of crab apples. A bit tired, we sat quietly in the sun, neither of us saying anything. Then he asked me, half-puzzled, half-incredulous, 'Where have you been, Lucy, all this time?'" Madeleva concluded, "No question has ever told me so much."[45]

Before his death, which occurred in January 1954, Madeleva wrote "To a Very Old Harness-Maker" in honor of her father. Printed on his funeral card, it served as his obituary and her farewell:

> Here are your harness shop, your world of leather,
> Collars and hames and harness on the wall,
> Summer-brown farmers come to town in fall,
> Or stamping snowy boots in winter weather;
> Here are your art of putting straps together,
> Stitching-horse, needled wax-threads, accurate awl,
> Your delicate ear, quick to the first bird's call,
> Your delicate eye, quick to its moulted feather.
>
> Here at your desk the day's accounts are ended,
> Your world resolved upon, your gardens planned,
> Your simple earnings totaled or expended,
> Leather goods bought and sold, poetry scanned.
> Here I remember you, smiling and quaintly splendid,
> A gathered moss rose in your wax-brown hand.

During a stay at an Arkansas sanatarium in October 1954, not long after her father's death, Madeleva composed a pair of poems, two of the last on subjects other than Christmas that she wrote: "Ballade for the Queen of the World" and "Ballade on Eschatology," the latter of which she dedicated to the Hero of the Habitually Relaxed Grasp. In both poems, she contemplated the interconnectedness of earthly life and transcendent reality.

Describing Mary, at once the humble mother of Jesus and a majestic Queen clothed in glory, Madeleva wrote:

> You wore mortality a little space,
> Lady of tears and laughter, myrrh and rue,
> Where seven swords of sorrow left sharp trace,
> Whence seven joys their flaming splendor drew.
> Bright as the sun from head to shining shoe,
> Your majesty is here, is everywhere,
> Too near to see, too palpable to view!

Although beyond change herself, the poet suggests, the eternal Queen has the power to confer "Beauty that can be beautiful and true" in "the world's wide, ever-changing place."

The same connection between natural and supernatural worlds defines the vision of the latter poem as well: "Time closes round me with impalpable net," Madeleva wrote. "I'll not advert to clay or crowns or wings./ I have no thing to lose, all things to get." She concludes:

> Lord, though by mortal tyrannies beset,
> Immortal freedom in my wild heart sings.
> A pauper comes to pay a pauper's debt.
> God, I shall not forget the four last things.

Madeleva did not construe the remembrance of the last things, traditionally defined as death, judgment, heaven, and hell, as negative; they reminded her of the Easter mystery, of death and sin transformed by eternal life and limitless love. The speaker of the poems redirects memory from a vain attempt to cling to the past (to recall, for example, "Your voice, your eyes,—or are they blue or gray?/ The day we said good-bye, the day we met;/Hills we have walked, birds, flowers, our work, our play") to mindfulness of "One ultimate matter," the presence of God, here, now, and always.

Loving life, Madeleva contemplated the last things both in her early and in her late poetry and, presumably, in her prayers. "My great preoccupation is death," she said both of her art and of her life.

In her opinion, "Next to birth and baptism, death is the greatest thing we can experience."[46] "Sister Death" was her familiar name for an experience that as a Christian and a nun she regarded as a homecoming, a time of reunion with the Father and of complete union, body and soul, with the divine Son, to whose service she had committed her life. In poems such as "Sister Death," "Details for My Burial," and "Concerning Death," as well as "Ballade for Eschatology," she contemplated the moment of final revelation that would answer all questions, dispel all doubts, and return her to the source of life.

In many respects, death represented to Madeleva what poetry always had: a natural way to the supernatural. Speaking of poetry, she said: "The person who loves poetry, who reads and writes it, looks out on an entirely different world than the person who never thinks above the level of prose. He sees in human beings a reflection of God. He looks out upon a transfigured, supernaturalized landscape, an immortalized vision of life."[47] Like poetry, death and its contemplation revealed to Madeleva the wholeness within herself and all created things.

Dame Julian of Norwich, the fifteenth-century mystic whose writings Madeleva had pondered since she first discovered them as a graduate student at Berkeley, recounted in the *Revelations of Divine Love* her discovery of God's love for and oneness with creation through her experiences of suffering and death, which paralleled those of Christ crucified. In one of the visions that came to her as, to all appearances, she lay on her deathbed, she saw something that she described as "no bigger than a hazelnut, lying in the palm of my hand, and I perceived that it was as round as any ball." Puzzled as to what it could be, God revealed to her that it was "all that is made." Julian wrote, "I was amazed that it could last, for I thought that it was so little that it could suddenly fall into nothing. And I was answered in my understanding: It lasts and always will, because God loves it; and thus everything has being through the love of God."

Julian's "showing" allowed her to put worldly things in perspective. So little and frail a thing offers no rest, Julian understood. God alone, "who is almighty, all wise and good" offers the only "true rest." In her text, she quotes God: "See, I am God. See, I am in all things. See, I do all things. See, I never remove my hands from my works, nor ever shall without end. See, I guide all things to the end that I ordain them for, before time began, with the same power and wisdom and love with which I made them. How should anything be amiss?"[48]

In an essay on Julian's life and work, Madeleva commented, "More than all else Dame Julian leaves a spiritual legacy to everyone who can enter into the mystery of love through the mystery of suffering. She understands and shares with her readers the epitomes of the universe in the Passion and Crucifixion of Christ; the intrinsic, solicitous presence of God in all things; the essential necessity of God's attributes, and [God's] essential intimacy with the universe."[49] In the writings of Julian, Madeleva found both a justification for and a powerful expression of the philosophy that guided her life.

16

GIVING BEAUTY BACK

Give beauty back, beauty, beauty, beauty, back to God, beauty's self and beauty's giver.

—Gerard Manley Hopkins

When she buried her father in 1954, Madeleva was close to her own sixty-seventh birthday and would soon mark the twentieth anniversary of her appointment to the presidency of Saint Mary's. Like her father, she resisted retirement. "The emptiest day of all our years will be the one in which we have to give up work for the last time," she said in one of her talks, possibly thinking of him; "when we are retired because of age if we are professional persons; when we have to be waited on by our grandchildren if we are parents; when we move to an infirmary or a nursing home. We will learn to fill the subsequent days with the rich activities of meditation, reading, prayer. We will not be able to reclaim the zest, the joy of our whole being that is the best reward of legitimate work well done."[1]

Surprising words, coming from a woman who had often spoken of her work as a distraction from her search for God. Her comments, published in *Conversations with Cassandra* in 1961, suggest an attitude that regards work neither as a punishment (the curse of Adam) nor as an escape from boredom or meaninglessness (a more modern interpretation) but as a vital expression of self. They signal a shift in perspective that occurred gradually, almost imperceptibly, over the years.

In the same talk, Madeleva went on to explain why she valued work so highly: "On the ultimate, the highest level we are children of God and about our Father's business. In any exegesis, the universe, existence itself began with the work of creation. That work is still in process: 'The Father worked until now, and I work,' Jesus said. . . . As Christians we are working with Him."[2]

"I feel hard work is necessary in doing a good, complete job, and I would be lost if I didn't work hard all the time," Madeleva told a

reporter in 1963.[3] Although such statements certainly betray something of the work ethic that inspired her parents and suggest a person who finds her meaning through work, Madeleva carefully distinguished work for its own sake from work as an expression of
Christian love. However pleasant or unpleasant the job (and Madeleva
regarded writing and gardening, which she loved, as well as administration, for which she cared less, as "hard" work), she valued the
willing gift of self that hard work represented. Done for the community in the spirit of Christ, it became an act of worship and a place
to meet God.

Madeleva spent her final years as president of Saint Mary's working harder than ever. Realizing that little time remained—the deaths
of her parents made that clear to her as nothing else had—she concentrated her energy on one last effort, what she referred to as the
"apostolate of beauty"; that is, the advocation of beauty as an expression of and a way to God. Specifically, in her last decade as president, she set for herself the task of creating a "home" for beauty at
the college. The project summed up all that had meant most to her
throughout her life, and she threw herself into it with passionate
conviction.

Madeleva had long regarded beauty as a tangible manifestation
of the divine, the most accessible to humans of all God's attributes.
Her devotion to beauty corresponded with her belief that the transcendent may be experienced through the senses as well as the soul;
that the love of God involves the entire person, including the body. "I
knew that of the trinity—goodness, truth and beauty, each an equation
for God—beauty is the most palpable, the most irresistible," she wrote.
"I have called it God's visibility."[4] She further explained, "We can 'see'
[Beauty] in a way we cannot see Truth or Goodness."[5]

Madeleva believed that beauty draws souls to God more effectively than preaching or proselytizing. Not that a beautiful aspect or
object in itself is God, but it can act sacramentally to reveal the reality
of God's presence both to the maker and to the partaker of beauty.

Madeleva's experience as a poet and as a nun had shaped her
ideas on beauty. As a young religious, she had seen what she referred
to as the "overwhelming beauty" of God through prayer, and her need
to express that vision resulted in poetry. As a graduate student at Berkeley, she defined the religious poet who writes from such experience
as "the soul satisfied by union" who sings, and wrote that this type of
poet, which she called "mystical," realizes that "Earth, life, the soul, the
Church, himself are wedded to God in a very ecstasy of love. All creation is a multiple mirror, dedicated to the reflection of these unions."[6]

As she grew older, Madeleva continued to associate poetry in a particular way with the vision of God and to describe the devotion to poetry as a form of worship, as when she described the poet as one who "looks out upon a transfigured, supernaturalized landscape," and sees in others "a reflection of God."[7]

Madeleva voiced her disapproval of much contemporary verse, which in her opinion was preoccupied with the ugly and the ignominious and induced at best a condition she called "emetic ecstasy." She devised a test of the "true" poet: "The test concerns the moon crescent sometimes visible in the early morning. If it's a 'thin crust of a moon' to you, you have something of the poet within you. But if it reminds you of a 'toenail' then you can't rise above prose, and you aren't much of a poet."[8] Too many poets, she said, suffered from disillusionment. "They lack faith and hope. They accuse others of being escapists, not realistic. Actually they are running away from the beauty and truth that is perennial."[9]

As she aged, Madeleva increasingly focused on enterprises devoted to the creation of beauty, which she intended as praise to match the best of her poems. Having established the college as a center of Christian education for women, she turned to gardening and church design as well as to her most ambitious project, establishing a center for the fine arts that would serve not only the college and the local community but the entire region. Satisfying for their own sakes, Madeleva trusted that these activities would put her in touch with a more profound reality. "Our own desire for and experience in creativity help us to understand why God created a universe and continues to create it," she wrote.[10] Time-consuming as they were, such activities freed her from what she referred to as a "thousand petty deities of clay" because they—like her poetry and prayer—centered her in the present moment, which she pointed out is as much time as anyone has.[11]

Since her days at the Wasatch, when she had been responsible for developing all aspects of the new campus, Madeleva had taken a keen interest in landscaping. At Saint Mary's, she personally designed several campus gardens and assumed responsibility for beautifying the grounds. As she had at the Wasatch, she set aside a small garden plot, which she tended with her mother's gardening tools. In it Madeleva grew her favorite flowers: "thoughtful, quietly beautiful" pansies; whimsical, "old-fashioned" nasturtiums; and stunning but "vilely expensive" tuberous begonias.[12]

After the war, she hired Joseph Bonadies, a master gardener who had been trained at Mount Vernon and at the New York Botanical Gardens. With Madeleva's imagination and taste as complements to his own, Joe transformed the already beautiful campus into a small Eden. Together, they devised massed plantings: of American beeches on the island in Lake Marian and a grove of pin oaks on the east side of campus. At her suggestion, he grafted a purple beech on a green one and planted it by the library, "to be seen in early spring," she advised. Hemlocks, with their soft needles, were planted to be touched, and Douglass firs for their scent.

Madeleva loved oaks, whose roots in ancient times were thought to link this world to eternity, and she saw that all varieties were planted in abundance. Once, when an old oak by the convent came down, Madeleva had Joe cut it into stumps and instructed him to place them by twos around campus to make conversation places "for lovers." According to Joe, she sometimes carried home in her suitcase seedlings gathered on her trips and returned with nuts and seeds from rare trees and plants, challenging him to realize her visions with the kernels on her outstretched palm.[13]

From a trip to Boston, Madeleva brought home several fine seedlings of European beeches. She had Joe put up fences around the young trees, thin as whips, to protect them. Every day she checked on them. When, in spite of the great care with which she and Joe tended them, they lost one, Madeleva regarded the shrivelled tree with sadness. "It happens with students, too," she said.

To commemorate her twenty-fifth year as president, Madeleva chose a pin oak, her favorite tree, to be planted close to the new fine arts building, and beside it she asked that a white burr oak be planted for Maria Pieta. One of the hardest things to detach herself from, Madeleva wrote in old age, was her desire to watch her seedling oak and birches grow into great trees.[14]

Madeleva thought of nature as a vast cathedral, a sacred space in which God dwelled, with the trees its pillars, arches, and spires. Inverting the metaphor, she thought of churches as gardens, wishing them to be as natural and bright as a forest glade. In "Easter Chronicle," a sonnet written during her sabbatical in Europe, she played on her sense of the sanctity of nature and the naturalness of worship, seeing in each the emblem of the other:

> Today is Easter; I am at Solesmes.
> The air is still and delicate and sweet.
> Violets cloud the path before my feet
> And edge the village with their purple hem.
> Alone, bemused with song, I gather them,
> Thinking how, on this morning, I should meet
> Blossoming sound, antiphonal, complete,

Blossoming color, leaf and flower and stem.
It has unfolded for me like a flower,
This great Gregorian chant: the solemn Mass,
The morning Office, hour by heavenly hour.
There shall remain, when lesser praise shall pass,
This music that is peace and prayer and power,
These April violets in the quickened grass.

To Madeleva's way of thinking, both cathedral and garden honored through imitation God's work as the Creator of Nature and the Architect of the Universe; they made conscious in human life the divine order and sacred message implicit in the world. Thus, it was not as big a leap as it may seem when, late in her career, Madeleva ventured into church design. In 1945, she took responsibility for transforming the academy library in Holy Cross Hall into a chapel. Disliking the traditional arrangement in the Le Mans chapel that distanced worshippers from the altar, she consulted liturgists and theologians and proposed that the altar have a central location, with the assembly gathered around it—a daring innovation at the time. Working with a manufacturer of church furniture, she negotiated the design for simple pews with open backs to create a sense of space.

According to Sister Miriam, Madeleva's vice president for development and a close friend to the older woman in her last years, "the outcome was a splendid bright room with light wood 'open' pews surrounding a square table altar with an altar railing on four sides. The crucifix over the altar with a corpus on two sides invited priest celebrants to offer Mass facing the assembly. The resident Dominicans of the faculty often presided there facing the congregation, thus preparing themselves and the college for the changes of Vatican Council II to come twenty years later."[15]

As early as 1908, while still a postulant, Madeleva had argued for and won the right to use a missal to follow the Latin mass in English, even though the practice was unusual at the time.[16] Whatever enhanced full participation in the liturgy won her unqualified endorsement; this concern with the liturgy coupled with her keen aesthetic sense explained her interest in a field of which she had much experience but little formal knowledge. Guided by the same principles that had motivated her design for the new library, she wished to create an uncluttered space, free of distractions, whose simplicity revealed beauty, so that beauty might lift the spirit.

In the early 1950s, Reverend Joseph Adams, OFM, cap., a distant cousin of Madeleva and the pastor of Saint Charles Borromeo parish in St. Louis, convinced Madeleva to design the eight master stained glass windows in the church on Locust Street. She went on to design a large rose window over the entrance; a mosaic over the main altar, which represented the apparitions of Our Lady; and the stations of the cross. According to Father Didicus Dunn, pastor at the church at the time of its closing in the late 1970s, she was also responsible for a life-sized nativity scene that was set up in the church and displayed year-round: a plausible suggestion, given her love of Christmas and of crèches.[17]

In her own community, however, most of Madeleva's suggestions for the Church of Loretto, the main place of worship at the Saint Mary's convent, were rejected. Built in 1885, the church was scheduled for reconstruction in 1955. Madeleva was asked to join a planning committee that consisted of Mother Rose Elizabeth, superior general at the time, three members of the art department at the college, all sisters, and three faculty members from Notre Dame, including two artists and an architect. The committee offered four recommendations to the general council of the congregation, which was responsible for making the final decision: tall mosaics with themes from scripture and literature; clear glass in the four main windows, because of the bright mosaics; the removal of all side-altars and their statues; and, most important, a central altar, both artistically and liturgically appropriate for the new building.

The forward-looking recommendations upset the more conservative sisters in the congregation, who put pressure on the members of the general council to reject them. By the time the reconstruction occurred, the stained glass windows from the old church had been installed in the new one, niches were provided for all the statues, and the altar "stayed where it belonged," along the west wall. According to Miriam, "Predictably Sister Madeleva, the committee, designer [Paul] Grillo and the college sisters were deeply disappointed to miss the experience of an aesthetically satisfying church building, along with the opportunity to educate a generation of worshippers at the Church of Loretto to sound theology of worship."[18] Madeleva accepted such setbacks with equanimity, biding her time. "By pushing things with even a shadow of prematurity we may damage the cause more than by a little delay," she cautioned in such circumstances.[19]

The same conservative element in the congregation came close to thwarting Madeleva's dream of a fine arts building that would also house a regional center for the performing arts. No matter that the arts, especially the dramatic arts, were regarded as morally and academically suspect by many Catholic educators at the time, nor that some of her superiors considered equipping such a facility to be inordinately expensive—Madeleva's mind was made up. She justified her desire by calling the fine arts "as old as human history" and identifying them as one of the best ways to give beauty back to beauty's giver.[20] Revising Eric Gill's statement: "Take care of goodness and truth, and beauty will take care of itself," she pronounced: "Take care of beauty, and goodness and truth will take care of themselves!" By building a home for beauty, Madeleva explained, she would create a space in which humans encountered the divine no less surely than if she built a church.

Madeleva began anticipating a fine arts building as early as 1941, as soon as ground was broken for the Alumnae Centennial Library. When she brought the matter up in 1947, once the war was over and construction again possible, Rose Elizabeth, her superior general and good friend, discouraged her; too many other projects, including a new convent building, took precedence. However, when Sister Francis Jerome O'Laughlin, who had served as vice president under Madeleva until her death, stipulated in her will that her share of a family inheritance be used for such a project, Rose Elizabeth gave way. "Build your fine arts building," she told her friend in 1952.[21]

Again the project was delayed when fire broke out in a chemistry laboratory in Holy Cross Hall. Madeleva reluctantly agreed with her trustees; a new science hall must come first. Not until 1956 was Moreau Hall finally completed. It housed art, music, and drama departments, including classrooms, faculty offices, and student practice rooms; two art galleries; a lecture hall; and an auditorium that seated 1,300 and contained the largest and best equipped stage in the region.

Decorating the exterior of the building were fifteen frescoes by Jean Charlot, a French artist who had lived for several years in Mexico and was teaching at Notre Dame at the time Madeleva commissioned him to do the paintings. She worked with him to design the frescoes, the largest of which depicted the fire of creation, with fourteen others portraying the fine arts through representative figures. From among the assembly of saints and literary titans depicted in the frescoes, the benign countenance of Saint Hilda of Whitby, Madeleva's inspiration for this project as for so many others, surveyed the campus, symbolizing poetry.

For the location of Moreau Hall, the highest spot on campus had been chosen, a hill between the convent and the college that overlooked the surrounding area. A lovely grove of trees had covered the site: old hemlocks, oaks, purple smoke trees, weeping beeches. When some of the sisters heard that Madeleva intended to cut them down to put a building in their place, they were outraged and fought her bitterly.

She found herself in the uncomfortable position of arguing that living beauty be sacrificed for beauty's sake—a clear indication of how much the building meant to her. According to Joe Bonadies, she said of her opponents, "If they want trees, let them go and live in the woods!"[22]

    Actress Helen Hayes, who came in November 1955 for the laying of the cornerstone of Moreau Hall, returned in the spring for its dedication. As a child, she had been educated by the Holy Cross sisters in Washington, D.C., a connection of which Madeleva had reminded her in her initial invitation to visit the college. With her sophisticated sense of symbol, Madeleva knew the value of having Miss Hayes present at these ceremonies. The "First Lady of the American theatre" epitomized the level of excellence Madeleva intended the center to uphold.

    Madeleva and the diminutive actress (she was just five feet tall) immediately warmed to each other. Miss Hayes was known for her shyness and reserve off the stage; Madeleva's air of quiet composure reassured even the most timid. In Miss Hayes, Madeleva recognized the signs of someone who longed for spiritual consolation and reached out to her. Like Clare Luce, she too had lost a child, her only daughter Mary, who died of polio in 1949, before she was twenty.

    Denied the sacraments of the church because of her marriage to playwright Charles MacArthur, a divorced man, Miss Hayes valued the acceptance Madeleva offered. In spite of numerous protests from church members when Saint Mary's announced its intention to award the lapsed Catholic an honorary degree in 1956 in recognition of her contributions to the college, Madeleva defended the choice, seeking the approval of church authorities, which she obtained.

    The following year, shortly after her husband's death, Miss Hayes reentered the church. She credited Madeleva's influence.[23] Thanking her, she wrote to describe her struggle between pride and stubborness on the one hand and her longing for the church on the other. After confession and penance, she wrote, she once again knew the peace and relief of reconciliation.[24]

    Madeleva wrote Ben Lehman that she and Miss Hayes had "wonderful plans for the future in our new and most beautiful fine arts building."[25] At her own suggestion, Miss Hayes cooperated to obtain publicity for the college and in particular for the new theatre. She was the drawing card for several fund-raising events of the college on the East Coast, and in 1960 returned to Saint Mary's for several weeks to star in a student production of Thornton Wilder's *The Skin of Our Teeth*, refusing to accept any compensation for her appearance.

Between the time of its completion in 1956 until Madeleva retired in 1961, the Moreau Center offered distinguished programs of performers and companies that brought Saint Mary's not only the "beauty" for which Madeleva said she had built it but also the national attention she wanted for the college. The world premiere of the NBC Opera Company's production of the *Marriage of Figaro*, which formally opened the new theatre in October 1956, attracted national press coverage as did a steady succession of first-rate dramatic and musical performances.

As Madeleva intended, the center offered outstanding theatre, opera, ballet, and orchestral and vocal music to the students and faculty of area colleges and universities as well as to local residents. She delighted to see people arrive regularly from Chicago and Indianapolis for performances. The facility was, she wrote, a "spiritual oasis"[26] that refreshed both body and soul with beauty.

A reporter and a photographer from *Life* magazine, which at the time had the largest circulation of any periodical in the United States, came to interview Madeleva for what she thought would be an article on the new fine arts center. She was nonplussed when the long-anticipated article appeared in the issue of June 10, 1957, focused entirely on her. Disappointed, she wrote several times to ask the reporter to return to cover what really mattered: the fine arts center itself.

During her last few years in office, Madeleva spread a cultural banquet at the college. Twice, for periods of several months each time, Robert Speaight came as an artist in residence, to lecture on drama and to stage student productions of *A Midsummer Night's Dream* and *Twelfth Night*. Through Speaight, Madeleva met British novelist Antonia White, who had recently returned to the church. The author of *Frost in May* and other autobiographical novels spent part of the fall and winter of 1959 and 1960 teaching creative writing at the college.[27]

Also through Speaight, Madeleva met E. Martin Browne, a friend from Speaight's Oxford days, and Henzie Raeburn, Browne's wife. Speaight and the Brownes had worked together on T. S. Eliot's *Murder in the Cathedral*, which the Brownes had staged and Martin Browne had directed. According to Speaight, the title was Henzie's idea. "She had an instinct for what would fetch the town," he wrote, "even if the town did not always know what it was in for—and there had generally been somebody in the audience who had come to the theatre wondering 'who had done it.'"[28]

Madeleva brought the Brownes, who specialized in religious drama, to Saint Mary's as guest artists. They offered workshops on medieval drama and directed students in a production of "The Mystery

of Mary," part of the Lincoln cycle of mystery plays, which was performed in March 1960. Madeleva hailed the couple as "the best contemporary exponents of medieval religious drama," which she regarded
as an embodiment of "the story of hope of our immortality."[29] Early in
her presidency, Madeleva had begun the practice of staging a medieval play annually, usually as the centerpiece of the Christmas program. The Browne's production she called "the finest thing we have
ever done here."[30] In her eyes, such drama embodied her ideal of art
raised to a level of praise.

In the summer of 1959, almost twenty-five years to the day after
she left Oxford, Madeleva returned to Europe. "The reason for which I
am going is not the reason for which I am going," she commented
cryptically in an interview.[31] Ostensibly scheduled for the purpose of
public relations and as a way to contact possible lecturers and professors for the college, the trip allowed Madeleva, at age seventy-two, to
revisit many of the places she had known twenty-five years before:
Oxford, London, Paris, Rome, Assisi, and parts of Austria and Germany.

Soon after her arrival in England, Speaight hosted an elegant
dinner party to which he invited her many English friends, most of
whom at some time or another she had welcomed to Saint Mary's.
There were so many that he had to move the event from his home in
Kent, where he originally planned to hold it, to London. She also
celebrated a reunion with Madge Vaison Mouton and her family, after
which she wrote Madge: "The joy of return has a charm that easily
matches the joy of discovery."[32]

Madeleva made plans to visit C. S. Lewis, although no record of
their meeting remains. "Please . . . do not let me intrude on leisure or
privacy that you may need much more than a call from a modern
Madam Eglantine," she wrote him.[33] "But of course you must call!" he
responded, inviting her to meet him in Oxford, where he still spent
vacations, even though he then taught at Cambridge.[34] Every few years
after leaving Oxford, Madeleva had reissued her open invitation to
Lewis to visit Saint Mary's and Notre Dame. "Please try to fit your
world into ours for at least some part of an academic year," she wrote
in 1954. In 1957, she again prodded him to come, even if only for a
"fortnight." He invariably refused, at first pleading hopeless stodginess
and then the illness of his wife.[35]

Her own poor health impeded Madeleva's trip, occasionally forc-
ing her to cancel plans and, a few times, to spend an entire day in bed,
unable to rise for mass or for meals. In a tiny travel diary, she dutifully
noted the places she and her companion stopped and the names of
some of the people she saw, but in contrast to the detailed, often

rhapsodic account of her 1933 and 1934 travels, her brief entries provide little more than an itinerary of her journey. Every now and then
she offered a vivid glimpse of her travels, as when she wrote that
while attending the opera in Vienna, a man seated behind her and her
companion indignantly requested that the two nuns remove their
"caps"—but she neglected to mention how they handled the situation.
She noted few other details, and in a general letter to the sisters at
Saint Mary's, promised to depict verbally "the delectable gargoyles"
on the "glorious structure of the summer of 1959" when she returned
home.[36]

At the festivities celebrating the golden jubilee of her entry into
religious life, Madeleva was radiant. But her weariness showed at
other times. Her bishop, the Most Reverend Leo Pursley, told her to
slow down, that she had looked "bushed" the last two times he saw
her.[37] After a visit to campus, her brother Vern was so concerned about
her condition that he wrote Fred: "I have no idea what their [the
congregation's] form of organization is or what provision they have
for replacing her but they had better do something along that line and
soon. Sis won't do it herself, and being a Wolff (and an Arntz) she
can't stop of her own volition."[38] Writing to Fred, Madeleva herself
admitted as much: "Temperamentally, I have the excessive drive to do
more and more, better and better. In such conditions, I exceed my
capacity."[39]

Looking back over her years in office, Madeleva wrote a friend,
"The past twenty-seven years has been a long time, hasn't it, but it
seems hardly a day as I look back at it."[40] By 1960 through 1961, her
last year as president of the college, she had quadrupled enrollment,
expanded facilities to include not only a new library but also a modern science hall and a center for the arts, and founded a graduate
school of theology for lay people. She had the satisfaction of seeing
Saint Mary's touted by *Time* as one of the best Catholic colleges in
America[41] and recognized by the *Chicago Tribune* as among the five top
colleges in the Midwest.[42] As the president of Saint Mary's, she had
published ten books of poetry, including three collected editions of
verse, three books of collected essays and speeches, an autobiography,
and scores of articles.

Although the circumstances of Madeleva's decision to retire never
became public, it seems clear that her local superior and the superior
general of the congregation finally intervened. Ironically, one of the
severest tests of her detachment came when she was forced to relinquish the office she had resisted twenty-seven years earlier. Once again
she submitted to the decision of her superiors, even though according

FIGURE 16.1

Madeleva on the Avenue into Saint Mary's, c. 1960

Courtesy Saint Mary's College Archives.

to some who were close to her she was hurt by the way in which she was ushered out of office—a plot to oust her had been launched behind her back during her summer in Europe—and troubled by the lack of a strong leader to replace her.[43]

Sister Maria Renata Daily, whom Madeleva had escorted to Yale over twenty-five years before, was named her successor. Madeleva relaxed her grasp. "Below the surface distractions there is a basic conviction that 'underneath are the Everlasting Arms,'" she wrote a friend. "The experimental knowledge of this will continue and be a place of rest in the years to come. This is one of the great realizations into which one enters as a fuller experience as one grows older."[44]

17

SISTER DEATH

"Welcome to the heaven of the retired, which one enters without going to the trouble of dying," Ben Lehman wrote Madeleva soon after she left office. "Do I see it? Poems, medieval studies, wise consultation without the responsibility of execution. Welcome, indeed."[1]

In retirement, Madeleva remained in the college, moving a few doors down the hall from the president's suite into another that included a bedroom, bath, and office. She described her new setting to a friend: "It consists of a charming outer office with a French door opening on to a little balcony, book shelves and book cases, a desk and chairs. An adjoining, smaller room is my little workshop [a room she sometimes called her 'anchorage,' or hermitage]. . . . There are two narrow perpendicular windows opening out to lovely vistas on our campus. A little alcove for books and various other built-in features comprise the room. Best of all, there are two beautiful solid oak chairs hand-carved and two hundred years old. I am sitting in one as I write."[2]

The shelves in Madeleva's room were filled with books, vases, statues, icons, and photographs, most of which were gifts, some rare and all beautiful, from friends and former students. "When I go to the infirmary," she told Sister Miriam, gesturing toward her things, "none of this goes along." She pulled open a small drawer in her cupboard and lifted out two seemingly insignificant treasures: a wooden statue from the Holy Land and a small ceramic figure of the Virgin and Child from Provence. "Only these go with me," she said.[3]

Not yet ready for that last stage of existence, Madeleva remained involved in the life of the college. Her official duties consisted of serving as a consultant to the new president, engaging in public relations and development work, and giving weekly talks to the young sisters in the community. A self-appointed duty was to arrange flowers she had cultivated in the college offices. "Please think of me in a rich and active retirement, doing a medley of jobs, all diverting, all different," she wrote a cousin. "This gives me an excellent opportunity to draw on my reserve of the past half century."[4]

Madeleva maintained a no less regular schedule than she had followed as president. After mass and morning prayers, she relaxed with a crossword puzzle—to keep her mind sharp, she said. She spent most of her work day writing and answering letters, or meeting with visitors to the college, with time set aside for gardening and a daily walk around the campus. "Sister Anastasia and I have just returned from a long walk among the wild flowers on the river bank," she wrote a friend. "The morning was perfect and the flowers carpet the ground for acres. Among the most exciting of our experiences was our interview with a rose-breasted grosbeak. He posed for us, sang for us and was a real star performer."[5]

Madeleva stayed out of the day-to-day administration of the college. In the eyes of her colleagues, one of her chief attributes had always been her willingness to delegate authority and allow others to do their jobs without interference. In retirement, she practiced the same detachment. Faculty and students complained as the quality and frequency of cultural activities declined. "Things are so arid around here," she acknowledged privately.[6] Publicly, she emphasized the smoothness of the transition and praised her successor's intelligence and competence, stressing her personal satisfaction with the new state of affairs.

Freed of the daily tasks of the presidency, Madeleva nevertheless remained "on wheels" as she put it, traveling often to give lectures on poetry or literature and to participate in various educational conferences. In her retirement, she took part in a study of Catholic education in the United States funded by the Carnegie Foundation and served on numerous advisory boards, one of which involved planning and conducting workshops in the humanities held each summer in Asheville, North Carolina.

In her dealings with the bishop in charge of the Asheville workshops, Madeleva proved that she still had the power to disconcert conventionalists when her avant-garde choice of books for the Asheville conference—namely, *Lord of the Flies*, *Animal Farm*, and *Rhinoceros*—elicited a caution from the sponsoring bishop, who feared they might be "a source of temptations" to the young nuns who would participate. Even though he conceded that sisters must maintain "relations with reality," he hesitated to encourage their "undue curiosity." Characteristically, Madeleva tactfully—and successfully—defended her choices, assuring the bishop that she had often used the books with sisters in her congregation, and with only positive results.[7] As Robert Speaight said of her, she fought her battles with an olive branch.[8]

During her presidency, Madeleva had introduced fund raising to the college, doing her best to placate those within the congregation as well as those among the alumnae who considered such activities beneath the dignity of women and especially nuns. At the request of Maria Renata, the new president, she continued her development work, not only because she believed in the cause of Christian and of women's education but also because she found the work stimulating and enjoyable. She wrote Clare Boothe Luce: "I spend my time practicing the 'relaxed grasp' with one hand and 'my hand in your pocket' with the other hand. Could any persons but Americans reconcile these activities?"[9]

As part of her public relations work, Madeleva maintained contact with hotel magnate Conrad Hilton, whose sister had been her classmate at Saint Mary's, and with Mrs. Fred Carroll, whom she called "Aunt Alice," a lonely, rich widow who had become interested in Saint Mary's through Madeleva's writing. Madeleva courted them and a few other important prospects with a mixture of high sentiment and conviviality, writing entertaining and uplifting letters to each.

Madeleva's efforts met with mixed success. In the opinion of Sister Miriam, who as Madeleva's vice president for development worked and traveled with her extensively during her last years in office, Madeleva was temperamentally better suited for public relations than for fundraising itself.[10] Although Hilton sent her many smaller gifts of stock, he refused to finance the "Hilton Hall" that she proposed to him (by letter rather than in person) at the urging of the development staff. However, Aunt Alice (with whom Madeleva exchanged letters almost weekly for more than five years) eventually endowed the college with funds for a liberal arts classroom building, constructed and named for Madeleva after her death.

In retirement, Madeleva's energy seemed boundless. In the fall of 1961, she traveled to the White House as part of a delegation representing the National Conference of Christians and Jews and met President John F. Kennedy, who had sent her a personal note at the time of her retirement. (She had a number of connections with the Kennedy family, beginning with her association as a young sister with Katherine Conway, a friend of Rose Kennedy's father.[11]) The following spring, as part of a public relations tour for the college, she spent a week with Clare and Harry Luce at their retreat near Phoenix, rediscovering the "crystal, sun-smitten" beauty of the desert, so different from the lush landscape of Indiana to which she had again grown accustomed. She traveled regularly to Boston for medical care, usually stopping in New York City to see Evarista Cotter, whose husband, Bill, had died in 1957. She also made several trips to Minnesota to visit her brothers and their ailing wives. Such personal visits were always part of an itinerary devoted to college business.

So ingrained was Madeleva's habit of hard work that she could no longer conceive of a satisfying existence without it.[12] In an almost complete turnaround from her former attitude that writing demanded solitude and contemplation, she said in an interview, "Writing comes from activity. If I hadn't the impact of new contacts and many places, I might atrophy. I would find there was nothing I cared to write about."[13] Most likely, Madeleva herself, always outgoing and energized by contact with others, had not changed; her self-knowledge, and self-acceptance, had deepened.

Scarcely a month went by without some sort of trip, often by plane in these later years. In demand as a speaker, Madeleva usually received transportation in return for her lectures, which she happily delivered to all who asked, not liking to refuse anyone. Having always returned the money she received as salary, honoraria, and royalties to the congregation—as did all members of the community—she had no money of her own, although the congregation met her needs with as much generosity as communal funds allowed.

Early in her retirement, Madeleva used her unaccustomed leisure to revisit the scenes of her youth, returning with cousins to the Arntz farm on the Wisconsin dells to climb the bluff where she had played as a child. She visited her maternal grandparents' graves as well as those of aunts and uncles buried nearby. Several times, she returned to Cumberland and to her parents' graves there. She also returned to the site of the Wasatch, which had finally closed its doors in 1959, a brief thirty-three years after she had founded it.

Madeleva's return to her roots had begun several years earlier, in the late 1950s, when her publisher, the Macmillan Company, proposed that she either authorize a biography of her life or write an autobiography. She reluctantly chose the latter, preferring to tell her own story, so she wrote *My First Seventy Years* during a two-week stay in a sanatorium; the legal-sized yellow pads on which she wrote it show scarcely a correction. "It is such a fragmentary little document," she confessed later. "Very much is omitted that I should like, if the time ever permits, to make of it a sequel to this first small volume."[14]

Written in a light, conversational style, full of humor and entertaining anecdotes, the autobiography described the events of Madeleva's early life and surveyed the public aspects of her life as a nun. It was an extrovert's autobiography, celebrating people she had known and places she had been, and said nothing of her religious feelings and experiences. Anticipating disappointment, she warned her reader: "The chronicle of my threescore years and ten is not a story of a nun on her 'prie-dieu. . . .It is quite free from devout aspirations."[15]

The autobiography was chosen as a main selection of a Catholic book club and sold well; Macmillan issued it in paperback—surely some sort of "ultimate," Madeleva joked, although she was pleased by the book's success.[16] *Reader's Digest* contacted her for further reminiscences, and although she agreed to consider the request, she delayed until nothing came of it. Nor did she write the sequel she proposed.

One of the chief effects of the book's publication was the steady flow of mail it brought, most of it from relatives, friends, and acquaintances, some of whom Madeleva had not heard from in years. Letters arrived from far-distant cousins, former classmates and students, and even the son of someone her mother had taught before her marriage. Several correspondents described their amazement when they discovered that the Eva Wolff they once knew had become Sister Madeleva the author. One of these was a ninety-year-old woman who had once been Madeleva's baby-sitter. Madeleva responded warmly to each letter, sharing further memories of times past.

C.S. Lewis wrote his praises of the autobiography: "What I really love is the early chapters. These set an old string vibrating—all the stories which a specially loved aunt used to tell me of her Canadian childhood. That lake, that Indian village. You give me a delicious nostalgia for places I have never seen. And all that smell of leather and wood. You do it, if I may say so, extremely well. And what a lucky girl you were."[17]

The imaginative journey into her past confirmed the old woman's contentment with her life. She proclaimed, "I can remember nothing that I have been engaged in that has been superficial. All my experiences have been vital."[18]

Among the assignments that meant most to Madeleva were her sessions with the postulants and novices of the congregation. She met weekly with more than three hundred young women to read and discuss poetry. As they listened, she intoned her own verse and that of others in a high-pitched chant that betrayed a noticeable quaver and the halting delivery of old age. She often paused to search for a word or phrase. For the newly professed nuns, she conducted poetry-writing workshops, critiquing their efforts and encouraging those with promise.

These sessions introduced the younger sisters to one of the most distinguished members of the congregation and allowed them to benefit from her talents. Through contact with the young nuns, Madeleva said that she hoped to "build into our community structure some of the opportunities and advantages that have come to me during the past fifty years."[19] Just as important, in Madeleva's mind, was the introduction of the young sisters to the beauty of the spoken and written word, which she hoped would transform their religious life as it had her own.

Because of the almost total segregation of the college sisters from others in the convent, Madeleva had grown distant from the larger group during her tenure as president, a situation that she trusted renewed contact with the community to improve. Ironically, while visitors both to Saint Mary's and to Notre Dame sought Madeleva out, many of the Holy Cross sisters who lived in close proximity tended to take her for granted, or in some cases, motivated by consideration, had preferred not to impose themselves on her busy schedule.

Madeleva's retirement served to remind others of her contributions to the congregation as well as of her professional achievements. "I want you to know that at the generalate, college, and convent I heard unqualified praise of Sister Madeleva. My heart rejoiced," one of the sisters wrote her after she retired. "There were times when I felt that you would have to die (and even rise again!) to be fully appreciated for your outstanding contribution to Holy Cross. We all tend to take for granted the greatness of our dedicated Sisters in religion. The fact that you, who have been an administrator for so long, have retired to the sidelines and have remained aloof from all administrative matters, speaks eloquently of the relaxed grasp."[20]

Madeleva wrote her brother Fred that she looked forward to doing "more writing of the kind that I can do best" during her retirement.[21] At the request of the Columbia Broadcasting System she wrote a script for a television play, "Praised Be My Lord," a story about Saint Francis of Assisi and the first Christmas crib, which was broadcast nationally on Christmas Eve 1963. She also faithfully composed the by then mandatory Christmas poems. One of the last of these, "Perennial," takes as its theme the impossibility of ever exhausting the topic of Christ's incarnation:

The final wild song of Your birth-night can never be written;
The last shining word of Your coming cannot be said.
Rough, slow-minded shepherds will run, angel-driven, forever
By night to a cave and a cattle shed.

Each year, Madeleva returned to the topic with fresh vision and vigor, celebrating some new aspect of the divine child, who for her symbolized the source of all life. "We grow young as we approach the source of life," she wrote in 1962.[22] In the mystery of the timelessness of those born into eternal life, she identified herself with the child born again in the darkness of winter and anticipated her own resurrection as she wrote.

But in darker moods, which descended periodically, Madeleva thought of all in life that she had left undone. Mocking her Martha-like devotion to duty, which she continued to fear had robbed her of the "the better part" reserved for Mary—a life spent contemplating God—she composed "Commitments," published posthumously in *A Child Asks for a Star* and probably the last poem she wrote:

> Did you notice that couple
> That we passed by?
> We might have helped them,
> You and I.
> The man, with his wife
> On their little dun ass,
> Turned aside on the road
> To let us pass.
>
> She was weaving small limbs
> For her unborn Child.
> She noticed our hurry
> But only smiled.
>
> Perhaps she guessed
> That we could not wait
> On this, our dynamic
> Apostolate.
>
> Also, persons who serve
> The world's great lacks
> Can hardly travel
> On donkeys' backs.

In her times of self-doubt, the thought of the wise men, finding at last the object of their quest, offered Madeleva comfort. As she put it in "Parables," another of her Christmas poems written late in life:

> Because we are wise as the wise men are,
> We find in every star a wild, prophetic star.
> Tonight we seek, way-worn, life-laden, one star's light
> Out of our night.

Madeleva meditated on Dante's *Paradiso* and returned to her favorite sources of inspiration: the Bible, the dictionary, and seed catalogues. She also discovered Teilhard de Chardin's *The Divine Milieu*, which she described as "one of the most completely luminous books that I have ever read. It is a volume to live in sentence by sentence for weeks and weeks. To me it is, in parts at least, another self."[23] In another letter, she elaborated: "This book speaks a language that I thought was peculiarly my own until I met it page after page in this small volume."[24]

Because of her continuing interest in the School of Sacred Theology, Madeleva kept abreast of theological and liturgical trends. In the early 1960s, she read and recommended to others the works of such progressive theologians as Hans Kung.[25] Calling his work "straightforward and courageous," she singled out *The Council Reform and Reunion* for special praise.[26] Welcoming liturgical changes, in particular, she called the mass celebrated with the priest facing the congregation "the most beautiful experience."[27]

Although she died before many of the changes initiated by the Second Vatican Council took effect, Madeleva enthusiastically approved of the transformation she saw coming in the church. Politically conservative (she favored Nixon over Kennedy in the 1960 election and Barry Goldwater over Lyndon Johnson in the presidential campaign of 1964[28]), she was progressive when it came to church reform. She expressed sympathy with and support for the approach of John XXIII, with whom she had three audiences (one of which was private) on her trip to Europe in 1959. After meeting him, she described him as "eminently a Father,"[29] spoke approvingly of his holiness and wisdom, and praised his vision for the church. In her private correspondence, she consistently criticized the retrograde attitudes of certain members of the clergy who fought to maintain the status quo. In 1964, she wrote: "Many of our bishops and priests are a bit intransigent and even resentful of change and the possibility of change. You know how the law of inertia can spread."[30]

Madeleva had spent her life as a religious and a professional woman combating "the law of inertia." The changes wrought in the Roman church and in American society in the early 1960s were coming about in part because she and others like her had used their measure of power to prepare the way. Working within traditional systems, she had pruned and grafted on established roots to promote new growth.

If Madeleva's life is any indication, liturgical reform and theological discussion did not begin with Vatican II; rather, the council recognized and built on decades of experimentation and innovation in local communities and churches, some of which had already produced—as in the case of the School of Sacred Theology—radical revisions of established practice. Not only in the way in which she and others like her modified traditional structures and systems but also in the way she interpreted and talked about them, Madeleva initiated change. During much of her life as a religious, she had pushed past the nonessential limits of community life conceptually as well as actually, struggling to achieve a balance between personal fulfillment and service to a larger ideal. Her poetry had bridged both needs, expressing her creative gifts and contributing to the Catholic revival of the first half of the twentieth century.

As an educator, Madeleva had managed to modernize and to reinterpret traditional institutions and values to a changing society. Through innovative programs of study (for example, the Trivium and Christian Culture as well as the School of Sacred Theology), farsighted decisions (such as early racial integration of the college), and a rich extracurricular mix of religious, intellectual, and aesthetic offerings, she discovered ways to incorporate Christian ideals and Catholic culture in the curriculum and the daily life of the college—ways that an increasingly secular society could understand and respect. She developed a rhetoric for talking about the education of women that drew upon her Christian heritage and at the same time anticipated key insights of the revitalized women's movement of the last quarter of the twentieth century.

Madeleva's life manifested all the benefits of an existence spent in a communal setting that unites its members with shared purpose and clearly defined goals and invests their actions with meaning. In developing and using her talents, she had at her disposal the support and resources of a wide-ranging network of individuals and institutions. As the church and her particular community of religious women made use of her talents to further its work and its witness, she enjoyed the personal benefits that come from a full and active life. Her rise to leadership shows the extent to which her community not only accepted but also encouraged creative, independent-minded women. Her limits—as a person, as a poet, as a leader—were as much a result of her own personal demons and imperfections as the circumstances in which she found herself.

Madeleva's life approached its close at the end of an era, marked in the Roman church by Vatican II and in American society by a series of "movements" (among them the civil rights movement, the anti-war movement, and the women's liberation movement), the consequences of which have been far-reaching and are still being played out. To a large extent, the choices she made and the institutions to which she devoted her energies have lost credibility not only in the eyes of a wider world but also among those within the institutions themselves. As a nun, and as an advocate for Catholic, private liberal arts education for women, she became something of an anomaly. Even in her lifetime, religious congregations and church-related schools began to decline in numbers, and many colleges for women closed or became coeducational. Poetry, too, had moved in a different direction from her pious, conventionally structured verse. Without the religious orders and the educational system they supported to sustain it, the vision of Catholic culture Madeleva had done so much to define and transmit would crumble. Her memory would fade with it, even though many of those who benefitted from her contributions to the status and education of women would carry on the work of reform.

Aware of the profound shifts underway, Madeleva declined to look too far into the future. She defined herself as a woman of the nineteenth and the twentieth centuries, not the twenty-first.[31] "How simple those old days were, though at the time they seemed complicated enough," she wrote ironically to Madge Vaison Mouton.[32] She saw how different the experiences and attitudes of her own generation were from those of the young women then entering college. "It is a little difficult for us to fit our worlds into theirs with any great effectiveness," she wrote Mother Rose Elizabeth in 1962.[33] To another friend, she wrote nostalgically: "Our loves are still in the old and beautiful world where our roots remain."[34]

Describing herself, Madeleva looked to the age that had shaped her ideals, as when, in a letter to a former classmate, she referred to herself as a "Victorian lady."[35] In a profile of Mother Angela, one of the early leaders of the congregation, Madeleva praised her as "eminently a lady," with "close contacts with the great men and women of her generation, [and] influences upon them," a person characterized by "manifold one-world-mindedness."[36] She might have been sketching her own self-portrait.

Still, the thought of the future excited Madeleva as memories of the past did not. She anticipated a coming age of "new frontiers and new explorations"[37] and exclaimed to a much younger friend, "What a world to be born in now! Its possibilities must thrill you deeply."[38] Cherishing tradition, Madeleva had sought through most of her life to preserve its essence through change and adaptation. She understood the paradoxical nature of her endeavor and its severity. The one who preserves through transformation must be willing to sacrifice not only the extraneous but also that which is loved, and must willingly accept the unfamiliar, often disconcerting shape of the new. One must also be prepared for one's own obsolescence.

In *A Lost Language*, a collection of essays on medieval literature, Madeleva depicted Chaucer and his contemporaries as speaking a language of prayer and of poetry, a "pleasant tongue," she wrote, which "has become almost a lost language." This language, she admitted, was full of conventions, and "conventions are a badly libeled lot. One knows they are devices; one concludes that they are deceits with an immediacy to be recommended rather for speed than for logic."

In defense of convention, Madeleva argued: "The fourteenth century writer probably used convention to say what he meant rather than to say the exact opposite of what he meant. That the form he used is, to us, artificial results not so much from his insincerity as from our own mode of expression. That, to him, would indicate something like savagery."[39] Setting herself up as a translator (similar to Chaucer, who had translated older writers for his contemporaries), Madeleva sought to interpret medieval writers to her own age. In her words, "They bring us to, and bring to us the great stabilities of existence, a world where a God of love and immortal man were realities and powers beside which atomic fission would have been a breath in the wind. They come to us from a world in which men's wills were free scientifically and experimentally, from a world in which men were not dissected; they were immortalized."[40]

In many ways, Madeleva herself speaks a lost language, not only of prayer and poetry but also of meaning and moral purpose. She inhabited a world distinguished by order, heightened by ritual, and lit by virtue, and lived a life devoted to the satisfaction of spiritual hungers and the gratification of immortal longings. Her voice recalls to us and calls us to that radical place.

On September 16, 1962, word came of Evarista Cotter's sudden death. She had spent most of the summer working as a volunteer at Lourdes, assisting the sick at the shrine and in the baths there. She and Madeleva had planned a reunion in New York City on September 19, where they had tickets to attend a matinee of *A Man for All Seasons*. Instead, Madeleva left for her best friend's funeral.

Other losses followed. A few weeks after Evarista's death, Helen Holland Voll, another close school friend, passed away, and on November 22, 1963, the day of President Kennedy's assassination, Madeleva's former teacher and long time friend C. S. Lewis died. Then, during that winter, both of her sisters-in-law passed away within a few months of each other. "It seems there aren't enough good people in the world ever to replace such splendid ones who leave it," she wrote.[41]

"There are, after all, ways of being very close without being in the physical presence of one another. If we did not know that we could hardly live through many of the separations that life asks of us."[42] With these words of consolation to a bereaved friend, Madeleva asserted her belief in the reality of spiritual life and the power of prayer. She called it "the one supernatural and omnipotent guided missile available to us."[43] But along with her faith in the ability of the spirit to transcend space and time, she continued to stress the importance of physical presence in human love and sought out those she loved.

After one of their last visits, Ben Lehman reflected on his friendship with his former pupil, which had lasted more than forty years. He called to mind: "The Berkeley times, the walk in the snow at the Wasatch and the long talks in room and corridor, Solesme and the office round the clock (though we were there at different times), Saint Mary's—in your curiosity shop [her name for her office], at table, and walking in the bend of the Saint Joseph's River. Then Lucy, of whom you told me before I read, and the Harness Maker—wonderful really. . . . For me, again personally, the enclosing idea is the relaxed grasp, of which at one time or another we have said so much. The conception has had a greater influence on my life than you would believe."[44]

When Lehman's former wife, Judith Anderson, performed at Saint Mary's in the fall of 1962, enacting the scenes from both *Medea* and *Macbeth* that had made her famous, she and Madeleva spent an evening together that stirred up potent memories in both of them. The actress was "beautifully gracious and cordial and reminiscent," Madeleva wrote Lehman afterwards. "How strangely our lives return upon themselves, tempered and luminous with the light of years and the goodness of us strange children of God. Just now I wish I could talk to you about so much of all this."[45]

Madeleva punned about her determination to grow old "gratefully."[46] She had much for which to be grateful: an active retirement, and in spite of its ups and downs, comparatively good health for her age. Early in 1964, she felt particularly well. At seventy-six, she looked years—even decades—younger. Her friend Robert Speaight wrote: "The passing years left no traces on her features," and quoted a friend who had once visited her in the hospital as saying her arms were still those of a young woman.[47] Another friend commented that Madeleva always reminded her of a girl—that even in old age she had "a young quality" about her.[48] Her eyesight remained sharp enough for her to read even the smallest print without eyeglasses.[49] Smooth-skinned, her glance as quick and as penetrating as ever, she showed her age only in the fine lines around her eyes and mouth and through her slower speech and movement. Some also detected about her an air of tiredness, an increased paleness, a more obvious fragility.

In January and again in March 1964, Madeleva traveled to the East Coast to visit her doctor in Boston, who gave her an encouraging report both times. While there, she delivered lectures to groups in New York and Connecticut and stopped to see Sister Mary of God at her convent. But by Easter, fatigue had set in and she spent two weeks in bed. She was well enough to welcome both her brothers to Saint Mary's in early May, when they spent a joyful weekend together. "It was good for the three of us to be together again," she wrote Fred afterwards. "We all share the signs of cumulative birthdays and must be prepared for the inroads they make upon physical health. But no matter what the coming years may bring, we have had a very blessed experience in at least three score and ten years in the past."[50]

As usual, Fred sent his sister two pots of flowers for what she referred to as her "oldest birthday" on May 24, 1964, when she turned seventy-seven. She placed them as she always did on the main altar of the college chapel. Writing to thank him, she mentioned that she planned to return to Boston in July for a thorough checkup and warned him that she would probably be hospitalized for observation.[51]

Before she left Saint Mary's for Boston, Madeleva put all her papers in order. Such meticulousness, unusual even for her, convinced her secretary of many years that Madeleva had a premonition that this trip would be her last.[52] Soon after her arrival, she had an attack of severe pain, and her doctors sent her immediately to the New England Baptist Hospital for tests.

When it seemed that Madeleva's stay would be longer than expected, Maria Pieta hurried to Boston to be with her. Several peaceful days passed. On July 22, Madeleva commemorated her feast day, the day on which the church celebrated the entry of her patroness, Mary Magdalen, into eternal life. Maria Pieta recalled: "It proved to be a gala day for Sister Madeleva. I spent two hours opening mail and reading messages to her. Saint Mary's had sent on little banners with appropriate decorations and messages. Sister received a very nice blue robe, which she immediately put on for the feast. She had many bouquets of flowers, many telegrams and many callers. Doctors and nurses dropped in to greet her for her feast day. She was in a most happy frame of mind."[53]

Surgery to remove Madeleva's gall bladder, diagnosed as the source of her problem, was scheduled for the following day, July 23— another special day in her calendar, the anniversary of Sister Rita's death (her "return to God," as Madeleva put it) fifty-four years before.

Mother Kathryn Marie, the superior general, and Mother Verda Clare, the provincial superior—the same Verda Clare who in her youth had been Madeleva's traveling companion through Europe—flew to Boston. They found Madeleva to be in good spirits, more concerned about finding a copy of Lewis Carroll's *Jabberwocky* for the children of one of her doctors than about the surgery itself.[54]

The procedure went smoothly, without complications, and the surgeon assured the sisters that he expected Madeleva to recover quickly and completely. The next afternoon, July 24, her general condition supported his prognosis. Her color was good, her mind keen, and she was resting comfortably. Reassured by her progress, her superiors left for Indiana later that day, leaving Maria Pieta to look after her.

In her poetry, her prayers, and her personal letters, Madeleva had long meditated on Sister Death. "She should not be so entirely a stranger and a fearful one to us who know that this is to be the one experience we all must have," Madeleva wrote late in life.[55] With her usual cool objectivity, she concluded: "The mystery of death is one for which the ultimate answer is our own experience."[56]

In one of her last letters to Lehman, Madeleva wrote, "You must not have missed in all of these years my great enthusiasm for death, my anticipation of it. With all our intellectual and spiritual quests we must look for answers. These I expect and so do you."[57] That point on which she had so long fixed her gaze, as on a lodestar, was no longer distant. Death, which she described as a "gentle gravitation to a great light," had drawn her on through life, to its conclusion.[58]

Everyone expressed surprise at how quickly death took Madeleva. Dr. Norcross, her physician, attributed her death early in the morning of July 25 to a "very rare complication of this type of surgery . . . a rare fulminating and overwhelming infection of the blood stream which occurred in spite of the large doses of antibiotic that she was receiving."[59]

News of her death confounded Kathryn Marie and Verda Clare, who assumed they had left her well on her way to recovery. A stunned Maria Pieta gathered up the new blue robe and the rest of Madeleva's belongings, made sure that a copy of *Jabberwocky*, which had finally been found, was delivered to the doctor's children, and accompanied her body home.

The poem that stands as a preface to *Knight's Errant*, Madeleva's first collection of verse, serves well as an epitaph for a woman who dedicated her life as well as her art to God. In the poem she titled: "To My Favorite Author," she becomes at last the word and the text, the story and the song, subsumed forever in the mind of God:

Dear God
Herewith a book do I inscribe and send
To Thee Who art both its Beginning and its End;
A volume odd,
Bound in some brief, allotted years,
And writ in blood and tears;
Fragments of which Thou art the perfect whole
Book of my Soul

Break Thou the sealing clod
And read me, God!

Notes

Preface

1. Madeleva, interview, *St. Louis Review,* Dec. 1961.

2. Marjorie Hall Walsh, "Sister Madeleva: Lyric Poet," master's thesis, Creighton University, 1962, 55.

3. From "Autumn," collected in *Knights Errant* (Appleton, 1923).

4. *Holy Cross Courier: Alumnae Quarterly of Saint Mary's College* (Summer 1964): 6.

5. John W. Norcross, M.D., letter to Sr. Verda Clare Doran, CSC, 10 Aug. 1964, Sisters of the Holy Cross Congregational Archives and Records (hereafter, General Archives).

6. *New York Times,* Mon., 27 Jul. 1964.

7. Collected in *A Question of Lovers* (St. Anthony Guild Press, 1936).

1. The Harness-Maker's Daughter

1. Werner Peter Wolff, ms.: "The Wolff Family" (1945), Saint Mary's College Archives (hereafter, College Archives), 7.

2. W. P. Wolff, 11.

3. Arntz Family History Committee, "A Chronological History of the Familie Arntz: Kellen to Kilbourn, the Story of the Migration of the Arntz Family from Westphalia to Wisconsin Dells and the West, 1600-1989," (privately printed, 1989 [hereafter, Arntz Family]), 151.

4. Arntz Family, 18.

5. W. P. Wolff, 13.

6. Arntz Family, 11.

7. W. P. Wolff, 12.

8. Sr. M. Madeleva Wolff, CSC, *My First Seventy Years* (New York: Macmillan, 1959 [hereafter, *MFSY*]), 2.

9. W. P. Wolff, 13.

10. Lucy Arntz Wolff, letter to Madeleva, 28 Jul. 1942, College Archives. Lucy's reminiscence was occasioned by what she regarded as a grandchild's lack of appreciation for the education she was receiving. She began the quoted passage with the exclamation, "What I would have given for her opportunity at her age!"

11. W. P. Wolff, 13.

12. This information, and much of the information that follows in this paragraph, differs significantly from the account of her father's family given by Madeleva in *MFSY* and from that recorded by W. P. Wolff. It was supplied by Carol Cooper Wolff (Mrs. James E. Wolff), a member of the Arntz Family History Committee, from notes she took during a personal interview with Cora Zickert, a granddaughter of Louisa and Christian Engelke, in Jul. 1981.

13. W. P. Wolff, 5.

14. Ibid.

15. Information on Cumberland and Barron County was obtained from an account of the history of Barron County on file at the Barron County Courthouse, Barron, Wisconsin. Some facts differ from accounts given by W. P. Wolff and by Madeleva in *MFSY*.

16. W. P. Wolff, 16.

17. See W. P. Wolff, 16, and Arntz Family, 47.

18. W. P. Wolff, 16. The choice of name seems strange if August Wolff knew his true history. However, that he would not have known it seems unlikely. According to Cora Zickert, his niece, Louisa Wolff Engelke Gamm (she married again after the death of Christian Engelke), was known as a "Schwartzfrau"—a "black woman" or "fallen woman"—in the Richwood community because of her past. August probably knew the truth but preferred to keep it secret, as did his wife and children, if they knew.

According to W. P. Wolff's account of his paternal grandfather, Julius Frederick Wolff (who he says happened to marry a woman with the same last name) fathered the first three of Louisa's children, dying soon after the birth of the twins. In *MFSY* Madeleva only obliquely refers to her paternal grandfather when she calls her grandmother a "young Pomeranian widow with ... three children" (1). But in every respect, Madeleva simplified and idealized her paternal grandmother's story, for example by leaving out any reference to Christian Engelke and his children, of whom she was certainly aware.

19. These and other early memories are recorded in the opening chapters of *MFSY* unless other sources are noted.

20. *MFSY*, 3.

21. W. P. Wolff, 17, and *MFSY*, 3.

22. W. P. Wolff, 2.

23. Ibid., 18.

24. Mrs. Frances R. Candio, letter to Madeleva, 25 Sept. 1961, College Archives.

25. *MFSY*, 14.

26. Madeleva in an unpubl. autobiographical statement (2). She also mentions this desire in a letter to Berenice and Thora Knutson, 7 Jan. 1964. Both are in the College Archives.

27. *MFSY*, 12–13.

28. Madeleva, letter to Sr. Kathryn Marie Gibbons, CSC, 26. Nov. 1962, College Archives.

29. Lucy Wolff, letter to Madeleva (no day), Oct. 1942, College Archives.

30. *MFSY* 3.

31. Ibid., 13.

32. Ibid., 16.

2. I Go to School

1. Madeleva, letter to Mrs. Richard Klee, 6 Apr. 1964, College Archives.

2. *MFSY*, 6–7.

3. Ibid., 18.

4. Ibid., 5–6.

5. Madeleva, letter to Ade de Bethune, 4 Jan. 1963, College Archives.

6. *MFSY*, 7.

7. Ibid., 6.

8. W. P. Wolff, 17.

9. *MFSY*, 7 and Marie H. Reilly, letter to Madeleva, 19 Mar. 1962, College Archives.

10. *MFSY*, 7.

11. Ibid., 18.

12. Ibid., 144.

13. Ibid., 18.

14. Walsh, 27.

15. *MFSY*, 21.

16. Ibid., 20.

17. Ibid.

18. Walsh, 12.

19. Ibid., 20.

20. Mary Lucia Wolff Stevenson, personal interview, 14 May 1988.

3. Away from Home

1. Louise Warwick Kelley, letter to Madeleva, 2 Apr. 1959, College Archives.

2. David Starr Jordan, "The Question of Coeducation," originally published in *Munsey's Magazine* Mar. 1906 and reprinted in *Portraits of the American University, 1890–1910*, compiled by James C. Stone and Donald P. De Nevi (San Francisco: Jossey-Bass, Inc., 1971).

3. Catalogue of the University of Wisconsin, 1905–06.

4. Merle Curti and Vernon Carstensen, *The University of Wisconsin: A History 1848–1925*, in two vols. (Madison: University of Wisconsin Press, 1949), 503.

5. *MFSY*, 23.

6. Madeleva, letter to J. Frederick Wolff, 4 Mar. 1960, College Archives.

7. Walsh, 3.

8. *MFSY*, 8.

9. Walsh, 1–3.

10. *MFSY*, 24.

11. Ibid., 25.

12. Walsh, 13.

13. M. L. Stevenson, personal interview, 14 May 1988.

4. Finding Peace

1. Collegiate Hall was renamed "Holy Cross Hall" in 1945.

2. *MFSY*, 26.

3. Ibid.

4. Ibid., 28.

5. Ibid.

6. Ibid.

7. Ibid., 26.

8. Ibid.

9. Madeleva, "The Madonna of the Lilies," published anonymously in *The Ave Maria*, 30 Jan. 1943.

10. Published under a pseudonym, "S. Marr" (Notre Dame, In.: The Ave Maria Press, 1911).

11. "The Madonna of the Lilies."

12. *MFSY*, 27.

13. For "On Memorial Day," Eva won a medal and the chance to recite the poem at a celebration at the University of Notre Dame on 30 May 1908. She published short essays in the Nov. 1906 issue of *Chimes* under the initials "E. W." and signed her name to essays published in Feb. and May 1907. Her first published poem, "From Death to Life," also appeared in the May 1907 issue.

14. Published in *Bookman* 49, no. 2 (Apr. 1919).

15. *MFSY*, 27.

16. Sr. Francis Jerome, CSC, *This Is Mother Pauline*. Vol. 7: Centenary Chronicles of the Sisters of the Holy Cross (Notre Dame, In.: Saint Mary's College, 1945), 128–29.

17. Walsh, 12.

18. This judgment is based on numerous personal conversations with family members, especially Carol Wolff and Mary Lucia Stevenson.

19. Bill Kavanaugh, a resident of Cumberland, personal interview, 24 Jul. 1989. He remembered that when the Wolffs ate at a local restaurant where he and his mother often dined, August always ate his food with his knife, much to his wife's chagrin.

20. *MFSY*, 31.

21. Walsh, 3.

22. *MFSY*, 34.

5. An Unlikely Candidate

1. *MFSY*, 29.

2. Ibid., 31–32.

3. *A Story of Fifty Years: From the Annals of the Congregation of the Sisters of the Holy Cross: 1855–1905* (Notre Dame, In.: The Ave Maria Press, 1905).

4. Ibid., 213.

5. *MFSY*, 34.

6. Ibid.

7. Ibid.

8. Ibid., 35.

9. Ibid., 34.

10. Lucy Arntz Wolff, letter to Madeleva, 26 Mar. 1946, College Archives.

11. "Concerning Certain Matters of Dress," collected in *Penelope* (Appleton, 1927).

12. Sr. M. Campion Kuhn, CSC, former archivist for the Congregation of the Sisters of the Holy Cross, letter to the author, 1 Oct. 1991.

13. *Constitutions of the Sisters of the Holy Cross* (Notre Dame, In.: The Ave Maria Press, 1896). Madeleva may have chosen this time to reveal her father's illegitimacy. Her paternal grandmother's reputation as a "fallen woman" suggests a plausible reason for her superiors' choice of Mary Magdalene as Madeleva's patroness and namesake in religious life.

14. *Chimes*, Dec. 1908: 50.

15. These words are prescribed in the *Customs and Reminders* of the Congregation of the Sisters of the Holy Cross.

16. *MFSY*, 35.

17. From "Chaucer's Nuns," in *Chaucer's Nuns and Other Essays* (Appleton, 1923).

18. Madeleva makes the point in *MFSY* (35) that canon law was not as explicit then as it became later on the formation of religious.

19. *MFSY*, 36.

20. Her experience of teaching without adequate preparation surely influenced her efforts in later years in the Sister Formation movement, which sought to ensure adequate professional training for sisters before they entered the classroom.

21. The head of the Congregation of the Sisters of the Holy Cross was referred to as "Mother General" when Madeleva entered the order, a term changed to "Superior General" in the 1930s. The latter title is used throughout this work. The designation "Mother" was customarily accorded to those who served as members of the general council of the order.

22. Walsh, 30.

23. *MFSY*, 22.

24. Ibid., 28.

25. See "Red Tulips" and "Unto the End" in *Knights Errant*. Forms of these poems were first published in *Chimes*. A letter from Theodore Maynard to Madeleva (Dec. 1912, College Archives) refers to the latter poem, dating it as among the earliest she wrote.

26. Walsh, 25.

27. Ibid., 29–30.

6. Learning Holy Indifference

1. *MFSY*, 38.

2. Madeleva's devotion to her mentor lasted all her life: more than thirty years later, she anonymously published her own memorial of Sr. Rita, "Madonna of the Lilies," and late in life wrote of her again, in her autobiography.

3. This editorial appeared Sat., 23 Jul. 1910, as quoted in the memorial leaflet distributed at Sr. Rita's funeral mass.

4. Madeleva, autobiographical statement, 14 Mar. 1940, College Archives.

5. Walsh, 46–47.

6. *MFSY*, 147.

7. *This Is Mother Pauline*, 22.

8. In *MFSY*, Madeleva gives 1912 as the date of the beginning of Miss Conway's residence at Saint Mary's. The General Archives, however, records the date as Sept. 1911, as do several college histories. It seems most likely that Madeleva's memory was faulty in this instance.

9. *MFSY*, 41.

10. Ibid., 169.

11. As quoted in ibid., 170.

12. *MFSY*, 169.

13. Sr. M. Eleanore, CSC, *The King's Highway* (New York and London: Appleton, 1931).

14. *MFSY*, 43.

15. Ibid., 44.

16. This exchange exists in letters dated 20 Mar. 1963 and 13 Jun. 1963, from Madeleva to Rev. Edward Maginn, and from him to her, respectively, in the College Archives. The occasion of the correspondence was her recently published autobiography, which mentioned him and their friendship.

17. In her curriculum vitae and various biographical statements, Madeleva and the college give 1909 as the date of her B.A. degree. Her official transcript leaves blank the date of graduation but lists undergraduate courses through 1912. It seems likely that she completed course work piecemeal over the four years following her entry into the convent and the degree itself was predated.

18. Madeleva's transcript of college credits lists a course titled "Essay" taken in 1911. This course was probably the one she took from Charles O'Donnell, since he later directed her M.A. thesis on the essay. (During the novitiate, she took only one other English course for credit, on the novel. It is possible but unlikely that she took a course on creative writing from Father O'Donnell for no credit.)

19. New York: Gomme, 1916.

20. *MFSY*, 45.

21. Ibid., 146.

22. Theodore Maynard, letter to Madeleva, Dec. 1912, College Archives, mentions these poems by name.

23. Sr. Bernadette Marie Downey, CSC (Madeleva's secretary for the last twenty years of her presidency), personal interview, 29 Oct. 1987. The envelopes are now on file in the College Archives. In fact, Madeleva may have been motivated as much by literary as by personal reasons for keeping these mementos of her friend.

24. *This Is Mother Pauline*, 230.

25. Madeleva, letter to Mother M. Vincentia Fannon, CSC, 21 Oct. 1933, College Archives.

26. Rev. Cornelius Hagerty, CSC, letter to Madeleva, 11 Jun. 1929, College Archives.

27. Cornelius Hagerty, "Canoe Trips" (privately printed, 1965), 16.

28. This information is recorded in the General Archives narrative for 1916.

29. Madeleva, letter to Rev. Charles L. O'Donnell, CSC, 1918, College Archives.

30. Hagerty makes this statement in his remarks about Mother Pauline in *This Is Mother Pauline*, 234.

31. Now the University of Portland.

7. Patrins

1. Madeleva, interview, *Montreal Star*, Wed. 23 May 1962.

2. Madeleva, letter to Hagerty, Feast of the Ascension (1920?), Indiana Province Archives Center (hereafter, Provincial Archives).

3. Madeleva, interview, *Montreal Star*, Wed. 23 May 1962.

4. *MFSY*, 47.

5. Ibid., 49.

6. Madeleva, letter to Sr. Mary of God, OP, 30 Oct. 1959, College Archives.

7. Madeleva, letter to Hagerty, Feast of the Ascension (1920?), Provincial Archives.

8. Madeleva, letter to Benjamin Harrison Lehman, Feast of Saint Timothy, Beloved of Saint Paul, 24 Jan. (no year), in the Benjamin H. Lehman

Papers, Bancroft Library, University of California, Berkeley (hereafter, Lehman Papers).

9. Madeleva, letter to Mother M. Aquina Kerwin, CSC, 28 Jul. 1920, General Archives.

10. Madeleva, letter to Mother Aquina, 31 May 1921, General Archives.

11. *MFSY*, 50.

12. The description of her trip occurs in a letter from Madeleva to Mother Aquina, 27 Jul. 1921, General Archives.

13. Madeleva, interview, *Catholic Poetry Society of America Bulletin*, Feb. 1944 (hereafter, *CPSA Bulletin*).

14. Madeleva, letter to Mother Aquina, Palm Sunday 1922, General Archives.

15. Ibid.

16. Madeleva, letter to Mother Aquina, 9 Jul. 1922, General Archives.

17. Verne A. Stadtman, *The University of California: 1868–1968* (New York: McGraw Hill, 1970), 509.

18. As quoted in David Littlejohn, "B. H. Lehman and the Central Concerns," *California Monthly* (Jan.-Feb. 1978): 10.

19. Madeleva tells the story in *MFSY*, 51.

20. *MFSY*, 52.

21. See John Livingston Lowes, letter to Madeleva, 3 Feb. 1923, College Archives.

22. See Lowes, letter to Madeleva, 1 Jun. 1921, College Archives.

23. Lehman, letter to Mother Aquina, 19 Aug. 1922, General Archives.

24. *MFSY*, 52.

25. The contract for this book was issued Jul. 1925; the book appeared the following year.

26. Madeleva, letter to Mother Aquina, 17 Jul. 1923, College Archives.

27. Hagerty, letter to Madeleva, 30 Sept. 1923, College Archives.

28. See Lowes, letter to Madeleva, 13 Jan. 1923, College Archives.

29. See Lowes, letter to Lehman, 4 Oct. 1924, College Archives. Lehman forwarded the letter to Madeleva.

30. O'Donnell, letter to Madeleva, 8 Sept. 1923, College Archives.

31. Madeleva, interview, *CPSA Bulletin*, Feb. 1944.

32. Hagerty, letter to Madeleva, 30 Sept. 1923, College Archives.

33. Madeleva, letter to Hagerty, 5 May 1922, Provincial Archives.

34. Hagerty, letter to Madeleva, 21 Oct. 1925, College Archives.

35. Hagerty, letter to Madeleva, 16 Jan. 1929, College Archives.

36. Madeleva, letter to Hagerty, 5 May 1922, Provincial Archives.

37. Hagerty, letter to Madeleva, 30 Sept. 1923, College Archives.

38. Madeleva, letter to Mother Aquina, Feast of St. Michael (1924?), General Archives.

39. Madeleva, letter to Mother Aquina, 1 May 1924, General Archives.

40. He refers in his letter of 23 Aug. 1924, College Archives, to hers, which he has recently received; hers is lost.

41. Hagerty, letter to Madeleva, 21 Oct. 1925, College Archives.

42. Madeleva, letter to Mother Aquina, Feast of St. Michael (1924?), General Archives.

43. Sr. M. Mercedes, CSC, letter to Sr. Conception, CSC, 28 Mar. 1925, College Archives.

44. Madeleva, interview, *Richmond Times-Dispatch*, 9 Nov. 1959.

45. From *St. Teresa, An Autobiography*, as quoted in *Pearl: A Study of Spiritual Dryness* (Appleton, 1925), 28.

46. As quoted in *Pearl*, 30.

47. Her letters to him, along with many copies of her poems, are collected in the Noel Sullivan Papers in the Bancroft Library at the University of California, Berkeley.

48. See Littlejohn, 11.

49. Lehman, letter to Madeleva, 30 June 1926, College Archives.

50. Madeleva, letter to Lehman, 3 Apr. (1925?), Lehman Papers.

51. Madeleva, letter to Mother Vincentia, 8 Oct. 1932, College Archives.

52. From *Chaucer's Nuns*, 6.

53. Walsh, 42.

54. *MFSY*, 50.

55. This copy, dated 6 Jul. 1926, is among the Lehman Papers.

56. Madeleva, letter to Lehman, 4 Jan. 1925, Lehman Papers.

57. Madeleva, letter to Lehman, 3 Apr. (1925?), Lehman Papers.

58. Madeleva, letter to Lehman, 4 Jan. 1925, Lehman Papers.

59. Madeleva, letter to Mother Aquina, Easter 1925, General Archives.

60. She writes of her feelings in *MFSY*, 54, and of her conversation with Lehman in a letter to him, 26 Sept. 1925, Lehman Papers.

61. Vernon Patterson, letter to Madeleva, 20 Apr. 1964, College Archives.

62. *MFSY*, 54.

63. Ibid., 55.

64. Lehman, letter to Madeleva (undated but apparently written in 1925, after he received a copy of *Pearl*), College Archives.

8. Penelope

1. Madeleva, letter to Lehman, 24 Jan. 1926, Lehman Papers.

2. See Lowes, letter to Madeleva (written to congratulate her on the completion of her doctorate), 17 Dec. 1925, College Archives.

3. O'Donnell, letter to Madeleva, 9 Nov. 1925, College Archives.

4. O'Donnell, letter to Madeleva, 5 Aug. 1926, College Archives.

5. Described by her in a letter to Lehman, 20 Sept. 1925, Lehman Papers.

6. Madeleva, letter to Lehman, 8 Jul. 1926, Lehman Papers.

7. Madeleva, letter to Hagerty, 12 Feb. 1926, Provincial Archives.

8. Hagerty, "Canoe Trips," 44.

9. M. L. Stevenson, personal interview, 14 May 1988.

10. Madeleva, letter to Lehman, 8 Jul. 1926, Lehman Papers.

11. Madeleva, letter to Lehman, 9 Nov. (1926?), Lehman Papers.

12. Madeleva, letter to Lehman, 24 Jan. 1926, Lehman Papers.

13. Madeleva, letter to Lehman, 9 Nov. (1926?), Lehman Papers.

14. *MFSY*, 56.

15. She specifically referred to this desire in a letter to Father Hudson, editor of *Ave Maria*, in an undated letter in the College Archives. She also apparently mentioned it to Father Hagerty in a letter now lost.

16. Madeleva, "Saint Hilda of Whitby," in *Saints for Now*, ed. Clare Boothe Luce (Sheed and Ward, 1952).

17. Madeleva, letter to Lehman, 13 Jun. (1927?), Lehman Papers.

18. These and other activities are described in a letter to Lehman, 7 Mar. 1927, Lehman Papers.

19. Hagerty, letter to Madeleva, 16 Jan. 1929, College Archives.

20. Madeleva, letter to Lehman, no date, Lehman Papers.

21. Madeleva, letter to Lehman, 12 Jun. 1928, Lehman Papers.

22. Madeleva, letter to Lehman, 20 Jul. 1928, Lehman Papers.

23. Madeleva, letter to Lehman, 29 Sept. 1928, Lehman Papers.

24. Hagerty, "Canoe Trips," 48.

25. Madeleva, letter to Lehman, 7 Mar. 1927, Lehman Papers.

26. See Harriet Monroe, letter to Madeleva, dated only 1926, College Archives.

27. O'Donnell, letter to Madeleva, 5 Aug. 1926, College Archives.

28. O'Donnell, letter to Madeleva, 24 Nov. 1926, College Archives.

29. O'Donnell, letter to Madeleva, 19 May 1927, College Archives.

30. As in *Conversations with Cassandra* (Macmillan, 1961; hereafter, *CWC*).

31. Walsh, 41.

32. Madeleva, letter to Lehman, 6 Jul. 1926, Lehman Papers.

33. Lehman, letter to Madeleva, 12 May 1927, College Archives.

34. Hagerty, letter to Madeleva, 16 Jan. 1929, College Archives.

35. Hagerty, letter to Madeleva, 11 Jun. 1929, College Archives.

36. Hagerty, letter to Madeleva, 16 Jan. 1929, College Archives.

37. Hagerty, letter to Madeleva, 19 Apr. 1929, College Archives.

38. Hagerty, letter to Madeleva, 11 Jun. 1929, College Archives.

39. Ibid.

40. Hagerty, letter to Madeleva, 20 Apr. 1929, College Archives.

41. Ibid.

42. Hagerty, letter to Madeleva, 11 Jun. 1929, College Archives.

43. Hagerty, letter to Madeleva, 20 Apr. 1929, College Archives.

44. Hagerty, letter to Madeleva, 10 Nov. 1931, College Archives.

45. Hagerty, letter to Madeleva, 13 Jun. 1933, College Archives.

46. Hagerty, letter to Madeleva, 21 Oct. 1925, College Archives.

47. *MFSY*, xii.

48. Hagerty, letter to Madeleva, 11 Nov. 1931, College Archives.

9. Procrustes' Bed

1. Lucy Hazard, letter to Madeleva, 4 Aug. 1929, College Archives.

2. Madeleva, letter to Lehman, 13 Apr. 1929, Lehman Papers.

3. Hazard, letter to Madeleva, 11 Jun. 1930, College Archives.

4. Madeleva, letter to O'Donnell, 29 Jun. 1930, College Archives.

5. Madeleva, letter to Mother Vincentia, 3 Jul. 1932, College Archives.

6. Madeleva, letter to Mother Vincentia, 8 Oct. 1932, College Archives.

7. Madeleva, letter to Lehman, 31 Aug. 1931, Lehman Papers.

8. Madeleva, letter to Mother Vincentia, 13 Jun. 1932, College Archives.

9. See Lew Sarett, letter to Madeleva, 1 Nov. 1931, College Archives.

10. See Louis Untermeyer, letter to Madeleva, 4 Jul. 1931, College Archives.

11. Jean Untermeyer, letter to Madeleva, 8 May 1931, College Archives.

12. Madeleva, letter to Lehman, 5 Dec. 1930, Lehman Papers.

13. Madeleva, letter to Lehman, 27 Feb. 1931, Lehman Papers.

14. Lehman, letter to Madeleva, 7 Mar. 1931, College Archives.

15. Madeleva, letter to Mother Vincentia, 8 Oct. 1932, College Archives.

16. Madeleva, letter to the Most Rev. John J. Mitty, Feast of Saint Joseph 1932, College Archives.

17. Madeleva, letter to Mother Vincentia, Palm Sunday 1933, College Archives.

18. O'Donnell, letter to Madeleva, 30 Oct. 1930, College Archives.

19. Madeleva, letter to Lehman, 9 Jul. 1932, Lehman Papers.

20. O'Donnell, letter to Madeleva, 13 Aug. 1930, College Archives.

21. Maynard, letter to Madeleva, 28 Feb. 1931, College Archives.

22. Madeleva, letter to Mother Vincentia, 8 Oct. 1932, College Archives.

23. Hagerty, letter to Madeleva, 11 Nov. 1931, College Archives.

24. Madeleva, letter to Mother Vincentia, 8 Oct. 1932, College Archives.

25. O'Donnell, letter to Madeleva, 12 Jan. 1933, College Archives.

26. Madeleva, letter to O'Donnell, 15 Jan. 1933, Records of President Charles L. O'Donnell, UPCO 5/62, University of Notre Dame Archives.

27. Madeleva, letter to Mother Vincentia, Passion Sunday 1933, College Archives.

28. Madeleva, letter to Mother Vincentia, 19 Jul. 1932, College Archives.

29. Madeleva, letter to Mother Vincentia, 19 Apr. 1933, College Archives.

30. Sr. Eleanore to Madeleva, 1 Feb. 1933, with a penciled note at the end from Mother Vincentia, College Archives.

31. *MFSY*, 59.

32. Madeleva, letter to Lehman, 13 Aug. 1933, Lehman Papers.

33. Madeleva, letter to Mother Vincentia, 23 Jul. 1933, General Archives.

34. Madeleva, letter to Lehman, 13 Aug. 1933, Lehman Papers.

10. This Other Eden

1. Madeleva, letter to Mother Vincentia, 29 Aug. 1933, College Archives.

2. Ibid.

3. Madeleva, letter to Marion McCandless, 18 Sept. 1933, College Archives.

4. Madge Vaison Mouton, letter to Madeleva, 23 Dec. 1933, College Archives.

5. Madeleva, letter to Mother Vincentia, 10 Sept. 1933, College Archives.

6. *MFSY*, 61.

7. Madeleva, letter to Lehman, Feast of Saint Lucy 1933, Lehman Papers.

8. Ibid.

9. Madeleva's journal of her 1933–34 European trip, 1 Oct. 1933, College Archives.

10. *MFSY*, 60.

11. Madeleva, letter to Mother Vincentia, 21 Oct. 1933, College Archives.

12. Ibid.

13. Ibid.

14. Ibid.

15. Ibid.

16. Ibid.

17. Madeleva, letter to Mother Vincentia, Easter 1934, College Archives.

18. Mother Margaret Williams, RSCJ, letter to the author, 3 Jun. 1988.

19. Madeleva, letter to Mrs. John D. Ross, 18 Feb. 1960, College Archives.

20. Madeleva, letter to Mother Vincentia, 21 Oct. 1933, College Archives.

21. Mother Williams, letter to the author, 3 Jun. 1988.

22. Madeleva, letter to Mother Vincentia, 21 Oct. 1933, College Archives.

23. Hagerty, letter to Madeleva, 7 Jan. 1934, College Archives.

24. Madeleva, letter to Lehman, Feast of Saint Lucy 1933, Lehman Papers.

25. Madeleva's journal, 1 Dec. 1933, College Archives.

26. Madeleva, letter to Mother Vincentia, 19 Dec. 1933, College Archives.

27. Madeleva, letter to Lehman, Feast of Saint Lucy 1933, Lehman Papers.

28. Madeleva, letter to Mother Vincentia, 19 Dec. 1933, College Archives.

29. Madeleva, letter to Mother Vincentia, 1 Jan. 1934, College Archives.

30. Madeleva's journal, 23 Nov. 1933, College Archives.

31. Madeleva's journal, 29 Jan. 1934, College Archives.

32. Miriam Marshall Hemphill, letter to the author, 25 Oct. 1987.

33. Madeleva, letter to Mother Vincentia, 24 Feb. 1934, College Archives.

34. Ibid.

35. *MFSY*, 72.

36. Ibid., 74.

37. Madeleva's journal, 11 Apr. 1934, College Archives.

38. *MFSY*, 75.

39. Madeleva, letter to C. S. Lewis, 1 May 1951, College Archives.

40. See Lewis, letter to Madeleva, 13 Mar. 1959, College Archives.

41. Madeleva, letter to Mother Vincentia, 9 Jun. 1934, College Archives.

42. Madeleva, letter to Mother Vincentia, Feast of Apparition of Saint Michael 1934, College Archives.

43. See Lewis, letter to Madeleva, 7 Jun. 1934, Marion E. Wade Center, Wheaton College.

44. These respective letters are dated 8 May 1957, 27 Apr. 1959, and 26 Sept. 1963, College Archives.

45. Lewis, letter to Madeleva, 3 Oct. 1963, Marion E. Wade Center, Wheaton College.

46. *MFSY*, 76.

47. Ibid., 78.

48. Madeleva, letter to Mother Vincentia, Jul. 1934, College Archives.

49. Rev. Conrad Pepler, OP, letter to Madeleva (late 1961 or early 1962?), College Archives.

50. Madeleva, letter to Mother Vincentia, 9 Jun. 1934, College Archives.

51. Ibid.

52. Madeleva, letter to Mother Vincentia, Jul. 1934, College Archives.

53. Ibid.

54. *MFSY*, 93.

55. Arthur J. Hope, CSC, *Notre Dame: One Hundred Years* (Notre Dame Press, 1943), 439.

56. Madeleva, letter to Mother Vincentia, 9 Jun. 1934, College Archives.

57. From a ms. later published in *Spirit* 3 (Jul. 1936): 88-91, College Archives.

58. Madeleva, letter to Lehman, 29 Jul. 1953, Lehman Papers.

59. *MFSY,* 87.

60. Madeleva, letter to Edward F. Murphy, 1 Jun. 1963, College Archives.

11. Harnessing Her Will

1. Madeleva, letter to Lehman, 7 Aug. 1934, Lehman Papers.

2. Madeleva, letter to Lehman, 2 Jan. 1935, Lehman Papers.

3. Madeleva, letters to Mother Vincentia, 4 Jun. 1934 and 23 Jun. 1934, respectively, General Archives.

4. *MFSY,* 93.

5. Madeleva, letter to Lehman, 2 Jan. 1935, Lehman Papers.

6. Madeleva, letter to Lehman, 15 Sept. 1927, Lehman Papers.

7. Hagerty, letter to Madeleva, 11 June 1929, College Archives.

8. *Constitutions,* 94–95.

9. *MFSY,* 94.

10. Sr. Mary Immaculate Creek, CSC, *A Panorama: 1844–1977* (Saint Mary's College, 1977), 106.

11. *Static* (Saint Mary's College Student Newspaper), Nov. 1934.

12. Ibid.

13. *MFSY,* 96.

14. Ibid., 120.

15. Ibid., 97.

16. Ibid., 94.

17. See, for example, Edward J. Power, *A History of Higher Education in the United States* (Milwaukee: Bruce, 1958), 149.

18. Madeleva, letter to Lehman, 2 Jan. 1935, Lehman Papers.

19. Madeleva, letter to Mortimer Adler, 5 Nov. 1962, College Archives. In the letter, written on the occasion of his sixtieth birthday, she reminded him of the circumstances of their first meeting.

20. Throughout the spring of 1935, Sr. Miriam Joseph Rauh, CSC, Sr. Maria Teresa Heineman, CSC, and Madeleva traveled regularly to Chicago to

study the trivium with Mortimer Adler. They were joined by three sisters from Rosary College, including Sr. Cyrill Gill, OP, whom the author interviewed by telephone 2 Apr. 1992. Srs. Miriam Joseph and Maria Teresa subsequently traveled to New York in the summer of 1935 to continue their work with Professor Adler, who was teaching in the summer program at Columbia College.

21. It seems likely that Madeleva's familiarity with the University of Wisconsin's commitment to continuing education inspired and influenced her many efforts to reach out to the larger community.

22. Mary Ellen Klein, "Sister M. Madeleva Wolff, CSC: A Study of Presidential Leadership 1934–1961" (diss. Kent State University, 1983), 34.

23. Klein, 34.

24. Madeleva, letter to Lehman, 22 Oct. 1935, Lehman Papers.

25. Lehman, letter to Madeleva, 26 Dec. 1934, College Archives.

26. Lehman, letter to Madeleva, 6 Jun. 1935, College Archives.

27. Lehman, letter to Madeleva, [no day] 1935, College Archives.

28. Ibid.

29. This was the comment of the reader, unnamed, for Macmillan, who subsequently published *Selected Poems* (1939). See the report of Theodore Purdy, Jr., to Madeleva, 9 Jun. 1938, College Archives.

30. Walsh, 48.

31. Hagerty is listed as a replacement for another Holy Cross priest on leave from Saint Mary's in 1935–36. He is subsequently listed as teaching in the 1937 summer session. The author found no record of further employment at Saint Mary's in the files either of Saint Mary's or of Notre Dame; however, careful records of part-time teachers were not kept.

32. See "Canoe Trips."

33. Hagerty, letter to Madeleva, 13 Jan. 1934, College Archives.

34. *CWC*, 97.

35. From a manuscript, College Archives, later published as "Saint Hilda of Whitby" in *Saints for Now*.

12. Narrow Gates

1. Madeleva, letter to Sr. Mary Francis, PC, 29 Aug. 1963, College Archives.

2. *MFSY*, 93.

3. Madeleva, letter to Lehman, Good Friday 1940, Lehman Papers.

4. For example, "David" and "Dialogue," which appeared in *American Twelfth Night* in 1955, but had been written sometime before 1912.

5. Walsh 34.

6. Ibid.

7. *Static,* Sept. 1936.

8. *MFSY,* 67.

9. Madeleva, letter to Lehman, 13 Jun. (1931?), Lehman Papers.

10. On 22 Oct. 1935, Madeleva wrote Lehman: "I know that you will be glad when I tell you that I received twenty-five-thousand dollars Sunday for the beginning of a new library here," Lehman Papers.

11. Madeleva, letter to Lehman, 11 Feb. 1941, Lehman Papers.

12. *MFSY,* 101.

13. Ibid., 96.

14. Speaight, *The Property Basket: Reflections of a Divided Life* (London: Collins and Harvill, 1970), 335.

15. See Charles Du Bos, letter to Madeleva, 3 Aug. 1937, College Archives.

16. Madge Vaison Mouton, letter to Madeleva, 19 Mar. 1934, College Archives.

17. Ibid.

18. Madeleva, letter to Sr. Ruth Adelaide, SC, 2 Oct. 1947, College Archives, in which Madeleva specifies that the conversations occurred on Sunday mornings only, not daily, as suggested in *MFSY*.

19. *MFSY,* 66.

20. Ibid.

21. Madeleva, letter to Madge Vaison Mouton, 24 Nov. 1938, College Archives.

22. Madeleva, letter to Madge Vaison Mouton, 23 Jan. 1941, College Archives.

23. *MFSY,* 67.

24. Madeleva, letter to Madge Vaison Mouton, 3 Nov. 1939, College Archives.

25. Madeleva, "Precepts of Peace," *Addressed to Youth* (St. Anthony Guild Press, 1944), 1.

26. Zezette Du Bos, letter to Madeleva, 17 Apr. 1942, College Archives.

27. Bruno P. Schlesinger, personal interview, 20 Mar. 1995.

28. L. A. von Simson, *Happy Exiles* (privately printed, 1981), 67–68.

29. Madeleva, letter to Lehman, 8 May 1942, Lehman Papers.

30. Madeleva, letter to Lehman, 24 Mar. 1937, Lehman Papers.

31. Madeleva, letter to Lehman, 26 Sept. 1936, Lehman Papers.

32. Madeleva, letter to Lehman, 26 Jun. 1945, Lehman Papers.

33. Ibid.

34. Madeleva, letter to Lehman, 8 May 1942, Lehman Papers.

35. *CWC*, 107.

36. See *MFSY*, 98–99.

37. See Ibid. for Madeleva's account of her decision, which she writes was made in 1941, and its consequences.

38. *MFSY*, 98–99.

39. Ibid., 99.

40. Sr. Gerald Hartney, CSC, telephone interview, 14 Aug. 1995.

41. "Report of the President," 1950, College Archives.

42. Madeleva, letter to Robert Heineman, 5 Jan. 1962, College Archives.

43. Madeleva, letter to Edward D. Hansford, Jr., 8 Jul. 1953, College Archives.

44. Madeleva, letter to Vernon Patterson, 11 May 1964, College Archives.

45. Madeleva, letter to Lewis, 27 Aug. 1957, College Archives.

46. Madeleva, interview, *Catholic Reporter*, 21 Oct. 1961.

47. See the file on the Gary Poetry Workshop 1961, and in particular, Madeleva, letter to Wilmot Graham, 25 Feb. 1961, College Archives.

48. See, for example, Madeleva, letter to Barbara Ward (Lady Jackson), 8 Oct. 1959, College Archives.

49. *A College Goes to School* (Notre Dame, In.: Saint Mary's College, 1945), 136.

50. Bruno P. Schlesinger, personal interview, 20 Mar. 1995.

51. Madeleva made the notation on a list of names and addresses, College Archives.

13. Educating Women

1. Sr. Maria Assunta Werner, CSC, *Madeleva: A Pictorial Biography* (Notre Dame, In.: Saint Mary's College, 1993), 283.

2. Madeleva, "Education for Immortality," in *A College Goes to School*, 162.

3. Viz., "The Madonna of the Lilies."

4. Walsh, 28.

5. See *CWC*, "What Are Mothers Like?" 63–64.

6. *CWC*, 65.

7. Ibid., 64.

8. See for example "We Work Our Way Through College," *CWC*, 66–71, in which Madeleva describes work as "a universal vocation, as a gift of God." She quotes the words of Jesus: "The Father worked until now, and I work."

9. Madeleva, autobiographical statement, 14 Mar. 1940, College Archives.

10. *MFSY*, 119.

11. Madeleva, interview, *Syracuse Herald*, Thurs. 16 Mar. 1939.

12. *MFSY*, 124.

13. *CWC*, 18–19.

14. Madeleva, interview, *Montreal Gazette*, 23 Jun. 1962.

15. Madeleva, letter to Mr. H. S. Latham, 31 Oct. 1944, College Archives.

16. *MFSY*, 128.

17. *Ibid.*, 126.

18. *Addressed to Youth*, 37.

19. Madeleva, interview, *Milwaukee Journal*, Thurs. 18 Apr. 1963.

20. *CWC*, 24.

21. See Martha Blocker, letter to Madeleva, 27 Aug. 1960, College Archives.

22. *CWC*, 19.

23. *MFSY*, 128–29.

24. Ibid., 128.

25. Ibid., 127.

26. Madeleva, interview, *Montreal Gazette*, Wed. 23 May 1962.

27. Ibid.

28. *MFSY*, 114–15.

29. *CWC*, 81.

30. Ibid.

31. Rev. Francis J. Connell, CSSR, quoting Saint Paul, in "The Theological School in America," in *Essays on Catholic Education in the United States*, ed. Roy J. Deferrari (Washington, D.C.: Catholic University Press, 1942), 219.

32. Connell in Deferrari, 225.

33. As discussed in Rev. William J. McGucken, SJ, "The Renascence of Religion Teaching in American Catholic Schools," in Deferrari, 329–51.

34. From a transcript, signed by Madeleva, of an interview, 24 Mar. 1964, conducted by Sr. Maria Concepta McDermott, CSC, and subsequently published in *The Making of a Sister Teacher* (Notre Dame, 1965), 160–61.

35. *MFSY*, 115.

36. Ibid., 114.

37. Archives narrative 1946–47, College Archives.

38. *MFSY*, 118.

39. Madeleva, letter to Thomas Merton, 8 Jul. 1953, College Archives.

40. Report of the president, 1960, 10, College Archives.

41. McDermott, 161.

42. Ibid.

43. The Most Rev. E. O'Hara, letter to Madeleva, 15 Mar. 1948, College Archives.

44. Most Rev. Edwin V. O'Hara, "Theology for Women," *Theology and the Teacher: Anniversary Addresses for the Tenth Anniversary of the Graduate School of Sacred Theology 1943-53*, College Archives.

45. Madeleva, letter to Rev. Francis McHenry, St. Columba's Abbey, Glenstal, Ireland, no date, College Archives.

46. Madeleva, letter to Sr. Mary Patrick, IHM, 29 May 1952, College Archives.

47. *MFSY*, 112.

48. McDermott describes the program and its evolution in detail in *The Making of a Sister-Teacher*, 167ff.

49. *MFSY*, 113.

50. The anecdotes that follow emerged from conversations with members of the faculty, staff, and administration at the college during Madeleva's presidency.

51. Von Simson, 69.

52. See, for example, Klein 69–72, and various reports of the president to the superiors of the Holy Cross Congregation, College Archives.

53. Report of the president, 1947, College Archives.

54. See for example the report of the president for 1950, College Archives.

55. Klein, 70.

56. *American Association of University Professors Bulletin*, Winter 1946, v. 32, no. 4, 719.

57. Report of the president, 1956-57, College Archives.

58. Report of the president, 1960, College Archives.

59. *CWC*, 119.

60. *Gabrielle* (Saint Mary's College), Apr.–May 1957.

61. Report of the president, 1960, College Archives.

62. *MFSY*, 129.

63. Ibid.

14. In the Country of the Soul

1. *MFSY,* 169.

2. Ibid.

3. Walsh, 35.

4. Madeleva, letter to William S. Miller, 25 Sept. 1963, College Archives.

5. Sr. Mary of God, telephone interview, 12 Apr. 1988.

6. Madeleva, letter to Robert Heineman, 7 Jan. 1953, College Archives.

7. Madeleva, letter to William E. Cotter, 19 Jun. 1963, College Archives.

8. Madeleva, letter to Winifred Feely, 24 Jul. 1962, College Archives.

9. Sr. Mary Emil, IHM, in the *Sister Formation Bulletin,* reprinted in *Courier* (Winter 1966).

10. Madeleva, letter to Mother Rose Elizabeth Havican, CSC, 24 Nov. 1961, College Archives.

11. Sr. Alma Peter, CSC, personal interview, 1 Feb. 1995.

12. Madeleva, interview, *Syracuse Journal,* Thurs. 16 Mar. 1939.

13. Madeleva, letter to Mary of God, 21 Apr. 1961, College Archives.

14. Madeleva, letter to Mary of God, 2 Jul 1951, College Archives.

15. Madeleva, letter to Mary of God, 28 Dec. 1957, College Archives.

16. Madeleva, letter to Mary of God, 30 Apr. 1957, College Archives.

17. Madeleva, letter to Mary of God, 31 Jan. 1962, College Archives.

18. Madeleva, letter to Mother M. Immaculata, PC, 12 May 1947, College Archives.

19. Madeleva, letter to Mother Immaculata, 28 Jan. 1947, College Archives.

20. Madeleva, letter to Mother Immaculata, 27 Sept. 1946, College Archives.

21. Madeleva, letter to Sr. Mary Francis, PC, 5 Sept. 1944, College Archives.

22. Madeleva, letter to Sr. Mary Francis, 11 Aug. 1950, College Archives.

23. Madeleva, letter to Sr. Mary Francis, 26 Jan. 1945, College Archives.

24. Ibid.

25. Madeleva, letter to Fr. Adelmo of Vernio, 6 Feb. 1964, College Archives.

26. Madeleva, letter to Rev. Daniel, OFM, 6 Feb. 1964, College Archives.

27. Madeleva, letter to Merton, 2 May 1949, College Archives.

28. Madeleva, letter to Merton, 24 Aug. 1949, College Archives.

29. See Merton, letter to Madeleva, 21 Oct. 1948, College Archives.

30. Michael Mott, *The Seven Mountains of Thomas Merton* (Boston: Houghton Mifflin, 1984), 225.

31. Mary of God, telephone interview, 12 Apr. 1988.

32. See Merton, letter to Madeleva, 4 Feb. 1950, College Archives.

33. Madeleva, letter to Merton, 2 May 1949, College Archives.

34. Madeleva, letter to Merton, 28 Nov. 1962, College Archives.

35. Madeleva, letter to Merton, 27 Feb. 1962, College Archives.

36. See Merton, letter to Madeleva, 9 Mar. 1962, College Archives.

37. Mary L. Norris, letter to the author, 4 Jan. 1987.

38. Carrie Powers Powell, letter to the author, 8 Nov. 1987.

39. Sr. Gerald, telephone interview, 14 Aug. 1995.

40. Sr. Miriam Patrick Cooney, CSC, personal interview, 31 Jul. 1995. Madeleva's comment suggests that she regarded every gift as from God, and the act of consecration as a conscious invitation to Christ to become present through it.

41. Edward Fischer, *Notre Dame Remembered* (University of Notre Dame Press, 1987) 117.

42. Madeleva, letter to Henry Luce, 22 Nov. 1957, College Archives.

43. *CWC*, 109–10.

44. Edward Fischer, personal interview, 4 May 1988.

45. *MFSY*, 158.

46. Madeleva, letter to Clare Boothe Luce, 3 Sept. 1947, College Archives.

47. See C. B. Luce, letter to Madeleva, 28 Oct. 1948, College Archives.

48. Madeleva, letter to C. B. Luce, 11 Dec. 1956, College Archives.

49. Madeleva, letter to Norman St. John Stevas of *The Wise Man Review*, 7 Nov. 1961, College Archives.

50. *MFSY*, 158.

51. Madeleva, letter to C. B. Luce, 7 Nov. 1961, College Archives.

52. Like Madeleva, Lehman was fascinated with the performing arts and artists. As a young man, he had followed the Italian actress Eleonora Duse around Europe, and all three of his wives were connected with the theatre, the first as a screenwriter for films, the second as an actress famous for her performances both on stage and on screen, and the third as a dramatic poet.

53. Lehman died in 1978 at eighty-nine.

54. Madeleva, letter to Lehman, 19 May 1948, Lehman Papers.

55. Madeleva, letter to Lehman, 22 Sept. 1949, Lehman Papers.

56. Madeleva, letter to Lehman, 21 Feb. 1955, Lehman Papers.

57. Madge Vaison Mouton, letter to Madeleva, 29 Aug. 1962, College Archives.

15. The Relaxed Grasp

1. *MFSY* 170–71.

2. Ibid., 172.

3. Madeleva, letter to Mary Cotter Millard, 28 Nov. 1962, College Archives.

4. Sr. Bernadette Marie, personal interview, 29 Oct. 1987.

5. Madeleva, letter to Mrs. John D. Ross, 21 Jan. 1960, College Archives.

6. *Panorama*, 107.

7. Helen Aschmann (Mrs. Charles), letter to Madeleva, 2 Jul. 1944, College Archives.

8. Letter from the Executive Director of CPSA to Madeleva, 25 Nov. 1961, College Archives.

9. Madeleva, letter to Arline Hagan, 27 Apr. 1962, College Archives.

10. Madeleva, letter to G. Bromley Oxnam, 6 Jun. 1950, College Archives.

11. Madeleva, letter to Mrs. N. E. Larsen, 11 Aug. 1961, College Archives.

12. Madeleva, interview, *CPSA Bulletin*, Feb. 1944.

13. Madeleva, letter to Lewis, 1 May 1951, College Archives.

14. Madeleva, letter to Mr. and Mrs. William Cotter, 10 Jan. 1948, private collection.

15. Madeleva, letter to Harry J. Cargas, editor of *Queen's Work,* 12 Jul. 1963, College Archives.

16. Madeleva, interview, *Richmond Times-Dispatch,* 9 Nov. 1959.

17. Madeleva, interview, *CPSA Bulletin,* Feb. 1944.

18. Walsh, 18.

19. Madeleva, interview, *CPSA Bulletin,* Feb 1944.

20. *MFSY,* 172.

21. Walsh, 47.

22. *MFSY,* 172.

23. Sr. Miriam P. Cooney, CSC, "Church Renovation Committee," a presentation to the faculty of Saint Mary's College, Mar. 1992. Quoted with permission of the author.

24. Walsh, 47.

25. Madeleva, letter to Lehman, undated, Lehman Papers.

26. Walsh, 46–47.

27. *MFSY,* 146.

28. Many sisters who worked closely with Madeleva or knew her well commented on her ways of meditating, which were unorthodox for the time, among them Srs. Bernadette Marie, Miriam, and Mary of God.

29. Madeleva, letter to Sue Sullivan, 27 Jul. 1962, College Archives.

30. Walsh, 130.

31. On Madeleva's view of art and its relationship to religion, see the author's *Madeleva: One Woman's Life* (Paulist, 1994) 18–20, and Madeleva's treatment of the topic in relation to other poets in "The Religious Poetry of the Nineteenth Century," collected in *Chaucer's Nuns* (Appleton, 1925).

32. Madeleva, letter to John Norcross, M.D., 21 Jul. 1949, College Archives.

33. Madeleva, letter to Norcross, 5 Jun. 1950, College Archives.

34. Madeleva, letter to Norcross, 8 Mar. 1950, College Archives.

35. Norcross, letter to Madeleva, 27 Jul. 1962, College Archives.

36. Madeleva, letter to John Daley, M.D., 22 Jul. 1949, College Archives.

37. Madeleva, letter to Daley, 9 Apr. 1951, College Archives.

38. Madeleva, letter to Madge Vaison Mouton, 27 Jun. 1938, College Archives.

39. Lucy Wolff, letter to Madeleva, 18 Dec. 1946, College Archives.

40. Lucy Wolff, letter to Madeleva, 11 Apr. 1947, College Archives.

41. Lucy Wolff, letter to Madeleva, 18 Dec. 1946, College Archives.

42. "Lucy Rehearses Her Funeral," *MFSY*, 139.

43. August Wolff, letter to Madeleva, 23 Nov. 1948, College Archives.

44. August Wolff, letter to Madeleva, Oct. 1949, College Archives.

45. *MFSY*, 143.

46. Madeleva, interview, *St. Louis Review*, Dec. 1961.

47. Madeleva, interview, *Syracuse Post-Standard*, 17 Mar. 1939.

48. Julian of Norwich, *Showings* (trans., Edmund Colledge, OSA, and James Walsh, SJ, Paulist Press, 1978) 130, 183–84, 199.

49. "Dame Julian of Norwich," reprinted in *CWC*, 131.

16. Giving Beauty Back

1. *CWC*, 67.

2. Ibid., 68.

3. Madeleva, interview, *Milwaukee Journal*, Thurs. 18 Apr. 1963.

4. *MFSY*, 104.

5. Walsh, 38. Of course, this idea of beauty is far from original with Madeleva. In "Phaedrus," for example, Plato expresses similar ideas on the apprehension of the good through beauty, and a beautiful body, in particular.

6. *Chaucer's Nuns*, 134.

7. Madeleva, interview, *Syracuse Post-Standard*, 17 Mar. 1939.

8. Ibid.

9. Madeleva, interview, *Montreal Gazette*, Wed. 23 May 1962.

10. Madeleva, letter to C. B. Luce, 29 Jan. 1962, College Archives.

11. Madeleva often spoke of the "sacrament" of the present moment, a concept she first discussed with Charles Du Bos. By centering oneself in the present, she believed, one might transcend time and experience the presence of Christ.

12. Madeleva, letter to Mrs. Fred Carroll, 10 May 1963, College Archives.

13. Joseph Bonadies, personal interview, 6 Jul. 1988.

14. *MFSY*, 172.

15. Sr. Miriam, "Church Renovation."

16. Sr. Miriam, "Church Renovation." Permission was granted on condition that Madeleva tell no one of the exception.

17. Rev. Didicus Dunn, OF, cap., telephone interview, 17 Jul. 1995.

18. Sr. Miriam, "Church Renovation."

19. Madeleva, letter to Sr. Mary Patrick, IHM, 30 Jun. 1952.

20. *MFSY*, 104–5.

21. Ibid., 102.

22. Joseph Bonadies, personal interview, 6 Jul. 1988.

23. W. P. Wolff to J. F. Wolff, letter repeating a conversation he had with Helen Hayes when they met at Saint Mary's, 15 May 1960, College Archives.

24. See Helen Hayes, letter to Madeleva, 12 Feb. 1957, College Archives.

25. Madeleva, letter to Lehman, 17 Nov. 1955, College Archives.

26. Madeleva, letter to Louisa Jenkins, 9 Jun. 1957.

27. Madeleva probably knew little of White's personal life and habits, including her unorthodox sexual exploits and heavy drinking. She most likely relied on Speaight's recommendation and her knowledge that White had recently returned to the practice of her Catholic faith.

28. Speaight, *The Property Basket*, 251.

29. From the brochure for the production, written by Madeleva, 1960, College Archives.

30. Madeleva, letter to Mother M. St. Stephen, IBVM, 23 Aug. 1962, College Archives.

31. *Courier* (Summer 1960).

32. Madeleva, letter to Madge Vaison Mouton, 28 Sept. 1959, College Archives.

33. Madeleva, letter to Lewis, 22 Apr. 1959, College Archives.

34. Lewis, letter to Madeleva, 27 Apr. 1959, College Archives.

35. Madeleva, letters to Lewis, 8 Apr. 1954 and 1 May 1957, respectively, College Archives.

36. Madeleva, general letter to the Holy Cross sisters, 18 Jul. 1959, College Archives.

37. The Most Rev. Leo Pursley, letter to Madeleva, undated (1961?), College Archives.

38. W. P. Wolff, letter to J. F. Wolff, 15 May 1960, College Archives.

39. Madeleva, letter to J. F. Wolff, 14 Nov. 1963, College Archives.

40. Madeleva, letter to Mrs. William T. Coholan, 23 Jun. 1961, College Archives.

41. *Time*, 9 Feb. 1962.

42. Along with Wabash, Earlham, DePaw, and Coe in Iowa. *Chicago Tribune*, Sat. 11 Feb. 1961.

43. Personal interviews with Srs. Maria Concepta, Miriam, Alma, and Bernadette Marie.

44. Madeleva, letter to Charles De Koninck, 25 Jul. 1961, College Archives.

17. Sister Death

1. Lehman, letter to Madeleva, 1 Aug. 1961, College Archives.

2. Madeleva, letter to Marian Newcomb, 5 Mar. 1963, College Archives.

3. Sr. Miriam, personal interview, 31 Jul. 1995.

4. Madeleva, letter to Julian Arntz, 1 Feb. 1962, College Archives.

5. Madeleva, letter to Anna Bird Stewart, 26 Jul. 1962, College Archives.

6. Bruno P. Schlesinger, personal interview, 20 Mar. 1995.

7. Madeleva, letter to the Most Rev. Vincent S. Waters, 26 Jun. 1963, College Archives.

8. Speaight, *The Property Basket*, 335.

9. Madeleva, letter to C. B. Luce, 21 May 1964, College Archives.

10. Sr. Miriam, personal interview, 31 Jul. 1995.

11. Madeleva and Rose Kennedy exchanged several letters during the spring and summer of 1960, prompted by Mrs. Kennedy's having read Madeleva's autobiography and recognized her friend, Miss Conway. The letters also refer to a proposed visit of J.F.K. to the Saint Mary's campus, which was later canceled. Another connection involved a Saint Mary's graduate who worked as a governess in the family of Robert Kennedy.

12. Madeleva, interview, *Milwaukee Journal,* Thurs. 18 Apr. 1963.

13. Madeleva, interview, *Montreal Star,* Wed. 23 May 1962.

14. Madeleva, letter to Mrs. Ronald Y. Levy, 6 Feb. 1964, College Archives.

15. Madeleva's approach struck some readers as superficial and opened her to sharp criticism. For example, Madeleine Jacqueline Savard wrote (18 Mar. 1959, College Archives): "[It is] an innocuous, name-dropping, unoriginal travelogue," lamenting that someone with Madeleva's "spiritual, intellectual, and moral resources should have shared so little of them."

16. Madeleva, letter to Lehman, undated, Lehman Papers.

17. Lewis, letter to Madeleva, 13 Mar. 1959, College Archives.

18. Madeleva, interview, a clipping identified only *St. Louis Review* (n.d.: 1962?), College Archives.

19. Madeleva, letter to J. F. Wolff, 6 Nov. 1961, College Archives.

20. Sr. Gerald, letter to Madeleva, 22 May 1962, College Archives.

21. Madeleva, letter to J. F. Wolff, 13 Jul. 1961, College Archives.

22. Madeleva, letter to C. B. Luce, 7 May 1962, College Archives.

23. Madeleva, letter to C. B. Luce, 16 Dec. 1960, College Archives.

24. Madeleva, letter to Norcross, 15 Nov. 1961, College Archives.

25. Madeleva, letter to Mr. and Mrs. Martin E. Browne, 8 May 1962, College Archives.

26. Madeleva, letter to Madge Vaison Mouton, 31 Jul. 1963, College Archives.

27. Madeleva, letter to Anna T. Starr, 4 Jan. 1962, College Archives.

28. Madeleva, letter to C. B. Luce, 20 Mar. 1964, College Archives.

29. Madeleva, notes dated 30 Jul. 1959, in "Correspondence: Europe, Summer 1959," College Archives.

30. Madeleva, letter to Mrs. Richard Klee, 6 Apr. 1964, College Archives.

31. Madeleva, letter to Lawrence F. Barmann, SJ, 3 Aug. 1962, College Archives.

32. Madeleva, letter to Madge Vaison Mouton, 2 Feb. 1950, College Archives.

33. Madeleva, letter to Mother Rose Elizabeth, 12 Nov. 1962, College Archives.

34. Madeleva, letter to Vincent McAloon, 25 Sept. 1959, College Archives.

35. Madeleva, letter to Leona Reemer, 24 Mar. 1961, College Archives.

36. Ms. copy of an entry on Mother Angela Gillespie, CSC, prepared for the *Biographical Dictionary of American Women*.

37. Madeleva, letter to C. B. Luce, 11 Jul. 1961, College Archives.

38. Madeleva, letter to C. B. Luce, 6 Dec. 1961, College Archives.

39. *A Lost Language and Other Essays on Chaucer* (New York: Sheed and Ward, 1951), 17.

40. Ibid., 143.

41. Madeleva, letter to Mrs. John D. Roth (about the death of Dr. Tom Dooley), 10 Feb. 1961, College Archives.

42. Madeleva, letter to Barbara Ward, 1 Mar. 1960, College Archives.

43. Madeleva, letter to Henry Luce, 28 Jun. 1957, College Archives.

44. Lehman, letter to Madeleva, 23 Mar. 1959, College Archives.

45. Madeleva, letter to Lehman, undated [probably 1962], Lehman Papers.

46. Madeleva, letter to Edward I. Wilkin, 17 Apr. 1964, College Archives.

47. Speaight, *The Property Basket*, 335.

48. Baroness E. Guttenberg, letter to Madeleva, 8 Jul. 1961, College Archives. In the same letter, the Baroness wrote that her secretary, who had met Madeleva on her 1959 European trip, asked why Madeleva should retire when she could be no more than forty-seven.

49. Madeleva, letter to Ada de Bethune, 4 Jan. 1963, College Archives.

50. Madeleva, letter to J. F. Wolff, 25 May 1964, College Archives.

51. Madeleva, letter to J. F. Wolff, 2 Jul. 1964, College Archives.

52. Personal interview with Sr. Bernadette Marie, who said that when word came of Madeleva's death, she locked the closet in which the files were

kept until she could transfer all the materials, just as Madeleva left them, to the College Archives.

53. *Courier* (Summer 1964): 6

54. *The Midwest Vineyard* (publication of the Sisters of the Holy Cross), 15 Aug. 1964, 1.

55. Madeleva, letter to Mrs. John D. Ross, 9 Mar. 1960, College Archives.

56. Madeleva, letter to C. B. Luce, 28 Oct. 1948, College Archives.

57. Madeleva, letter to Lehman, 8 Feb. 1962, College Archives.

58. Madeleva, letter to Wallace Leland, 30 Jan. 1962.

59. Norcross, letter to Sr. Verda Clare, 10 Aug. 1964, General Archives.

Selected Publications

Sister M. Madeleva Wolff, CSC. *Knights Errant and Other Poems*. D. Appleton and Co., 1923.

——. *Chaucer's Nuns and Other Essays*. D. Appleton and Co., 1925.

——. *The Pearl: A Study in Spiritual Dryness*. D. Appleton and Co., 1925.

——. *Penelope and Other Poems*. D. Appleton and Co., 1927.

——. *A Question of Lovers and Other Poems*. St. Anthony Guild Press, 1935.

——. *Ballad of the Happy Christmas Wind*. St. Anthony Guild Press, 1936.

——. *Gates and Other Poems*. The Macmillan Co., 1938.

——. *Christmas Eve and Other Poems*. St. Anthony Guild Press, 1938.

——. *Selected Poems*. The Macmillan Co., 1939.

——. *Four Girls*. St. Anthony Guild Press, 1941.

——. *Addressed to Youth*. St. Anthony Guild Press, 1944.

——. *A Song of Bedlam Inn*. St. Anthony Guild Press, 1946.

——. *Collected Poems*. The Macmillan Co., 1947.

——. *A Lost Language*. Sheed and Ward, 1951.

——. *American Twelfth Night*. The Macmillan Co., 1955.

——. *My First Seventy Years*. The Macmillan Co., 1959.

——. *The Four Last Things*. The Macmillan Co., 1959.

——. *Conversations with Cassandra*. The Macmillan Co., 1961.

——. *A Child Asks for a Star*. Dimension Books, Inc., 1964.

Index